AF506244

WORLDING THE WESTERN

WORLDING THE WESTERN

Contemporary US Western Fiction and the Global Community

NEIL CAMPBELL

UNIVERSITY OF NEVADA PRESS | *Reno & Las Vegas*

University of Nevada Press | Reno, Nevada 89557 USA
www.unpress.nevada.edu
Copyright © 2022 by University of Nevada Press
All rights reserved
Cover design by Louise OFarrell
Cover photographs: © iStock (background: ImagineGolf, Insets: Quardia, PeskyMonkey, taviphoto); © Shutterstock (HQ Vectors Premium Studio, eddie-hernandez); leather detail: The Lyda Hill Texas Collection of Photographs in Carol M. Highsmith's America Project, Library of Congress, Prints and Photographs Division.

LIBRARY OF CONGRESS CATALOGING-IN-PUBLICATION DATA ON FILE
LCCN 2022002730
ISBN 978-1-64779-055-4 (paperback)
ISBN 978-1-64779-056-1 (e-book)

The paper used in this book meets the requirements of American National Standard for Information Sciences—Permanence of Paper for Printed Library Materials, ANSI/NISO Z39.48-1992 (R2002).

FIRST PRINTING

Manufactured in the United States of America

Contents

Acknowledgments

I started this book in very different times. However, I completed it during the COVID-19 pandemic under strict lockdown, following Brexit and the election of Boris Johnson in the United Kingdom and, in the United States, the arrival of Joe Biden at the White House following four years of Donald Trump. The world felt strange. Before travel restrictions, I was fortunate to share some of this book with scholars in Italy, Spain, the United Kingdom, and the United States, and their comments and discussions have helped me shape it over time. Grateful thanks to Nancy Cook, Michael Johnson, Susan Kollin, Kathleen Stewart, Stephen Tatum, and O. Alan Weltzien. Specific thanks for kind invitations and friendship go to Stefano Rosso, David Rio, Amaia Ibarraran-Bigalondo, Ángel Chaparro Sainz, and Jesús Ángel González.

Coincidentally, almost precisely at the moment of this book's completion, Paul Greengrass's western *News of the World* appeared, reminding us once again of the power of stories to make worlds, build bridges, and heal. This has always been a book of worldings.

As always, this is for Jane. *Everything I am, you are.*

WORLDING THE WESTERN

INTRODUCTION

Enter West

Storying cannot any longer be put into the box of human exceptionalism.
—Donna Haraway, *Staying with the Trouble: Making Kin in the Chthulucene*

This earth is anything but a sharing of humanity. It is a world that
does not even manage to constitute a world; it is a world lacking
in world, and lacking in the meaning of world.
—Jean-Luc Nancy, *Being Singular Plural*

A HUNDRED OTHER WESTS

As long ago as 2002 in *Western American Literature*, James Maguire called
for a new relationship between western American literary studies and
globalization, quoting Stephen Greenblatt:

> To write literary history, we need more a sharp awareness of acci-
> dental judgments than a theory of the organic; more an account of
> purposes mistook than a narrative of gradual emergence; more a
> chronicle of carnal, bloody, and unnatural acts than a story of *inevi-*
> *table progress* from traceable origins. We need to understand coloni-
> zation, exile, emigration, wandering, contamination, and unexpected
> consequences, along with the fierce compulsions of greed, longing,
> and restlessness, for it is these *disruptive forces, not a rooted sense of*
> *cultural legitimacy*, that principally shape the history and diffusion
> of languages. (62; emphasis added)[1]

Since then critics have moved to explain, in Susan Kollin's words, the
"constructions and circulations of the Western" (2015a, 29) as a traveling
genre or "routed" form whose origins, development, and metamorphosis
deny Greenblatt's "rooted sense of cultural legitimacy" and challenge
"inevitable progress." Western American literature, or "westerns" as I will
refer to fiction discussed in this book, is, despite appearances, a hybrid
form crossed and recrossed by multiple traditions, transnational influences, and complex relations, with "roots" twisted and interspliced,

rhizomatic, and entangled betwixt and between many cultures, languages, and traditions. In this sense, the western genre has always belonged to the world just as, in Janne Lahti's words, the American West "is not just a distant land out there, but part of our collective, global history" (2019, 2).[2] Increasingly, texts referring to the American West dramatize the impact of "colonization, exile, emigration, wandering, contamination…fierce compulsions of greed, longing, and restlessness," producing a more fully rounded and critically engaged representation of what I term *regionality-as-worlding*. In so doing, such texts acknowledged complex transnational routes disrupting taken-for-granted assumptions and established exceptionalist discourses of the West's intimate connection to US nation building. To read against this tradition through the prism of *worlding* westerns is, in Paul Giles's words, to note how "cultural formations overlap and interfere with each other in surprising ways, thereby giving the map of the subject a new cartographic and conceptual twist" (2013, 18).

My aim is to show how in westerns, or in recent fiction of the West, such conceptual twists emerge as *worlding*, whereby tropes and assumptions are indeed "overlapped and interfered with," opened up to different entangled visions of the region as a space of multiple relations with its outside and, in turn, its formations made, remade, and dismantled from diverse perspectives. In Jean-Luc Nancy's words, "The unity of the world is not one: it is made of a diversity, including disparity and opposition. It is made of it, which is to say that it is not added to it and does not reduce it. The unity of the world is nothing other than its diversity, and its diversity is, in turn, a diversity of worlds" (2007a, 109). Through examining western fiction broadly chronologically, this book will explore these relations of disparity and opposition to show how a seemingly closed, heterogeneous region, like the West, might indeed be constituted of a "diversity of worlds." Through a critically recursive style, *Worlding the Western* places this fiction in dialogue with philosophy and criticism so that each chapter loops back and connects rhizomatically, revealing a type of globalization with a difference, "filled with human potential…a form of political action being done through culture… worlding, with emphasis on the whirl" (D. Watson x, xi). According to Rob Wilson, "If the global is not the world, worlding is not or should not be equated to globalization as it sometimes still is.…[W]orlding is not just a gesture or tactic in the given world but helps to create a world, *to world the world* in an active gerundive sense" (2018, 9).[3] Another useful definition comes from Jimmy Fazzino: "Worlding is interested in transgressive acts, whether they involve borders internal or external, textual or otherwise; worlding seeks to be transgressive: that is to say, counterhegemonic, reading against the grain, writing against empire and globalization transcendent" (2016, 26). As Kollin explains, such an approach adds to our understanding of "Westness" by "connecting stories of the American West to global contexts, extending postcolonial criticism to literary histories of the region, placing previously marginalized groups at the center of this work, and questioning what counts as the beginnings and ends of regions themselves" (2015a, 4). In addition, to emphasize Wilson's point, it is always also about the *active* creation of worlds that refuse to deny relations with others, in order to acknowledge and build interdependent, shared communities that are both local and global, or *regionality-as-worlding*.

Although, due to the scale and speed of its conquest and settlement, America has been traditionally viewed as exceptional, it is important to recognize, as this book will do, that the American adventure in the West had much in common with parallel settler-colonial processes taking place across the globe. As Lahti puts it, "Every expanding colonial empire had its own 'West' somewhere…[with] its scale of opportunity, process of conquest, fierce Natives, characteristics of its settler communities" (2019, 160). These frames and parallels have been largely overlooked in favor of the exceptionalist narratives of the frontier and thereby neglected the transnational, postwestern nature of westward expansion and its consequences on the region's histories. As Giles argues, "To relocate US cultural geography transnationally…is to move away from the identification of the United States itself as an enclosed territorial site and instead, to track ways in which its discursive dispersal around the globe is *introjected back uneasily* into the privileged home domain" (2013, 33; emphasis added). In other words, it is critically limiting to think about the US West as essentially an *American* phenomenon, but instead to always refract its stories, factual and imaginary, through what we might think of as a prism of worldliness.

Such *introjecting back* is characteristic of authors discussed in this book, many of whose works move back in time, tracing historical journeys into the West from other nations, drawing diverse peoples into the melee of westward expansion, and doing so through transnational authorial perspectives.[4] This is evident from Obreht's Ottoman Turk arriving in America in the 1850s and Zhang's Chinese migrants coming to "Gold Mountain" in the 1840s to Hamid's futuristic vision of a new western settlement of "Marin" on the Pacific Coast. Consequently, Giles's "privileged home domain" is undone by worlding, de-exceptionalized, and simultaneously understood as redolent of vital contemporary political themes and issues.[5] To borrow a phrase from Hernan Diaz, the writing I examine "walk[s] in circles wider than nations" (2017c, 269), reflecting differently upon the West and America as deeply imbricated in the world. Thus, this fictional "dispersal" of territory *worlds* the western, shifting its focus between the local and global, the everyday and the universal, the proximate and the distant, or, as Susan Stanford Friedman puts it, the "bird's eye and ground-level views that can inform and complement each other" (2018, 94). This is exemplified in Diaz's *In the Distance* (see chapter 2), employing what he calls "radical foreignness" through his central character, Swedish giant Håkan, whose actual foreignness makes him feel out of place, with no English language, and cut adrift in the West. Diaz "tried to make genre and even language itself feel foreign" so that the reader felt as disorientated as Håkan, until ultimately these strategies emphasize that, contrary to genre expectations, "this is a very American story, which makes us remember that foreignness is part of the American experience to begin with" (Pinckney 2017).

Sounding like Deleuze and Guattari, the westerns I discuss are "minor literature" in the sense that they *"send the major language racing"* and their authors "are foreigners in their own tongue," working against the "standard measure" of dominant literary and political forms with a force of "potential, creative and created becoming" (1996, 105–6; emphasis in the original). This latter point, above all, gives these "minoritarian" novels a contemporary political relevance, underlining the necessity of immigration and cultural mixing to the American story at a point in its history when, as Diaz puts it, referring directly to the Trump administration, the old questions are as vital as ever: "Who has a voice, and who doesn't? Who gets to tell their story, and who is silenced? Is there really room for everyone in a country as vast as this? All of these questions are part of our history" (Pinckney 2017).[6] This one example shows how the *dispersed* and *worlding* westerns discussed here engage, dramatize, and "foreignize" historic assumptions and myth while imbuing them with intense political resonance. In Deleuze and Guattari's terms, "By using a number of minority elements, by connecting, conjugating them, one invents a specific, unforeseen, autonomous becoming" (1996, 106). Ultimately, such deterritorialized writing of "silence, the interrupted, the interminable" runs counter to "one single dream" in order "to express another possible community and to forge the means for another consciousness and another sensibility" (Deleuze and Guattari 1986, 26, 27, 17).

This possible worlded community is "the opposite of separatism…the reverse of exclusivism" and explored best through Edward Said's notion of "worldliness" (2000, 382). Henry Giroux defined it as "an ethical and political stance" that is "a critical and engaged interaction with the world we live in mediated by a responsibility for challenging structures of domination and for alleviating human suffering." "Worldliness," according to Giroux, "required not being afraid of controversy, *making connections* that are otherwise hidden, *deflating the claims* of triumphalism, *bridging* intellectual work and the operation of politics…an act of interpretation linked to the possibility of *intervention in the world*" (2007, 8; emphasis added). My emphases above broadly track the critical process undertaken in this book, forging an active worldliness or worlding that is "a kind of border literacy in the plural" where multiple perspectives are at work in the creation of a world made of worlds (Giroux 2007, 8). In worlding the western, to riff on a phrase from Iain Chambers, "a hundred other Wests now open up" (2018, 15). What this means will, ultimately, be the focus for this book.

THE WEST AND THE WORLD

Writing in the foreword to *The West as America*, Elizabeth Broun explained how "America's creation myth," as she calls the story of westward expansion, "was ushered into the world" (Truettner 1991, ix) during the nineteenth century, framed by a desire to project a coherent national identity built upon the frontier experience. In so doing, the "ushered-in" myth controls history, modeling it as a particular and precise chain of events until "the world is rendered pure in the process; complexity and contradiction give way to order, clarity, and direction…an abstract shelter restricting debate" (40). Thus, myth constructs a "world" of ideological values, images, and stories functioning within the wider world and, in many ways, separating these two worlds from one another. The West (as America) was, therefore, represented as entirely exceptional: different because it was as if chosen to fulfill its destiny through ordained expansion, heightening and honing newly forged values translated from the world beyond. As Frederick Jackson Turner put it in "The West and American Ideals" (1914), "The world was to be made a better world" through the example of the West, comparing it to "vital germs which impinging upon a dead world would bring life to it" (1961, 109, 99). The destiny of the West under these terms was to regenerate a "dead world," infusing it with new blood and new values while simultaneously *absenting* the indigenous population as "past tense presences…destined to disappear with the frontier itself" (Byrd 2011, xx).

Turner summarized western exceptionalism in a passage of potent images haunting the United States to the present day: "The West offered an exit into a free life and greater well-being among the bounties of nature, into the midst of resources that demanded manly exertion, and that gave in return the chance for indefinite ascent in the scale of social advance" (1961, 91). Turner argued the West made America great and, in so doing, created a template for its future-defining exceptionalist traits. In *exiting* one world, America constructed another that would become not just western and American, but intimately connected to the *idea of the West* more generally. "The West" as a global idea was a historical construction, not a geographical one, dividing the world into "the West and the Rest" at the time of the Enlightenment. Often, however, this underestimated or overlooked "the role which 'the Rest' played in the formation of the idea of 'the West' and a 'western' sense of identity." This seems as true for the wider use of the term "West" (the Occident) as it does for the specific American West examined in this book. As Stuart Hall argues, under the ultimate weight of Eurocentric values, "separate and distinct worlds became…harnessed together in the same historical time-frame… [and] became different parts of one global social, economic and cultural system" (Hall 1992, 279). This book examines how these often forgotten "separate and distinct" stories might be acknowledged and celebrated, not to reinforce Turner's vision of the "indefinite ascent" of America, nor to presume "one global system," but rather to question both and propose alternative *worlded* histories of the American West.

Turner's positivism, as historian Greg Grandin explains, transformed America's frontier story into a tale of one distinct world of exceptional unanimity: "Frontier expansion would break every paradox, reconcile every contradiction, between say, ideals and interest, virtue and ambition. Extend the sphere, and you will ensure peace, protect individual freedom, and dilute factionalism; you will create a curious, buoyant, resourceful people in thrall to no received doctrine, transcend regionalism, spread prosperity, and move beyond racism. As horizons broaden, so will our love for the world's people. As boundaries widen so will our tolerance, the realization that humanity is our country" (2019, 270). Accordingly,

Turner's frontier provided a "soothing processional" vision trumpeting a "public anthem of a nation *moving out in the world*, not as a conquering race, much less a woodland Germanic tribe, but in the name of humanity" (Grandin 2019, 129; emphasis added). Grandin, however, while recognizing the initial democratic promise of the Turner thesis as a spreading of gritty capitalist values, or "American universalism" (129), to the world, also recognizes that such an idea, "along with its imagined suppression of extremes, could only be maintained through ceaseless expansion" (131) and the inevitable consequences on Native peoples and the environment. Rather like the wider discussion of the "West and the Rest," the development of the American West was made at the cost of the "Rest" as the process of internal colonization took hold. Under this process, "Society, nature and man—*the world as a whole*—is subjected to manageability and instrumentality. The world seems no more than an object outside of us that can be controlled and manipulated. Such a view implies a vantage point from where the world can be represented" (Meurs, Note, and Aerts 2009, 35; emphasis added).

Ironically, rather than beneficial to humanity, this grand vision of *moving out in the world* came with a high price in which other "worlds" were, consequently, diminished, displaced, or destroyed as a dominant male, white settler, colonial worldview gained ground. As Lahti puts it, the rapidly surpassed dream of the West as a "syncretic meeting ground" became instead "a realm where settlers came to stay, take the land, substitute the Natives, and instigate racial hierarchies and policies of exclusion. In short, the early West of shared worlds and middle grounds [associated with Turner's positive democratic hope], gradually and unevenly made way for a settler colonial West as the nineteenth century progressed" (2019, 46). Indeed, in this spirit, while suggesting the longevity of the frontier ideal, Anna Tsing terms westering "an imaginative project," "a zone of not-yet—not yet mapped, not yet regulated," where "some—and not others—may reap its rewards" (2005, 32, 27, 28).

Central to this imaginative project, Grandin argues, was Turner's essay "The Significance of the Frontier in American History" (1893), conveniently manipulated by politicians and businessmen into an "ideology of limitlessness," "to justify foreign wars" (2019, 168), aid capitalist market expansion, and, at the same time, avoid dealing with social troubles closer to home (like racism and inequality). As David Harvey explains, after the Civil War, the US government "broadly reflected corporate and industrial interests," exploiting the "abundant space for internal expansion" and promoting "the theory of manifest destiny [that] fuelled its own particular brand of expansionary racism and international idealism" (2003, 46–47). The endlessly recycled idea of the ever-expanding frontier sustained an "imagery of the world as the American West" (Grandin 2019, 187), with available "free" land, people, and markets to exploit economically, politically, and ideologically. Hence, a new narrative of American universalism hijacked and repurposed the early democratic thrust of Turner's ideas: the *West as America, the world as the American West.* Drawing the world into the United States' arc of influence concealed, as Harvey puts it, "the explicitness of territorial gains and occupations under the mask of a spaceless universalization of its own values, buried within a rhetoric that was ultimately to culminate in…'globalization'" (2003, 47). Thus, Turner's Americanization of a continent prepared the way for globalization as a view of the world because it is "to do with the way we consider the world, act upon it, and relate to it: practice it. Globalization in this sense is nothing more than the ambition to provide a way of thinking and forming the world" (Meurs, Note, and Aerts 2011, 14).

A hundred years after the Turner thesis, Gayatri Chakravorty Spivak commented on a similar global colonial process as "the worlding of a world": the "imperialist project which had to assume that the earth that is territorialized was in fact previously uninscribed. So then, a world, on a simple level of cartography, inscribed what was presumed to be uninscribed." As in Turner's sense of an "uninscribed" territory or "free land" waiting to be written over by pioneer-settlers, Spivak's notion of "worlding" is about imposition, surveying, or naturalizing what was, in reality, inscribed there already. As she continues, "This worlding actually is also a texting, textualising, a making into art, a making into an object to be understood" (1990, 1). Through worlding in Spivak's (and Turner's) sense, colonized natives and territories are "objectified" and defined in Eurocentric terms, translated through dominant colonial language, and designated as subject to Euro-imperial authority. As a result, "the worlding of a world" is an "epistemic violence" that "generates the force to make the 'native' see himself as 'other'" (1985, 267, 254), thus "denying its own 'worlding'" (Byrd 2011, 64). Examining this process through Native eyes, Jodi Byrd summarizes it as one in which "indigenous nations colonized by the United States are continually worlded into the more perfect union, the United States" (124) and, as a result, find their own worlds diminished or erased in the process.

As if responding to Turner's imagery of "indefinite ascent" and Spivak's negative colonial worlding, while questioning the supposed outcomes of expansion described by Grandin and Lahti, Elizabeth Broun argues that the ultimate legacy of *The West as America* art exhibition was in recognizing "that American society *still struggles* to adjust to limitations on natural resources, to grant overdue justice to native populations, to locate the contributions of ethnic minorities within a mainstream tradition, and to resolve conflicts between unbridled personal freedom and the larger social good" (1991, vii; emphasis added). In other words, the urgent critical path opened by the exhibition was to understand the lasting consequences of the American West as exceptional and isolated from the "rest" of the world and to recognize the blinkered limits of Turner's frontier vision. As I will suggest throughout this book, this critical path is as urgent as ever, ushering diverse worlds *back* into western stories whether indigenous or migratory and consequently reopening histories of the West to multiple and complex relations with region, nation, and world. The counterworlding (or *reworlding*) explored in this book "talks back" to the prior injurious worlding proposed by Turner and Spivak through various acts of imaginative retrieval and critical reinscription. As John Muthyala writes, reworlding is "discursive contestation that places migration, border crossing, transnational exchange, cultural translation, and colonial modernity at the center of debates and discussion regarding American literature and culture" (2006, xiv). For the purposes of this book, I reclaim the term "worlding," following Edward Said, Édouard Glissant, Jean-Luc Nancy, Rob Wilson, and others, as a potent and active "discursive contestation" (see chapter 1 on my use of "worlding").

Reclaiming worlding in this context envisages an entangled process by which the intimate, small-scale, and local everyday worlds of people, place, and nonhuman species relate to and dialogize with larger global concerns. Walter Mignolo describes this vital process as creating "macronarratives told from the historical experiences of multiple local histories (the histories of modernity/coloniality)," which collectively *interrupt* accepted narratives (such as Turner's) until "the imaginary of the modern world system cracks" (2000, 22, 23). With echoes of Said's "border literacy in the plural," Mignolo calls this transgressive approach "border thinking," which he closely aligns with "worldly culture"—"the multiplication of epistemic energies in diverse local histories" (39). As Rebecca Solnit has written in a similar vein, "The embrace of local power doesn't have to mean parochialism, withdrawal, or intolerance, only a coherent foundation from which to navigate the larger world," creating a "sense that you have an identity embedded in local circumstance and a role in the global dialogue" (2004, 113, 114). What is required, as Judith Butler points out, is an "altered state of perception, another imaginary, that would disorient us from the givens of the political present" and insist on "a social and global obligation we bear toward one another…interdependent…relational, fragile, sometimes conflictual and unbearable, sometimes ecstatic and joyous" (2020, 64). This is the seemingly "impossible world…that exists beyond the horizon of our present thinking," yet still a world worth striving toward because it is about the "affirmation of this life, bound up with yours" (64–65). Once again, it is what I mean by *regionality-as-worlding*.

It is the exploration of these multiple epistemic energies and their prior masking behind the myth of the frontier West that this book aims to unravel, not primarily through historical documents or political speeches, as Grandin and Lahti have both undertaken, but rather through literary *worlding*. As Nancy argues, "Once myth is interrupted, writing recounts our history to us again" (1991, 69). In doing so, fiction becomes the "active, critical, and imaginative process of worlding" (Wilson 2007, 210), reopening the West to its complex and multiple relations with the world rather than simply reiterating an American project as regional and inward looking, like an enclosed story it tells itself about itself. Western American literature might, therefore, become what Pheng Cheah calls "world literature as literature that is of the world, not a body of timeless aesthetic objects or a commodity-like thing that circulates globally, but something that can play a fundamental role and be a force in the ongoing cartography and creation of the world" (2014, 326).

By looking at *worldly relations* (see also chapter 1), we see the West differently, transversally, cutting across the lines that so often divide and demarcate it as exceptionalist, inward looking, and isolated. My chosen texts engage with the West in such a manner, "making worlds" not to stand apart or disconnected from others, but precisely to point toward their mutual and diverse relations, connections, and differences. As Bruno Latour points out, like Mignolo and others, globalization *might* mean the positive relations between the local and the global, "*multiplying* viewpoints, *registering* a greater number of varieties, *taking into account* a larger number of beings, cultures, phenomena, organisms, and people" (2018, 12–13). "Yet," he continues, it has tended to come to mean "*a single vision*… proposed by a few individuals, representing a very small number of interests…imposed on everyone and spread everywhere" (13). It is what Mignolo calls "global designs" (2005, 21).[7] The struggles examined in the chapters that follow are against such a reductive view of globalization and moving toward what Latour terms the "Terrestrial," meaning "bound to the earth and to the land, but…also *a way of worlding*, in that it aligns with no borders and transcends all identities" (2018, 54).

For Rebecca Solnit, "this other globalization," as she calls it, is the "antithesis of the homogenization and consolidation brought by the spread of chains and brands and corporations," being much more about "the globalization of communication and of ideas" (2010, 114). Global connections, as Anna Tsing points out, are not smooth, easy processes, but more often they "come to life in 'friction,' the grip of worldly encounter" (2005, 1). The meaning of the term "world" here shouldn't be confused with its use in everyday speech: "World as the *there* of being does not mean the space in which being takes place, but is the taking place of this being. It is not simply the place in which we live, but through which we live as well" (Meurs, Note, and Aerts 2009, 32). To comprehend what "through which we live" might mean, I deploy Rob Wilson's notion of worlding as a critical practice that "enacts openings of time and consciousness to other values and multiple modes of being, projection, and survival. Spatially, a worlded criticism seeks new and emergent connections to and articulations with region, place, area and trans-species forms" (2018, 8). Thus, to return to Tsing's comment above, worlding is never smooth flowing, but rather *interruptive*, both *gripping* and *frictional*, showing how the American West has been "continually co-produced" in its multiple frictional interactions with other cultures and traditions (or worlds), "shaped and transformed in long histories of regional-to-global networks of power, trade, and meaning" (Tsing 2005, 3). As the next section suggests, worlding is relevant to the present, and in a time of what Amitav Ghosh calls "the great derangement" (2016, 2), we need it more than ever. As I argue throughout this book, there is a type of fiction that emerged in this era of great derangement (or the Trump era) that is hybrid, epic, and imaginative without being defined purely as science fiction or speculative fiction (as Ghosh does), even though it might borrow from these traditions. American literature, according to LeAnne Howe (Choctaw), has learned from Native storytelling, by employing a "community of characters," a "splintered storytelling style with multiple characters and multiple points of view," and, vitally, understood the possibilities of narrative as "not linear," forging a deeper response so that "the land [is] teaching people here how to understand and talk through that space" (Squint 2010, 216–17). The goal of such *worldly* writing is to find alternative routes of worlding in different, relational, and entangled ways to stand against reductionism and uncover "change through exchange with each other, by way of inexorable clashes, pitiless wars, but also of advance in consciousness and hope" (Glissant 2020b, 6).

In an age of increasing global interconnectedness, despite many governments' attempts to adopt a closed-border isolationism, such as under the Trump presidency, "the body of the nation can no longer be conceived of as consisting of a territorialized human population: its very sinews are now revealed to be intertwined with forces that cannot be confined by boundaries" (Ghosh 2016, 144). Facing a global COVID-19 pandemic in 2020–21 reinforced the recognition of interconnectedness and the need for cooperative and mutual action to combat a virus that recognizes no borders. Similarly, Donna Haraway has written of "intertwined worldings" and all kinds of "knotting" that are consequent upon "worldly subject-and-object-shaping entanglements," which defy any notion of "human exceptionalism and bounded individualism" (2016, 13, 30). As she argues poignantly, "We become—with each other or not at all" (4), or, in the words of Gloria Anzaldúa, chiming perfectly with the direction of this book, "we're in each other's worlds…affected by the other…dependent… on the other" (2000, 215).

THE TRUMP ERA AND ITS FICTIONS—FLOATING IN DREAMLAND

> Barbed wire used properly can be a beautiful sight.
> —Donald Trump, Bozeman, Montana, November 3, 2018

Donald Trump announced his campaign for president in June 2015 and was elected the following year. As British novelist Carys Davies wrote, Trump's appeal to voters had a weird echo of the westering story of America because it was as if "the migration story has gone through another cycle, except the descendants of yesterday's winners now feel like today's losers, and they have made that very, very clear." As she explains, "He won the presidency partly by persuading the white indigenous natives of today's United States that he understands their sense of loss, their sense of dispossession; that he is listening to them when no one else is; that he understands their fears that their world is threatened by alien technology and robotics, by alien moral values like same-sex marriage and transgender bathrooms, and by alien people, like Mexicans and Muslims"

(2017). There is, of course, deliberate irony in Davies's use of "indigenous natives" to describe Trump's largely white electoral base, for it underlines the ways by which his narrative of reclaiming America excluded many Americans, including Native Americans. However, what Davies pinpoints is the sense of alienation and loss felt by what we might think of as the descendants of settler-colonial Americans, *dispossessed* of what Manifest Destiny had promised them in perpetuity.

Most of the fiction discussed in this book comes after 2015 and responds directly or indirectly to this era and its resonance with the American West. Indeed, one reviewer of Valeria Luiselli's *Lost Children Archive* (discussed in chapter 7) went as far as calling it "a road story for the Trump era." Trump's slogan "Make America Great Again" (MAGA) defined a vision of the world in which the United States has a closed, parochial, and limited notion of worldly relations, expressed most clearly in his UN speech in 2019: "The future does not belong to globalists. The future belongs to patriots."[8] Forged, above all, from a particular vision of the past, Trumpism clung to an exceptionalist notion of the United States, embodied emphatically in western expansion and settlement as the fundamental foundational myth of the nation. Jean-Luc Nancy refers to the nostalgic "horizon behind us" inevitably constructing a particular worldview like "a lost age in which community was woven of tight, harmonious, and infrangible bonds and in which above all it played back to itself, through its institutions, its rituals, and its symbols, the representation, indeed the living offering, of its own immanent unity, intimacy, and autonomy" (1991, 9). Trump's "projection" (9) was imbued with a similar nostalgia for older and simpler solutions to issues like immigration, foreign policy, and trade shackled to a desire for Americans "to shelter themselves from the world" (Latour 2018, 2). However, it is also a vision dependent upon what Aimee Bahng calls "a neoliberal fantasy of a seamless world unified under the sign of global capitalism for the global (financial) citizen" (2018, 8). As Trump wrote on the first page of his book *The Art of the Deal* in 1987, "Other people paint beautifully on canvas or write wonderful poetry. I like making deals, preferably big deals. That's how I get my kicks" (Trump and Schwartz 1987, 1).

However, having benefited financially from a unified world of global capitalism, the Trump presidency instead presented the United States as a beleaguered nation whose "deals" with the world have diminished its status. As a result, Trump instigated increased economic nationalism, sought to close the nation's borders, and retreated from wider political groupings such as NATO, the Iran Nuclear Deal, the Paris Climate Agreement, the Trans-Pacific Partnership, and the World Health Organization. The individual nation, under such a worldview, is sovereign and its relations with others relevant only when absolutely required or beneficial. Trump claimed his policy was about national renewal and, therefore, involved a move away from "globalism," the world, and being international in outlook and toward a reinvigorated "Americanism." As Mimi Yang has written, "By building and raising cultural, racial and religious walls, Trumpism incarnates an exclusionist, isolationist worldview, which disregards and disrupts the vital symbiosis of the vertical and the horizontal at the core of American culture, disfiguring Americanism" (2018). There is no room for "symbiosis" in this worldview, for it insists upon stark "us and them" politics, like that once portrayed in mainstream mythic westerns as the good sheriff taking on the black-hatted bad guys.

Thus, Trumpism managed, according to Bruno Latour, to "link, in a single gesture, first the *headlong rush* toward maximum profit while abandoning the rest of the world to its fate" and "the *headlong rush* backward of an entire people toward the return of national and ethnic categories ('Make America Great Again' behind a wall!)" (2018, 35). In so doing, despite the attack on "globalism," Trumpism "conflated" two once-opposed forces, the "advance towards globalization" and the "retreat toward the old national terrain," enabled, Latour contends, because it denies any conflict between "modernization" and "being terrestrial" (35–36). The effect of this strange "fusion" dissolves "all forms of solidarity, both external (among nations) and internal (among classes)" (36), until Trump's United States was positioned "outside of all worldly constraints, literally *offshore*, like a tax haven," "never having to share with others a world that they know will never again be a common world," and managing this "while maintaining the American ideal of the Frontier" (36).[9] Appositely, Latour terms this position as being *"Out-of-This-World"* [italics in original] (34).

Trump's America, therefore, "rejects the world it claims to inhabit" (38), becoming a fortress threatened by outside forces, such as immigrants and refugees who have, according to his analysis, "flooded in" and are continuously associated with crime, violence, drugs, and terrorism. This framing of the nation-as-a-container that must be closed off and protected from a threatening and malicious Other is also typically nationalistic and, of course, reflected most obviously in Trump's mission to build a wall on the Mexican border. The world, under such a philosophy, stands opposed to the United States rather than existing as mutually cooperative and interrelated communities.[10] As Trump said, "We have been taken advantage of by the world. That is not going to be happening anymore" (quoted in Grandin 2019, 291). His disengaged America became more like "a besieged medieval fortress" or, perhaps more fittingly to this book, like a twenty-first-century Alamo (Grandin 2019, 274; see Latour 2018).[11]

With his grandfather Friedrich's fortune made in the Klondike gold rush, perhaps it was no surprise then to find Donald Trump during his 2016 election campaign aligning himself with John Wayne, pictured embracing his daughter Aissa, in front of a life-size cutout of the "Duke" in his full Ethan Edwards costume. The ideological implications were spelled out by Trump to the audience: "When you think about it John Wayne represented strength, he represented power, he represented what the people are looking [for] today because we have exactly the opposite of John Wayne right now in this country."[12] What the United States had was Barack Obama representing for Trump Wayne's antithesis. In other words, the United States lacked the spirit of tough, masculine, white single-mindedness because it was, according to Trump, a weakened nation under siege from the demands of the world outside.

Developing this point before Trump's election, Eric Bolling wrote in the *Washington Post*: "Love him or hate him, agree with him or disagree, nobody can deny that The Donald has that swagger any cowboy of the Old West would recognize. He refuses to apologize for being a man, refuses to apologize for his opinions, and refuses to tone down or 'feminize' his style…. [H]e blazes his own trail" (2016).[13] In Trump's vision of America, its greatness had dwindled because the nation had lost sight of these rudimentary "truths," moved too far from such sustaining principles of "Americanism," and engaged too much in appeasing other cultural stories and experiences, consequently weakening the core of US certainty, power, and authority in the world. However, as early as 1987 in *The Art of the Deal*, Trump expressed his view on "hyperbole" to reclaim this mythic sense of American greatness: "The final key to the way I promote is bravado. I play to people's fantasies. People may not always think big themselves, but they can still get very excited by those who do. That's why a little hyperbole never hurts. People want to believe that something is the biggest and the greatest and the most spectacular" (Trump and Schwartz 1987, 58).

Sounding Turnerian, Trump's 2020 State of the Union address employed hyperbole to combine the legacy of the frontier and his vision of a new, but exclusive, nationalism, claiming, "The American Nation was carved out of the vast frontier by the toughest, strongest, fiercest, and most determined men and women ever to walk on the face of the Earth. Our ancestors braved the unknown; tamed the wilderness; settled the wild west." "This is the country," he continued, "where children learn names like Wyatt Earp, Davy Crockett, and Annie Oakley.... We are Americans. We are pioneers. We are the pathfinders. We settled the New World; we built the modern world; and we changed history forever by embracing the eternal truth that everyone is made equal by the hand of Almighty God.... Our grandest journeys are not yet made. The American age, the American epic, the American adventure has only just begun."[14] The *absences* of nonwhite Americans in this speech are breathtaking and, of course, tell a story of exclusion, erasure, and bias in his definition of the "we" in "the American epic." Following this speech, Patricia Nelson Limerick wrote in the *Denver Post*, "When a powerful national leader turns the people of the past into caricatures and thereby drains their lives of dignity and meaning, the response of a conscientious Western American historian condenses into four words: 'Just cut that out'" (2020). Similarly, Solnit defined Trump as a privileged figure, remote from others' stories and from the world: "When you don't hear others, you don't imagine them, they become unreal, and you are left in the wasteland of a world with only yourself in it, and that surely makes you starving, though you know not for what, if you have ceased to imagine others exist in any true deep way that matters" (2017a). The argument of this book is that fiction might enable a recomplication of the American epic by putting back stories so often forgotten or overlooked and in so doing find a "true deep way that matters," a worlding way.

For Grandin, any trace of frontier optimism is misplaced, and the reality of Trump's presidency was very different: "All the things that expansion was supposed to preserve have been destroyed, and all the things it was meant to destroy have been preserved. Instead of peace, there's endless war. Instead of critical, resilient, and progressive citizenry, a conspiratorial nihilism, rejecting reason and dreading change, has taken hold. Factionalism congealed and won a national election" (2019, 270). There is an inherent fear that by letting in the world, in all its diversity, difference, multiplicity, complexity, and challenge, this mythic American foundation story—"West after West, this rebirth of American society," as Turner called it (1961, 63)—is diluted and threatened until its very pillars of security would be undermined and enfeebled. The Trump era supplanted the iconic frontier of this earlier national origin story with the border wall, which, Grandin argues, had become "a monument to disenchantment, to a kind of brutal geopolitical realism: racism was never transcended; there's not enough to go around; the global economy will have winners and losers; not all can sit at the table; and government policies should be organized around accepting these truths" (2019, 272).

Solnit calls this worldview, with a delicious irony, "Trumpworld," in which "nothing is really connected to anything else, so no one has any responsibility for anything else" (2020). As Doreen Massey argued in 2005, long before the Trump presidency, there was a tendency to curtail and limit space through "a protective pulling-up of drawbridges and a building of walls against the new invasions," producing a "locus of denial, of attempted withdrawal from invasion/difference," creating a "politically conservative haven" (5). Latour put it more directly, arguing that Trump's administration, rather than confronting issues such as immigration or the climate emergency, "decided to keep America floating in dreamland" (2018, 7).

In contrast, Massey argues that "places are collections of…stories, articulations within the wider power-geometries of space" (2005, 130), integrating space and time in complex relations that cannot be simply drawn on a map or divided by walls. What is special about such "events of place" is "precisely that throwntogetherness [*sic*], the unavoidable challenge of negotiating a here-and-now (itself drawing on a history and a geography of thens and theres); and a negotiation which must take place within and between both human and nonhuman" (140). Massey sees place (region, nation, world) as a *constellation* of processes rather than a thing" (141; emphasis added), and certainly not a thing as bounded and inward looking as Trump's nation-state. The politics required of Massey's constellation denies notions of settled coherence and simple binary thought (good/bad, North/South, winners/losers, and so forth) and would rather recognize "a world which demands the ethics and the responsibility of facing up to the event; where the situation is unprecedented and the future is open. Place is an event in that sense too" (141). Trump's State of the Union address denied the existence of others' stories, refuting any sense that, in LeAnne Howe's words, "America is a tribal creation story, a tribalography" born out of the many contacts and exchanges between peoples (2013, 13). In her view, echoing Massey's idea of constellation, America is the active worlding of many tribes, a plurality of voices, a "symbiosis" that functions to "connect…in past, present, and future milieu…bringing things together…making consensus…one thing to another" (20, 31).[15]

Unlike Trump's "America floating in dreamland," Howe's words, like Massey's spatial politics, necessitate negotiation and "invention," ethics, responsibility, and a sense of care for the world in all its elements, "implicat[ing] us, perforce, in the lives of human others, and in our relations with nonhumans" (Massey 2005, 141). Trump-era politics endorsed bounded stories of a self-interested United States contained within a metaphorical and literal wall, whereas what Howe and Massey define, and this book also argues, is that places (regions and nations, the West, and the World) are more porous, "woven together out of ongoing stories, as a moment within power-geometries, as a particular constellation within the wider topographies of space, and as a process, as unfinished business" (Massey 2005, 131). According to Howe, such "unfinished business," with all its stories, "continually bring us into being" (2013, 31), possessing the imaginative power of *bringing worlds back* into view, *bringing down walls*, and *weaving together threads* that just might connect us rather than divide us. This recalls Said's "worldliness" and builds what Gloria Anzaldúa once called "the bridge to the world," because "staying 'home' and not venturing out from our own group comes from woundedness, and stagnates our growth. To bridge means loosening our borders, not closing off to others. Bridging is the work of opening the gate to the stranger, within and without" (Anzaldúa and Keating 2002, 574, 3).

◄ 1 ►

ON WORLDING

But to dream the world is not to live it. For us, beauty does
not grow from the dream, it explodes in the entanglement.
—Édouard Glissant, *Treatise on the Whole-World*

You think our country's so innocent?
I think our country has plenty of killers.
—Donald Trump, quoted in David Shields,
Nobody Hates Trump More than Trump: An Intervention

WORLDING STORIES

W.G. Sebald wrote, "I think of how little we can hold in mind, how everything is constantly lapsing into oblivion with every extinguished life, how the world is, as it were, draining itself, in that the history of countless places and objects which themselves have no power of memory is never heard, never described or passed on" (2001, 24). The fiction discussed in this book imagines worlds to counter such a narrowing vision epitomized by the values of the Trump era outlined in the introduction. Rather than "draining" the world of its "countless" stories, these novels bring them forth to challenge established myths, constructs, and rhetoric that hold a dominant single world *in place*—for example, the world of frontier mythology, patriarchal control, white supremacy, and violent repression in the US West ("Americans…pioneers…pathfinders," as Trump put it). The works considered, in contrast, *bring forth* worlds from within and without America, often historical, sometimes surreal and jarring worlds that reopen and dialogize the closed, presumed world that many in contemporary US culture and politics portray as a healthy and acceptable norm. As Grandin argues, "Trumpism is an extremism turned inward, all-consuming and self-devouring" (2019, 7), because although the old ideal of the frontier as a space where Americanism defined itself through Manifest Destiny, conquest, or regenerative violence was over, its ideology persisted. Expansion became contraction and reduction, a resettling around prescribed limits and closed definitions of what it meant to be

21

American in the twenty-first century. Instead, a new power geometry arose recognizing that "the world's horizon is not limitless; not all can share in its wealth; and the nation's policies should reflect that reality" (8). Rather than a "humane" understanding of limitation (of resources, wealth, or opportunity) and the consequential appreciation of necessary shared international responsibilities, what transpired instead was "that recognition of limits requires domination" (8). This meant a virulent gathering up of power into the hands of the few and, with it, a genuine suspicion of engaging collectively with the world outside.

Iain Chambers once commented that postmodernity is concerned not with the "end of the world," but rather with "the potential ending of *a* world: a world of European, enlightened rationalism and its metaphysical and positivist variants." Its function was "to contest a world that is white, male and Eurocentric" and to put the notion of such a single dominant world *under pressure* until it is "cracking apart as both internal and external forms of history, knowledge and power multiply [and] Old meanings do indeed find themselves meaning-less" (1996, 202). As the introduction argued, such a unanimous worldview, heightened under Trumpian ideology, has the effect of stultifying the sense of worlds (of possibility, of becoming, of imagination) and presenting instead something limited and contained until what emerges is a feeling of being "worldless" (Cheah 2016, 177) or "floating in dreamland." Central to this is a "linear understanding of universal progress with its temporality of endless succession in which time becomes a perpetually self-renewing resource" (Chambers 1996, 200). The time-space compression of globalization intensifies this process of enclosure, "levelling the world's opening to the other, because its fundamental imperative is the mastery of finitude through the management and appropriation of time" (Cheah 2016, 179). Globalization's efforts to control and manage time "[destroy] the worlds to-come" (179–80) by reducing alternatives, constraining difference, and "levelling the world's opening to the other." Following Heidegger in this argument, Cheah sees globalization as a force of "unworlding" with the world reduced to a "picture" or "worldview" with beings as static objects framed and ordered as in a painting. Hence, "The world is no longer a meaningful whole but merely what we create through subjective representation" (121), enclosed by the language that defines it and the power behind those words. The product of such a worldview is what Heidegger calls "the certainty of representing" and "an objectivity that has become flat and devoid of background" (2013, 127, 142). In Cheah's words, it "destroys the worlds to-come."

Nevertheless, these forces of unworlding might be interrupted and subverted by what Cheah calls "an other immanent force of worlding" (2016, 180).[1] As Muthyala stated earlier, literature has the capacity to "reworld" through "discursive contestation," and, for Cheah, fiction's "peculiar ontological status" challenges this reductive process of "unworlding." It is literature's "undecidability that opens the world," interrupting linearity and introducing alternative temporalities, shifting the vertical and the horizontal structures of narrative, to unsettle the established and defined "world" (180, 212). Literature *makes* worlds as it reaches beyond authorial presence to connect with others (readers), thereby engaging affects and reason, while stimulating further "undecidable" and unpredictable imaginative creativity. As Cheah remarks, fiction is a "structural setting-adrift of meaningfulness" that functions "by tearing the succession of time and interrupting the continuity of past, present, and future" (182). Thus, for example, in Téa Obreht's *Inland* (see chapter 4), different temporalizations, migrations, and cultures collide in the nineteenth-century West, bringing Syrian Turks, Greeks, Anglo-Slovenes, and English together, revealing what she calls "the world in all its workings" (2019, 80). As we experience this turbulent mix, temporality shifts until the living and the dead, the past, present, and the future, take voice to speak through the book. Obreht's *worlded* West is far removed from Heidegger's enclosed world, "flat and devoid of background," and has more in common with LeAnne Howe's (see chapter 6) tribalography, as a complex space of interlocking histories, myths, native stories, travelers' tales, immigrant pasts, spiritualist séances, ghostly presences, and dramatic visions. As Latour has written, to counter reductionism, one must "*generate alternative descriptions*" because "without doing this we could perhaps utter astute opinions or defend respectable values, but our political affects would be churning in a void" (2018, 94). "Now more than ever," as the Native writer Tommy Orange has said, "I believe fiction can change minds, build empathy by asking readers to walk in others' shoes, and thereby contribute to real change" (2018a).

Worlding is a positive, critical concept through which to put the notion of *a world* under pressure until it cracks apart. As discussed in the introduction, diversity, disparity, and opposition are central to the dynamic *frictional* fiction I consider in this book, where a unanimous conceptualization of *a world* is disrupted by *worlding* bringing into the frame multiple and different worlds colliding—like the "city swollen by refugees" in Mohsin Hamid's *Exit West*. As he writes, with an astute sense of contemporary relevance, "The news in those days was full of war and migrants and nativists, and it was full of fracturing too, of regions pulling away from nations, and cities pulling away from hinterlands, and it seemed that as everyone was coming together everyone was also moving apart. Without borders nations appeared to be becoming somewhat illusory, and people were questioning what role they had to play" (2017, 155). Under such conditions of friction, questioning and contestation emerge as generative worldings. Rob Wilson summarizes the worlding explored in the chapters that follow as

> an active force gerund, [that] would turn nouns (world) into verb (worlding), thus shifting the taken-for-granted and normal life-forms of the market and war into the to-be-generated and remade. As such a *gerundive* process of situated articulation and world-making, "worlding" thus would help deepen and show how modes and texts of contemporary being and uncanny worldly dwelling (as in reading the language of first-world novels against the imperial grain, for that matter) can become a historical process of taking care, and setting limits, entering into, and making the world-horizon come near and become local and informed, situated, instantiated as an uneven/incomplete material process of *world-becoming*. (Wilson and Connery 2007, 212)

Worlding the Western employs this "process" as a critical locus to interrogate the assumed goals of Manifest Destiny, of empire, of neoliberal expansion, of patriarchal, gendered, and racial dominance in the West, seeing instead how small worlds matter, how lived worlds have value outside the sweep to homogeneity, patriarchal norms, and the broadly agreed targets of global capitalist accumulation. The fiction analyzed opens doors into worlding—an *Exit West* (to borrow from Mohsin Hamid)—taking us outside these long-held associations, historical indicators, and recent political recuperations to exit *this* West through worlding, putting back the "differential, transnational, mongrel, and situated" (Wilson and Connery 2007, 210). As Hamid has said, and as the novels in this book illustrate, "the West is just an idea, and that idea is changing, dissolving, reforming" (2018a).

As if responding to these ideas, toward the end of Diaz's *In the Distance*,

Håkan, having traveled across Europe, America, and out into the world, sees a globe for the first time in the house of a wealthy California wine-maker. He "walked around it, trying to track his long journey and seeing how all those lands came together in a circle" (2017c, 328), as if in this moment of interconnectedness, worlds overlap and energize one another, their many different stories countering what Sebald earlier referred to as "the world…draining itself." In such revelatory moments emerging in stories, worlds form through relations as a sense of hope and challenge announced by Édouard Glissant: "Rhizomatic thought is the principle behind…the Poetics of Relation, in which each and every identity is extended through a relationship with the Other" (1997, 11).

MYTH INTERRUPTED, COMMUNITY SHARED

The epigraph to David Shields's book *Nobody Hates Trump More than Trump: An Intervention* (2018) comes from the voice-over to Adam Curtis's 2016 BBC documentary *HyperNormalisation*. It examines the unfolding political and cultural events that led to recent world history: "We live in a strange time. Extraordinary events keep happening that undermine the stability of our world.… [O]ver the past forty years, politicians, financiers and technological utopians, rather than face up to the real complexities of the world, retreated…constructed a simpler version of the world in order to hang on to power. As this fake world grew, all of us went along with it because the simplicity was reassuring." The creation of a "simpler version of the world" as a "reassuring" balm that Curtis links to twenty-first-century politics might also relate to earlier constructions of myth in the manner defined most eloquently by Roland Barthes as far back as 1957. For Barthes, myth puts all the world's "richness at a distance" until "meaning loses its value, but keeps its life" in order to create a simplification wherein the fullness of history is emptied out (1976, 118). With echoes of Sebald's draining of the world, Barthes goes on, "The function of myth is to empty reality: it is, literally, a ceaseless flowing out, a haemorrhage, or perhaps an evaporation, in short a perceptible absence." According to Barthes, myth is "depoliticized speech" where we understand *political* as "the whole of human relations…their power of *making the world*." Within myth, such richness of relations is hollowed out until *making the world* is presented as much more straightforward and natural, and so, as he puts it, it "*goes without saying*" (143; emphasis added). Myth "abolishes the complexity of human acts, it gives them the simplicity of essences…it *organizes a world without contradictions* because it is without depth, a world wide open and wallowing in the evident, it establishes a blissful clarity" (153; emphasis added).

This book takes recent fiction of the US West as a site for an examination of the consequences and continuation of such mythology in the Trump era, tracing this emptying of reality, or "ideological abuse" (Barthes 1974, 11), through recurrent tropes of Westness, such as expansionism, exceptionalism, racism, violence, gender inequality, and border struggles.[2] Barthes wrote that myth "evaporates" the entanglements of history, allowing us to "enjoy this beautiful object without wondering where it comes from" (151). Myth obscured "the ceaseless making of the world" like the ink of a cuttlefish and, in so doing, "fixated this world into an object which can be for ever possessed, catalogued its riches, embalmed it, and injected into reality some purifying essence which will stop its transformation, its flight towards other forms of existence" (155).

Following Barthes, Nancy wrote in 1986 how myth "takes on a whole series of values that amplify, fill, and ennoble this speech, giving the dimensions of a narrative of origins and an explanation of destinies" (1991, 48). For Nancy, myth is foundational because it creates and bonds, closes off rather than opens up, and ultimately defines community through sameness. As discussed in the introduction, frontier myth "founded" America's sense of itself and its world, and then, subsequently, as Grandin argues, its renewal underpinned its contemporary political relevance. Nancy could have been writing of the American West when he said, "The idea of myth alone perhaps presents the very Idea of the West, with its perpetual representation of the compulsion to return to its own sources in order to re-engender itself from them as the very destiny of humanity" (46). This process of *re-engendering* based on the traits of frontier and the myth of American character (via Turner and most presidents until Trump) endlessly asserts a view of natural "destiny": "Myth is not simple representation, it is representation at work…it is *fiction that founds*. And what it founds is not a fictive world, but fictioning as the fashioning of a world" (56; emphasis added). For Nancy, therefore, myth is without end and can only ever be "interrupted" and exposed at its limits: "The myth does not end, nor is it lost, but in fact, because it itself does not disappear, it must be interrupted, its mything or fictioning diverted" (Biro 2019, 68). Interruption, therefore, "disrupts by sending myth's propriety astray, bringing into play fragmentation and variance, it suspends 'fusion and communion' and in this interruption 'something makes itself heard, namely, what remains of myth when it is interrupted'" (Biro 2019 citing Nancy 1991, 61–62). *Worlding the Western* shows, following Nancy's argument, that literary fiction can indeed interrupt or divert myth's "fictioning," using its own stories to disrupt "myth's propriety" and present alternative or errant worlds.[3]

At a time of market capitalism, bounded individualism, new nativism, climate emergency, and migration crises, all seemingly justified by mythic thinking, fiction *puts worlds back* to challenge this "embalmed" and fixed vision and its concomitant dark globalization. If, as Barthes puts it, the goal of myth is "to immobilize the world" (1976, 155), then the work of this book is to counter such stasis, fathoming how and why contemporary fiction might remobilize worlds as complex, relational, and layered. *Worlding* (Barthes's "making the world" or Nancy's "world-making") is a diverse and more open form of cultural politics.

Sounding very much like Édouard Glissant, whose work sustains this book's theoretical approach and will be discussed more fully later, Nancy asserts, "A world is a multiplicity of worlds…and its unity is a sharing out [*partage*] and the mutual exposure in this world of all its worlds" (2007a, 109).[4] The reductionism of globalization, capitalism, and centralized power and the curtailing of ethnicities, histories, and stories conspire to obstruct this "sharing out" of the world, whereas Nancy's sense of justice involves a very different proposition. As he puts it, "Contact, juxtaposition, porosity, osmosis, frictions, attraction and repulsion" redraw "the sharing of community…to each and to all, to each as to all, to each insofar as all," because "it is coexistence by which existence itself and a world in general are defined" (110). For Nancy, crucially, any community (such as those of the American West in our case) should not be defined by mythic territory or as a "worked" or imposed spatial ideal, "be these homeland, native soil or blood, nation, a delivered or fulfilled humanity, absolute phalanstery, family, or mystical body" (15).[5] Instead, it is a *resistance* to such national "completion," or what Nancy calls "the impossibility of community" when viewed as a "fusion" or "project" (81, 15). Community is rather "a gift to be renewed and communicated…not a work to be done or produced" (35). Nancy's writing is about "unworking" established and nostalgic views of a lost community where the individual is its vital component whose destiny defines the "people" and the nation. As Devisch reminds us, "For Nancy, 'being' is 'with,'" and so *community unworked* is seen as always "with," "relationality," and "the between" rather than "One, the Other, or the We" (2000, 244).

Community is, therefore, not a gathering or fusion of people into one but singular beings in more mobile, unfixed relations, because "community is always beyond" this pull to the center or the "congregation."[6] It is "a contact, it is a contagion: a touching, the transmission of a trembling at the edge of being, the communication of a passion that makes us fellows, or the communication of the passion to be fellows, to be *in* common" (Nancy 1991, 61). This sense of community as "infinite, indefinitely open, circulating and transforming" is also a *worlding* that exists "on this edge, destined to this edge and called forth by it, born of interruption, there is a passion" (110, 61). What Nancy calls "passion" here is, therefore, "the voice of the interrupted community, the voice of the incomplete, exposed community speaking as myth without being in any respect mythic speech." At this critical moment of interruption, "one hears just at that instant something else…a kind of echo, but one *that does not repeat that of which it is the reverberation*" (62; emphasis added), which stands apart and singular. This echo *that does not repeat* its source is like the fiction I discuss, which interrupts western myth in order to go beyond it, articulating new forms of shared incomplete community.[7]

Resisting the mythic center, "communication takes place on the limit, or on the common limits where we are exposed and where it exposes us" (67), and once again the difference is between exposing or imposing, where the latter is reductive and mythic. Through exposed and vulnerable communication, as in fiction, something is opened up, not closed down, something "inaugural" takes place, "from you to me, from silence to speech, from the many to the singular, from myth to writing," and, in so doing, "once myth is interrupted, writing recounts our history to us again…without its unfolding being imposed upon us" (67, 69). For Nancy, literature that interrupts myth "inscribes being-in-common, being for others and through others," because "to write for others means in reality to write because of others," and "we would not write if our being were not shared" (66, 69). Once more, this articulation of being-in-common, for and with others, is a form of politics, but one resisting completion and instead "opening community to itself, rather than to a destiny or to a future" (80).[8]

The American West provides a powerful test case (a laboratory of the future, to borrow a phrase from Charles Bowden), in which many of these ideas have been ever present yet historically masked or denied in the rush toward unanimity and nation building, overriding a just world of sharing, mutuality, and coexistence. Rather than the myth of a closed, unified community, of "America Great Again" in contemporary parlance, Nancy hopes "to open the bad infinite of globalisation, that first and foremost still is a reductionist desire to unify the world under the form of capitalist economics" (Meurs, Note, and Aerts 2009, 43). He points toward "coexistence whose indefinite intertwining is the sole ground on which the 'form' of existence rises…[but] there is only the 'with,' proximity and its spacing, the strange familiarity of all the worlds in the world." It is the "with" that joins, connects, relates individual "existents" (as Nancy calls them) into "coexistence," but without any univocal presence "that would loom over the world" and restrict its multiplicity. Ultimately, this sense of world is inscribed by "common impropriety…non belonging and…non dependence, the absolute errancy of the creation of the world" (Nancy 2007a, III).

The *errant* or *errancy* is a concept central, as we shall discover, in Glissant's writing, signifying among other things Nancy's sense here of the interrupted, mobile and unfixed, because, vitally, "the thought of errantry is a poetics…the tale of Relation" (Glissant 1997, 18).[9] For both Nancy and Glissant, errant thought "challenges and discards the universal [or mythic]—this generalizing edict that summarized the world as something obvious and transparent, claiming for it one presupposed sense and one destiny," favoring instead opacity, relations, and diversity (20). As problematic as errancy sounds, it reminds us most obviously of Nancy's resistance to fusion, communion, and foundational fictions and his preference, like Glissant's postcolonial mind, for "the movement, the agitation of the general diversity of the worlds, which make the world (and which 'unmake' it as well)" (Nancy 2007, 112). Barthes wrote that "errantry does not align— it produces iridescence: what results is the nuance" (2002, 103), and, ultimately, worlding too, like changing angles of refracted light, produces prismatic plays of iridescent color, altering our ways of seeing and being.

TO WRITE IS TO SAY—THE WORLD

Worlding is, therefore, a positive, "iridescent," critical concept through which to put the notion of *a* single unanimous world under pressure. Glissant explained reductionist thinking in terms of the experience of the American frontier in his book *Faulkner, Mississippi*, while noting, at the same time, its potential for change: "What is at work, then, is the formidable enterprise of reduction, from the Diverse to the Same. For participants as well as onlookers, the frontier is the place that includes all that and where, paradoxically, an opening (a transformation, a change) is available at every moment" (1996b, 225). For Glissant, Faulkner's fiction was about the "questioning of the legitimacy of this closed place [the American South]" (2020c, 49), just as the authors examined in this book follow a similar course in relation to the West. As evidenced in his study of Faulkner, Glissant saw literature at the heart of his poetics of Relation and the drive against reductionism: "It is literature that illustrates this movement of freeing up, which leads from our place to the thought of the world… using the powers of the imagination…raising up the network, the rhizome of open identities, who talk and listen to one another" (154). As if directly addressing the very cultural political focus of *Worlding the Western*, Glissant states that "any culture that isolates and closes itself gradually falls into malaise and discomfort, into this imbalance." The danger of this process of closing in is the assumption of an "everyday 'normality'" in which "statements of exclusion and rejection of the other" become acceptable and approved, as under the Trump presidency. Literature, however, has the capacity for countering such "normality" through opening up worlds, connecting people with each other and with places, as an active rebalancing of culture: "To speak of one's surroundings, one's country: to speak of the Other, of the world" (156). In so doing, literature is *errant*, following a "trajectory of wandering" (112), from place to world and back.

Glissant's ideas derive from a close consideration of the Caribbean as a site or crossroads of cultures, a colonial frontier where, through the horrors of slavery and the plantation system, many different uprooted people, cultures, and traditions came into contact. Rather like Mary-Louise Pratt's conceptualization of the contact zone, Glissant saw the Caribbean as a space of complex, rhizomatic relations that gave rise to his important term "Relation" (always capitalized in his writing).[10] As John Drabinski has asked, "What comes after that, the New World, is Relation: the creation of meaning, significance, and connection at the crossroads of the world" (2019, 157). Although not precisely parallel, Glissant's ideas translate to the experience of the American West with its expansionism, migration, and cultural collisions, another "crossroads of the world," but one often masked, as we have seen, by the intensity of a drive toward unanimity, nation building, and racial dominance. Glissant's Caribbean, where "Relation names the culture work at and inside that meeting space,…[is] a tortured geography but also home, place, and site of deep belonging" (1996a, 191), might equally be true of the West but for the powerful mythical constructs managing its narrative and downplaying "Relation" in favor of homogeneity. For Glissant, the geography of the Caribbean islands as an "archipelago" initiated his sense of the world as multiplicity: "unity as fragmentation, fragmentation as a fecund principle" (158). For him, the "newness of the New World is pain, violence, and atrocity, but it is also the making of a world with meaning, language, and possibility" (161).

Central to this process of "world making" (or what Nancy calls *mondialization*) is an awareness of cultural difference (racial, sexual, gendered) and political considerations (on violence, coloniality, and exploitation of environment) working to reopen accepted (and normalized) notions of the *world of the West* (exceptional, patriarchal, white, capitalist, colonial, unanimous, mythic, and so forth). As discussed in the introduction, this accepted world is linear and "horizontal," intimately tied to progress and modernity, or what Glissant calls "filiation," "setting out upon the fixed linearity of time, always toward a projection, a project." It is a "genealogical sequence," implying a line of descent that roots the legitimacy of a people to a particular "creation of the world" or origin story, "by describing in reverse the trajectory of the community, from its present to this act of creation" (1997, 47). This is the narrative arc of Frederick Jackson Turner's "project," examined earlier, drawing a line of filiation across the continent east to west, legitimizing the rights of territorial control and Americanization in the bold, epic portrayal of the creation of a world. Of course, such a line dismisses or erases many different voices, histories, and perspectives and thereby reduces what Glissant terms the potential "expanse of the world" (55).

In western terms, as discussed in the introduction, Howe's tribalography is an example of addressing such erasure, employing indigenous knowledge to "inform ourselves, and the non-Indian world, about who we are" (2013, 3). With echoes of Glissant's errant thought, Jodi Byrd argues tribalography starts from a native base, but "*looks out toward* a region, a hemisphere, to a world," offering "an invitation to improvise and connect" (2014, 56; emphasis added). Ultimately, it is "a powerful analytic tool through which to confront, challenge, and reconfigure the stories colonizers like to tell about themselves and their place in the world" (62). For Howe (see chapter 6), as for all the writers considered in the chapters that follow, stories must continue to be told and reinvented as reminders of what the world means, not as the territory owned and used by the few, but rather as land shared actively and mutually by all living things. As Glissant writes, "It is through the imagination that we will ultimately conquer these derelictions that attack us," through the sharing of stories and the exchange of knowledge, since "it is the whole world that is speaking to you, through so many gagged voices" (2020c, 9, 7).

Thinking of coloniality more generally ("these derelictions that attack us"), Glissant set out how territorial conquest worked as a powerful interlinked system: "The absolute of ancient filiation and conquering linearity, the project of knowledge and arrowlike nomadism, each used the other in its growth" (1997, 56).[11] Cecilia Sjöholm explains succinctly Glissant's struggle against filiation and why in the context of this book it is relevant to the US West: "If we are to succeed, we need to observe the stories, the literature, and the witnessing that tears the horizon of filiation apart, supplanting our expectations of successive orders with a receptive capacity to meet with the entangled web of relations that would arise among those who are ruled over rather than rulers, those that are made invisible rather than seen, and those that are proud of their loss rather than their origin." Hence, this "entangled web of relations" as opposed to the exact line of filiation demands "responding to the voices, the lives and the desires of those who remain obscure in the eyes of history" (Bydler and Sjöholm 2014, 67).

Filiation is played out via the horizontal, linear form most obviously associated with the structures of myth and the epic, like those championed in American stories of westward expansion and Manifest Destiny.[12] Traditionally, the epic is, according to Mikhail Bakhtin, aligned with "the national heroic past" and presents "a world of 'beginnings' and 'peak times' in the national history, a world of fathers and of founding families, a world of 'firsts' and 'bests'" (1990, 13). Thus, Bakhtin coheres with Glissant's sense of filiation. To this extent, the epic appears "walled off from all subsequent times," representing the past as "absolute and complete…as closed as a circle," where "everything is finished, already over," with no room for "any openendedness, indecision, indeterminacy" (16). As a result, the "epic world is constructed in the zone of an absolute distanced image, beyond the sphere of possible contact with the developing, incomplete and therefore re-thinking and re-evaluating present" (17).

Glissant, however, revised theories of the epic in 1990, bringing to the fore this precluded sense of contact and incompleteness to interrogate the closed circle of distance embodied in the traditional form in which "Epic thought is close to that of Myth" (1997, 16n).[13] In 1999 Glissant developed his concept of a new epic literature to challenge this "mythic" form and "establish relation and not exclusion…[and] do without the concept of being, in order to remain astounded by the imagination of becoming, of all the possible becomings of the world, of all possible existings. The question of being is no longer asked in that profitable solitude to which the thought of the universal had been reduced. The universal has been upset and toppled by the diverse" (2002, 292). Rather than a literature of exclusion, distance, and universality, the new epic could be more inclusive and local, giving voice to those lives previously omitted or subordinated to the dominant narrative of epic tales. As with the idea of myth discussed earlier, Glissant argues that epics were put to work as national narratives when, in truth, they were more complex "books of errantry, going beyond the pursuits and triumphs of rootedness required by the evolution of history" (1997, 16). To reiterate, such works were errant and concerned with "the imagination of becoming," not rooting communities into fixed, invariant, and homogeneous states, and existing "without having to merge the Other (the expanse of the world) into a reductive transparency" (55). As Glissant explains, the "thought of errantry is also the thought of what is relative, the thing relayed as well as the thing related. The thought of errantry is a poetics, which always infers that at some moment it is told. The tale of errantry is the tale of Relation" (18). For Glissant, whose critical impetus came from colonialism's grip on Martinique, this new epic was an opportunity to talk back to the dominant culture, stressing the value of "Relation," with the "epic voice retying into the weft of the world, beyond any imposed solitude, exaction, or oppression." In a key phrase defining the function of the new epic and recalling Nancy's notion of *partage* (sharing out), Glissant writes not of exclusion and imposition, but of "sharing in the life of the world" (35).

Worlding the Western applies Glissant's work to the West, finding within recent fiction exemplary *errant* texts that reinterpret these elements of the epic to tell different, challenging stories of region, nation, and world. So rather than the horizontal form associated with myth and the epic, many of the novels I discuss move differently, as discussed in the introduction, following nonlinear, errant trajectories, moving "vertically," circling, or in reverse, unsettling space and time and throwing new light onto established views of the West and the world.

In short, this new epic fiction *worlds* to challenge the single fixed concept of the world as taken for granted and unanimous. As Amitav Ghosh puts it in *The Great Derangement*, epics bring "multiple universes into conjunction" with settings to "the world beyond" and embracing the expansiveness of time and space (2016, 59). In times of global climate change, for example, which is Ghosh's motivating point, or in an era where the nation-state is turning increasingly inward and bounded, there is a greater need to see the world as dramatically and vitally connected, without a "delimited horizon" (61), where texts are more than local, regional, or national, but rather sweepingly and imaginatively worldly. In Wilson's words from the introduction, echoing Glissant, worlding "enacts openings of time and consciousness to other values and multiple modes of being, projection, and survival" (2018, 8). What this book shows is that fiction of the American West has too often been interpreted as a "vessel for the exploration of…the nation-state," whereas Ghosh suggests that hybridity in the novel is often commonly found in the "outhouses of genre," such as science fiction, fantasy, and the gothic (2016, 59, 66). In the worlding westerns discussed here, such "outhouse" genres developed in novels like *In the Distance, Lost Children Archive, Inland, There There,* and *Exit West* expand regional concerns with global reach and depth.[14] As Ghosh writes, "New hybrid forms will emerge and the act of reading itself will change" as worlding opens up the "dwindling world" (84) to varied and contrary views.

In these new epics, therefore, the process of westering is reimagined as *errant* and relational, and by placing them side by side in the chapters that follow, I deliberately evoke a relational practice, like that approved by Glissant as "Relation" or what he later called "tout-monde" ("Whole-World" or "world-mentality"), "chaos-monde," and "mondialité." Thus, these chapters "sit together as sites of insight, sites of poetry, sites of inter-ruption, and so sites of relation as Relation" (Drabinski 2019, 165).[15] After all, as C Pam Zhang commented, "I think that literature set in the West has always reminded us that ordinary people can lead epic lives. And so that's part of the duality of living here. Life was hard but also beautiful" (Simon 2020).

POSSIBLE WORLDS IN THE WORLD

With Glissant in mind, I wish to return to Jean-Luc Nancy, whose ideas intersect with many explored earlier, such as Solnit (other globalization), Tsing (frictional global connections), and Latour (the Terrestrial). Build-ing on his earlier work on myth and community discussed above, Nancy contrasts the term "globalization" with "mondialization" (world-forming), arguing that the former is the "idea of an integrated totality," while the latter "would rather evoke an expanding *process* throughout the expanse of the *world* of human beings, cultures and nations." For him, mondialization suggests "keeping the horizon of the 'world' as a space of possible meaning for the whole of human relations (or as a space of possible significance)" in contrast to globalization's "different indication…of an enclosure in the undifferentiated sphere of unitotality" (2007a, 28). This book's exploration of worlding is related closely to "world-forming" or mondialization, echoing Nancy's differentiation of terms, teasing out the different ways in which imaginative work constantly reminds us of the world as a "space of possible meaning for the whole of human [and non-human] relations," while countering globalization's insistent and negative pull toward sameness and "unitotality." In an era of closing borders, extreme nationalism, and increasing ecological damage, creative work must find different ways to remind us of such "relations" and direct us toward a greater ethical sense of the world as a still "forming" shared space of possibility and hope. In Nancy's words, we must "give ourselves (open ourselves) in order to look ahead of ourselves," making worlds of habitation and coexistence. In *The Creation of the World; or, Globalization*, Nancy develops these ideas more fully and suggestively, starting with the very title's structure, with its "disjunctive, substitutive, or conjunctive senses." Indeed, each possible interpretation is a provocation to think about what globalization might "do," or, as he asks, can it "give rise to a world, or to its contrary?" (29).

Globalization for Nancy is "agglomeration," a piling up, a conglomeration and accumulation that benefits the few while eroding possibility and "worsening…inequalities" for the many, producing an "un-world" in which "the convergence of knowledge, ethics, and social well-being dissipated, and the domination of an empire made up of technological power and pure economic reason asserted itself" (34). Echoing Nancy's own warnings about myth in *The Inoperative Community* (1991) and Grandin's specific comments on the American myth of frontier discussed earlier, globalization, contrary to its promise of interconnectedness and prosperity, is described by Nancy as "circumscribing the earth more and more in a horizon without opening or exit" (47).[16] Permeated with a "death drive," the world of globalization has to be confronted: "We must ask anew what the world wants of us, and what we want of it, everywhere, in all senses, *urbi et orbi*, all over the world and for the whole world, without the capital of the world but with the richness of the world" (35). The world viewed as a world market, therefore, reduces it to an accumulation and circulation of capital, diminishing its potential richness and difference.[17] Since the publication of Nancy's book in 2002, this ethico-philosophical struggle seems ever more prescient with the increased influence of neoliberal ideology, deregulation, and the various new nationalisms arising across countries from the United States and Brazil to Hungary and Poland, from the United Kingdom to India and Afghanistan.

As discussed in the introduction, one might consider this unworlding process typified by the era of Donald Trump whose "capital" outlook asserted accumulation and retrenchment as central to his slogan of "Making America Great Again," while denying climate change, militarizing the border, and showing no desire to share or open America to the world. As Grandin put it, "Trumpism cultivates an enraged refusal of limits… [where] 'freedom' means freedom from restraint," while recognizing not everyone can be free—hence the wall and the "cruelty, domination, and racism" that maintain this freedom (2019, 275). In Nancy's terms, the sense of the world has been lost, as the West (in the wider meaning) has become globalized. "Our time is thus one in which it is urgent that the West—or what remains of it—analyze its own becoming, turn back…to examine its provenance and its trajectory, and question itself concerning the process of decomposition of sense to which it has given rise" (2008, 30). His words reflect the process undertaken by this book, analyzing the "becoming" of the American West through a "turning back" to examine histories, trajectories, and national "provenance." Think for a moment of Zhang's *How Much of These Hills Is Gold* as an analysis of American provenance (from the French *provenir*, "to come from/forth"), drawing together the overlapping worlds of China and Europe to explore the painful "coming forth" of the West and America.

Nancy argues, "A world is precisely that in which there is room for everyone: but a genuine place, one in which things can genuinely *take place* (in this world)" (2007a, 42). It is, therefore, not an imagined or dreamed space in which things are longed for; it is "genuine," active ("taking place"), and by extension related to creativity. In Nancy's view, the world is "not a [fixed] unity," it "does not presuppose itself," nor is it "given in advance," but a world is a space of "resonances," where things *take place*, "arrive and happen," forming "a totality of places: of presences and dispositions for possible events" (42, 43, 59).[18] Note the plurals here and Nancy's sense of the world as always about *possibility* rather than certainty or fixture: "A world is an ethos, a *habitus* and an inhabiting: it is what holds to itself, following to its proper mode" (42). Applied to the West, these arguments situate it as what I have called elsewhere a critical regionality, not as a "fixed unity" of American values, like those proposed by Manifest Destiny, frontier theory, or contemporary Trumpism, but rather something constantly in production, "a totality of places," humans, nonhumans, and things that "genuinely *take place*" actively and communally.[19] The world seen in this way is not simply the place in which we live, but through which we live as well, ethically and responsibly.

Hence, "*To create the world* means: immediately without delay, reopening each possible struggle for a world, that is, for what must form the contrary of a global injustice against the background of general equivalence" (54). The idea of "general equivalence" is the dangerous leveling off of globalization or the belief in cultural or ideological homogeneity so that all things and all people become interchangeable objects in the marketplace until, as Nancy suggests above, "global injustice" becomes more likely. World-forming (*mondialization*), however, is aligned with "what cannot be accumulated or what is not equivalent," for it has a "value" derived from creation in which "sharing singularity (always plural) means to configure a world, a quantity of possible worlds in the world" (46).[20] The world, therefore, has to be experienced as "singularities, without their plurality constructed as a unitotality," as "unceasing activity and actuality," characterized by "creation as bringing forth…a world—an active sense that is nothing else than the first sense of *creatio*" (61, 65). As discussed earlier, a world is always, therefore, a multiplicity of worlds, a "nontotalizable totality": "The world is always the plurality of worlds: a constellation whose compossibility is identical with its fragmentation, the compactness of a powder of absolute fragments" (Glissant 1997, 155). With this in mind, and recalling Doreen Massey in the introduction, politics becomes a matter of articulating the world in its pluralized "constellation" without either granting a divinely mandated superiority to the human subject or falling into a delusional all-encompassing point of view. As Nancy put it in an interview: "I believe in particular that right now a profound movement is taking place, a continental drift of sense or thought, between the thoughts of yesterday and those still to come, between those of the old West and those coming from the diverse elsewheres that are no longer elsewhere, and it is there that we discover plenty of tasks for thought" (2007b, 534). Although talking of the broadest sense of the West here, Nancy's remarks allow us to return to the subject of this book and how in our example of the US West there is also "a profound movement…taking place" in which fiction "coming from…diverse elsewheres" creates worlds to challenge the "centrifugal spiral" of American empire (2007a, 47).

WHAT WORLDING DOES

In my discussion of Rebecca Solnit's *Infinite City* in *Affective Critical Regionality* (2016), I stressed how her creation of a new atlas of region understands that San Francisco contains layered, active, and mobile worlds within itself. Her vision is of a *worlded* and *worlding* space, echoing Nancy's "diverse elsewheres":

> Places are leaky containers. They always refer beyond themselves, whether island or mainland, and can be imagined in various scales, from the drama of a back alley to transcontinental geopolitical forces and global climate. What we call places are stable locations with unstable converging forces that cannot be delineated either by fences on the ground or by boundaries in the imagination—or by the perimeter of the map. Something is always coming from elsewhere, whether it's wind, water, immigrants, trade goods, or ideas. The local exists—an endemic species may evolve out of those circumstances, or the human equivalent—but it exists in relation, whether symbiotic with or sanctuary from the larger world. (2010, vii)

Within her sense of the local is a measured reminder of its dialogic relations with everything around, below, and above, in the "various scales" that together constitute its being. In the key line "Something is always coming from elsewhere, whether it's wind, water, immigrants, trade goods, or ideas," she locates the local as relational and dynamic, bound to all manner of human and nonhuman forces that function collectively in its construction. Any one apparent space, Solnit reminds us here, is, in reality, constituted of ever-forming and -deforming interrelated human and nonhuman worlds. *Worlding the Western* builds from such recognition, tracing how any space, and in this case in particular the American West, is both worlded and worlding, or, as Martin Heidegger might have put it in a different context, the West "worlds." As Heidegger explains, "Wherever those decisions of our history that relate to our very being are made, are taken up and abandoned by us, go unrecognized and are rediscovered by new inquiry, there the world worlds" (1975, 45). These are the very processes of worlding examined in this book, of history "made," "taken up," and "abandoned," "unrecognized" and then "rediscovered" through different forms of writing, becoming new inquiries into the West and the world.

Pheng Cheah expands on Heidegger's suggestive remark: "A world is precisely what cannot be represented on a map. Worlding is not a cartographical process that epistemologically constructs the world by means of discursive representations, but a process of temporalization. Cartography reduces the world to a spatial object. In contradistinction, worlding is a force that subtends and exceeds all human calculations that reduce the world as a temporal structure to the sum of objects in space. Imperialist cartography is such a calculation in the sphere of geopolitical economy" (2016, 8). Rather than the tendency to "reduce the world as a temporal structure to the sum of objects in space" to be defined, ordered, and controlled, Solnit's atlas of San Francisco, to return to that example, is an "opening" of all the "unstable converging forces" that constitute place and region as a complex site of contrariness, deep layers of time, and an awkward, immeasurable hauntedness. This tracing of worlds, through the "opening up of a world," like that of the American West, in multiple and different ways, is the focus of this book, since, as Heidegger understood, "the work opens up a *world* and keeps it abidingly in force" (1975, 44).

My aim here is to achieve a consideration of the West as what Heidegger terms a "setting forth" (45), showing how it has always been and continues to be a *worlded* space of *worlding*, where people, nations, languages, habits, species, and energies entangle. Plainly, I am not arguing for the uniqueness of the West or its exceptionalism, since these assumptions are bound to what Cheah called above "imperialist cartography," driven by the old myths and narratives spun to establish and reinforce dominant ideologies that contributed to a narrowing down of place and space, promoting unhealthy nationalism, racism, sexism, exploitation, and bigotry. Solnit expresses this entanglement of worlded western space through a specific example: "Pocatello, Idaho has had its inventions and tragedies: a heartbreak that can be mapped out in six blocks, with bars and slammed doors and a bedroom; the tale of what happened to the lands of the Shoshone and Bannock; a gold rush; the larger forces of geology and climate and animal migration and watersheds" (2010, vii). This sweeping line explicitly draws the relations of place from the intimate to the planetary, local to worldly, human to nonhuman, but in such a nonhierarchical way that what emerges is an edgy composite of an entangled, shared, alternative cartography. This is, as Solnit points out, a "mapping," but one unlike that associated with imperial, linear, reductive, or grid-like constructions, described by Valeria Luiselli as "a spatial abstraction; the imposition of a temporal dimension" (2013, 19). "In essence," she continues, "an anatomist and a cartographer do the same thing: trace vaguely arbitrary frontiers on a body whose nature it is to resist determined borders, definitions, and precise limits" (22). The mapmaker sees the world like a cadaver, reducing its liveliness to arbitrary lines, scales, and measurements that fail to convey the actual depth and variety of Solnit's worlding Pocatello, for example. "A map," Luiselli writes, "like a toy, is an analogy of a portion of the world made to the measure of the eye and the hand. It is a fixed superimposition on a world in perpetual motion" (26). Alternative cartography, like that created in Solnit's *Infinite City*, is an attempt to capture the spirit of what Luiselli calls "a world in perpetual motion," always overflowing, like her description of Mexico City, as "a stain, a trace, a distant memory of something else" (28). This is what Cheah meant earlier by "worlding [as] a force that subtends and exceeds." As we shall see later, such alternative, *overflowing* cartographies—alternative mappings—have become an increasing aspect of so many of the worlding westerns examined in this book.

As stated earlier, Rob Wilson's work has helped to define worlding, and his persuasive arguments and political integrity have a specific relationship to the American West, for, as he explained, the "crucial first trajectory of *The Worlding Project* as a critical-poetic emergence" grew, he says, "out of William Everson's west-coast and post-Beat Big Sur commitment to forge a critical-poetic regionalism here, a consciousness of sea and coast and redemptive Eros in which 'God finds you in the landscape,' as well as the Albert Hofstadter translation project of 'Building, Dwelling, Thinking,' that came out of Heidegger but took far different, more, vulgarized postcolonial turns (as Spivak urged), as situated in consciousness-transforming, and place-making turns here in this 'borderlands'/place of holy crossings Santa Cruz" (2008).[21] Like Solnit's western emphasis, Wilson's hybrid "critical-poetic regionalism" was born from the colliding borders of North and South and the urgent presence of the Pacific Rim, as well as an engagement with Heidegger and a response to postcolonial critics like Spivak. The product was an active sense of worlding as a method for questioning an overly dominant and static worldview tied to capitalism, corporate globalization, bounded individualism, and their deep-seated values and ideologies. As native botanist Robin Wall Kimmerer puts it, a scientific perspective that separated "knowledge from responsibility" (2013, 346) too often bolstered such a view.

Since *The Worlding Project* (2007), the political impetus of Wilson's work has accelerated in the light of "the devastating consequences of Trumpism (cum Putinism) in the United States," calling it "an authoritarian amplification of statist capitalism that embraces profiteering regimes, anti-multiculturalism, financial deregulation, refugee hostility, sporadic and anti-terrorist war, and counter-factual spectacle to create social chaos, reterritorialization, capitalist capitulation, and planetary indifference" (2018, 4–5). Faced with such powerful political shifts and their consequent narrowing of worlds, despite the "promises" of globalization, it is perhaps no surprise, as this book will argue, that there is an ever-greater need for sustained processes of imagination and action seeking to extend our capacity for worlding to interrupt this increasingly static, one-dimensional worldview. As Glissant and Nancy asserted above, and Wilson reiterates, worlding is "world-making," "mysteriously gerundive, a world-forming verb more than any pregiven noun, suggesting actions or tactics to counter the norms and ruses of 'globality achieved.'" Worlding enacts creative relations of becoming so that the one-dimensional or closed mind is opened up to "other values and multiple modes of being, projection, and survival," removing boundaries between subject and environment, seeking "emergent connections to and articulations with region, place, area, and trans-species forms" (11). Ultimately, as multiple and emergent, worlding necessitates "a projection of body, community, and place creatively keeping open the present for the future" (12). Like Ghosh, Wilson recognizes a time of "great derangement" wherein worlding is even more urgent, because "we are living through the crisis of everyday de-worlding, meaning a dismantling of the life-world threatening multi-species endangerment, environmental destruction, extreme weather events, dismantled health plans and work regimes, resource plundering, and far-flung precariousness and cruelty as norm" (4).

This "de-worlding" seems bound up with the US West's myth of endless "modernization and progress," as Tsing terms it, and "the assumption that the trope of progress is sufficient to know the world" (2015, 20, 21). Under this process, time moves inexorably into the future like an arrow that we follow, but if this rhythm is altered, if the "forward march" is interrupted, then we become sensitive to different, unnoticed patterns and types of "world-making"—"the divergent, layered, and conjoined"—that "has been ignored because it never fit the time line of progress" (21, 22). Thematic and formal *interruptions* of this kind recall Nancy, who claimed they functioned by "sending myth's propriety astray, bringing into play fragmentation and variance," and are pivotal to many of the texts discussed in this book. For example, *In the Distance*'s central character, Håkan, is displaced from his mythic linear quest for wealth, opportunity, and progress, redolent of the classical westward journey, and plunged into a different, parallel, and alternative temporal experience, taking him *into* the earth, *circling* in time, and seeing the world through *nonhuman* eyes. By interrupting "the modern human conceit" (22) of linear westwardness embedded in Turner's frontier directive and time's arrow, he becomes a figure of "circulation," which, as Friedman argues, "is the archive of mobility…seeing linkages, networks, conjunctions, creolizations, intertextualities, travels and transplantations" (2018, 77). Exposed to such "worlds," Håkan becomes vulnerable to others, precarious, open to unpredictability, unable to rely on the stable structures of community, often out of control, yet these worldly encounters throw him into the world all over again, "remaking" him "as well as others" (Tsing 2015, 20). A world limited by individualist dreams and narratives of progress is here destabilized and opened up, remade instead as multiple interacting *worlds* that "show us how to look around rather than ahead" (22).

Håkan's diasporic circling reopens and redefines culture and identity as spatial and temporal, "as moving, not in a line but through different circuits" (Hall 1995, 207), emphasizing relations beyond the self and beyond the human, connecting with the widest "circuits" and flows of the natural and human worlds. Worlding articulates these processes: following, connecting, knotting, but also interrupting a horizontal or linear worldview with a vertical one that is transversal, cutting through and digging down through layers of accumulated history and myth (symbolically carried out by Håkan or through the alternative archive, in Valeria Luiselli's *Lost Children Archive*). In this process, the world is revealed not as a single totality, but rather as "worlds," complex, messy, and troubled, because, as Donna Haraway puts it, "We cannot denounce the world in the name of an ideal world" (2016, 12). Håkan's journey (like all the other characters' journeys in the novels I discuss)[22] shifts him from "an ideal world" imagined as the immigrant dream of American success to an experiential series of worlds—"the business of being"—that collides with him "against the current of settlers" (Diaz 2007c, 282, 121). As Barthes put it, "The other is in a condition of perpetual departure, of journeying; the other is, by vocation, migrant, fugitive" (2002, 13).

Crucially, as Wilson declares, "Worlding…opens up different ways of being with others and being in the world, connecting to other worlds, opening life to other 'lived local temporalities'…and ways of dwelling (or 'being with') above or below the nation-state or the heavily bordered world system." Worlding has the capacity to critique the nation-state's one-dimensional politics of patriotism and nativism, by questioning notions of belonging, borders, and division. Thus, in Pheng Cheah's work, which Wilson refers to in the quotation above, and in keeping with Mignolo's ideas mentioned earlier, the attention is upon the role of postcolonial literature "as a remaking project" (2018, 14) that takes what colonialism and globalization have created and remakes it through the prism of postcolonial world-making power.[23] In such literature, Cheah argues, alternative voices, histories, and "worlds" interrupt the seamless flow of globalization and its tendency toward the reproduction of a single agreed-upon, unanimous world (globality), or "the totality of the world-becoming market," as Wilson puts it (6–7). In many regards, the novels discussed in this book follow a similar "postcolonial" course, interrupting and coming after the "colonial" dominance of such a unanimous world-view: white, male, entrepreneurial, and locked into a Turnerian notion of individualism, progress, and conquest. As Alex Hunt has written, "Post-colonialism holds a mirror to the American West that forces the recognition that it is, more than a regional or national tradition, part of a global literature of colonization, indeed a literature of the Age of Imperialism." Consequently, the West has never actually been a single place, but is rather "crisscrossed, torn, and stitched" (2011, 231) with the traces of empire: indigenous peoples, Spanish, Mexican, Africans, and Anglos woven into its history, literature, and geography. In the chapters that follow, I explore worlding as a critique that enacts "the excavation and connection of alternative histories and their different temporalities that cannot be contained by the progressive narrative of Western developmentalism" (Lowe and Lloyd 1997, 5). Once exposed, these traces are the very matter of worlding.

"What West?"

Hernan Diaz's *In the Distance*

We cannot denounce the world in the name of an ideal world.
—Donna Haraway, *Staying with the Trouble: Making Kin in the Chthulucene*

THIS BOOK OF THE WORLD

Describing the geography of the American West, Lucy Lippard's *Under-mining* establishes a crucial framework for my approach to Hernan Diaz's novel *In the Distance*: "The horizontal is iconic in the western landscape, representing the onward and outward expansion, or Manifest Destiny. First came footpaths, then exploratory trails, most following those made by the First Nations—a history unfolding 'as a geometry of interruption and yearning.'...Then came wagon roads, railways, highways—extended construction leading to sprawl. We are drawn through American land-scape on 'the fingers of imperialism'" (2014, 15). Diaz proposes an inter-ruption to such an "iconic," linear, and progressive mapping of the West, marked in contrast by verticality, discontinuity, and what I will call, fol-lowing Édouard Glissant, *errantry*. As this chapter will show, such an approach replenishes a sense of world, seen not as a predictably defined imposition, but rather as a "huge entanglement...where the voice of every community is heard. The accumulation of common places, of dis-placed cries, of mortal silences" (Glissant 2020c, 15). Robert Macfarlane's *Underland* (2019) amplifies this shift from the linear to the relational fur-ther as a way of "countermanding...quick greeds and furies with older, slower stories of making and unmaking" (15): "When viewed in deep time, [that is, moving beyond horizontal/"flat ontology"] things come alive that seemed inert. New responsibilities declare themselves. A convivi-ality of being leaps to mind and eye. The world becomes eerily various and vibrant again. Ice breathes. Rock has tides. Mountains ebb and flow. Stone pulses. We live on a restless Earth" (15–16). Such a "conviviality of being" allows us to see ourselves as "part of a web of gift, inheritance and legacy" stretching across time, caught within an ever-changing network of responsibility, care, and relationality that Glissant would call *"tout-monde"* (Whole-World).[1]

These approaches intersect with Bruno Latour's *Down to Earth* (2018), discussed in the introduction, linking together the election of Donald Trump, Brexit, and the migration crisis as symptoms of and reactions to a New Climatic Regime in which the earth has become too remote and detached from our lives. Politicians want "to shelter themselves from the world" (2), building walls to isolate nations from other nations, looking after individual and national interests rather than seeing the Whole-World as a shared and related enterprise of care and attachment. Latour redefines migration as a more "generalized" (worldly) concept made up of forces "sweeping across all our borders…migrations without form or nation that we know as climate, erosion, pollution, resource depletion, habitat destruction," and, as he argues, "Even if you seal the frontiers against two-legged refugees, you cannot prevent these others from crossing over" (10).[2] He therefore proposes an approach that bridges contradictions: first, *"attaching oneself to a particular patch of soil,"* and, second, *"having access to the global world"* (12; emphasis in the original).[3]

However, echoing the dominant *horizontal* perspective sketched above, the shift from local to global under globalization seems only to have reduced the world to a "single vision" rather than fulfilling its initial promise of *"multiplying* viewpoints, *registering* a greater number of varieties" (12). Because this form of globalization benefits a "small number of interests" and is "imposed on everyone and spread everywhere," such positions, according to Latour, must be *interrupted* and the "limited view" they present challenged (13). Any simple sense of the local (or "Local-minus"[4]) alone cannot achieve this. A move to the Global (capitalized in Latour), however, "delineated scientific, economic, and moral horizons," creating "a pioneering frontier of modernization" and driving people away from (local) homelands "to profit from the world."[5] Those who deviated from this path, according to Latour, were "the (neo-) natives, the antiquated, the vanquished, the colonized, the subaltern, the excluded," simply "dregs, rejects" (27), all sharing much with the contemporary representations of migrants and the marginalized.

In the example of the American West, Latour's line of modernization equates to Frederick Jackson Turner's frontier demarcation between savagery and civilization or to Lippard's definition of Manifest Destiny above. As discussed in the introduction, Latour views Trumpism as having maintained "the American ideal of the Frontier" while "abandoning the rest of the world to its fate" (36). In Trump's call to "Make America Great Again," his followers have put themselves "*Out-of-This-World*," "outside of all worldly constraints, literally *offshore*, like a tax haven" (34, 36), viewing the earth or the "Terrestrial" as an endless depository of raw materials, and, therefore, not sharing with others any responsibility for a common world. For this reason, Diaz's novel about nineteenth-century migration and frontier expansion in the West has a particular resonance for readers today. Amid this bundle of *contemporary* contradictions about freedom, opportunity, individualism, and deregulation (the frontier dream) looms an "offshore" or remote approach to the world, the earth, and its inhabitants—the latest example of the flat/horizontal perspective discussed above. As Latour puts it, Trumpian politics is "post-politics" because it is "literally, a politics *with no object*, since, it rejects the world it claims to inhabit" (38).

Latour proposes instead a shift to the *Terrestrial*, whereby "space has become an agitated history in which we are *participants among others*" (42; emphasis added). So modernization's push toward an "infinite horizon…a limitless frontier" of the Global has to change, but so also does the desire for any *unquestioning return* to the Local with its attachments to "ethnic homogeneity, a focus on patrimony, historicism, nostalgia, inauthentic authenticity" (42, 53). This is the "negotiation" Latour advocates. "Whereas the Local is designated to differentiate itself by closing itself off, the Terrestrial is designated to differentiate itself by opening itself up" (51). Latour advocates a move "down to earth": "For the Terrestrial is bound to the earth and to the land," but, critically for the relevance of this to my argument, "it is also *a way of worlding*, in that it aligns with no borders, transcends all identities." Key to this shift to the Terrestrial as an action of worlding is that the linear perception of the Local and the Global "as successive sightings along a single trajectory has never made any sense" (54). The Global "grasps all things from *far away*, as if they were *external* to the social world and completely *indifferent* to human concerns. The Terrestrial grasps the same structures from *close up*, as *internal* to the collectivities and *sensitive* to human actions, to which they *react* swiftly" (66–67). Such remote thinking distorts our perception of the earth—it is the earth known only from the outside (equivalent to the "offshore" view [72])—and speaks only of rationality, science, and reality. The *inside view* is dismissed as "traditional, intimate, archaic" with the Global as the "horizon of modernity," rather than paying attention to the "subjective and sensitive positions" dismissed only as Local (71).

Echoing Macfarlane above, Latour proposes a "system of engendering" rather than "production," seeing the Terrestrial as full of participating "actors" with various dependencies and relations across time, "cultivating attachments…constantly overlapping, embedding themselves within one another" where "points of *life* proliferate" (83, 88). The Terrestrial (earthbound or worlded) is not archaic or belonging to some lost moment, but relevant and alive, living in deep time and drawing the past into the present and future, *multiplying*. For Latour, it is about being able to attach oneself to the soil and being attached to the world *at the same time* in "a balancing act" (92, 93). Vitally, the Terrestrial does not push people back inside boundaries of nation, region, ethnicity, or identity, nor does it withdraw from such struggles to a position above and grasp the earth as a whole: "The subversion of scales and of temporal and spatial frontiers defines the Terrestrial." Latour, sounding like Glissant, argues that worlding "is not unifying," but instead "atmospheric" and a complex weave of "its entanglements with others" (93). Equally, with a strong echo of Latour's ideas, as a call to arms, Glissant writes, "Let us open up in us this book of the world" (2020c, 104).

BECOMING TERRESTRIAL

With these ideas in mind, I turn now to Hernan Diaz's *In the Distance* (2017), a Trump-era novel that although set in the nineteenth century explores the historical sweep of modernization and ecology through the prism of the American West, dramatizing a migrant journey toward the Terrestrial. To this end, I will also use Édouard Glissant's work to provide a framework of ideas tracing relations between colonization, expansion, the local, the global, and the ecological. Predating Latour, Glissant shares many of his views, particularly on the relations of local and global. As noted in chapter 1, he strives outward (and back again) from specific places (such as his home island of Martinique), engaging with and expressing the world, stressing at every stage the multiple and diverse relations that constitute what he terms "composite cultures," the products of colonization, migration, and unpredictability. He is interested in the "trace" ("a wandering that guides us") left by such processes, both as a path and as formative expressions of culture. What matters is the "common-place" (2020, 9), a place we all have in common and from where we come (broadly, the Local), but which also exists in relation to the world we have in common too (like Latour's Terrestrial). This ultimately defines Glissant's concept of the "Whole-World," experienced in terms of relationality. As in Latour, this is the "exact opposite of globalization, which is seen in entirely negative terms as suppressing difference" by insisting on a crippling sameness—"the birthright, the purity of the race, the integrality, if not the integrity, of the dogma"—whereas Glissant's Whole-World acknowledges instead the messy potentiality of analogy, "creolization," "chaos," or "Chaos-world" (2, 8).

As discussed in the introduction, much engaged writing about the American West today comes from outside, bringing with it new and different perspectives of *worldliness*.[6] What this "outside" might mean, however, is by its very nature diverse, ranging from authors themselves as non-Americans to some who are naturalized citizens born elsewhere or to novels that engage with "Westness" transnationally. Through such outlooks, the world finds its way back into the West at a time when there has been a move in US politics "Out-of-This-World," as Latour has it. Glissant provides a wonderfully expanded explanation of such "fragile knowledge": "Those who meet up here always come from an 'over there,' from the expanse of the world, and here they are, determined to bring to this 'here' the fragile knowledge that they have taken from over there. Fragile knowledge is not imperious science. We sense that we are following a trace" (9). In Diaz's case, he was born in Argentina, grew up in Sweden, was educated in England, and is now an American citizen, but without doubt these varied perspectives present what Glissant called "the weave of illegitimate diversity, the daring of fragmented knowledge" as a direct challenge to "total and systematic" forms or, as I termed it earlier, "horizontal" thought (62).

In the Distance begins echoing Macfarlane's "world…eerily various and vibrant again": "The hole, a broken star on the ice, was the only interruption on the white plain merging into the white sky. No wind, no life, no sound" (Diaz 2017c, 3). Pointedly, this is an "interruption" of something—of a landscape certainly—but I would contend something *more than* a landscape too, a whole mythology of the American West, of Manifest Destiny and expansionism, or what Latour termed "a pioneering frontier of modernization." Diaz deliberately breaks with horizontalism since the seamless whiteness of plains and sky, like the endless vistas of the classical western desert, is *interrupted* by a small vertical event, a broken star, a hole in the silent space, a hole in myth itself. From this point of interruption, the novel continues to disturb established, mythic frameworks: moving its central character along a paradoxical journey from west to east, from movement to stasis, and from the horizontal to the vertical, literally down into the earth itself (from which, as we have seen, he emerges in this opening scene). In Latour's terms, it is becoming Terrestrial.

Recalling my discussion of Jean-Luc Nancy in chapter 1, like all the novels considered in this book, *In the Distance* is an *interruptive* western, a postwestern and postexceptionalist novel that reverses, breaks, stretches, and questions our expectations of the genre while still holding on to its elements, *inhabiting* and *haunting* the form both surreally and provocatively. The novel also interrupts because, as Diaz has said, he wanted "to translate different genres into each other" (Bady 2017); hence the adventure story, bildungsroman, captivity narrative, nature tale, western, and science fiction (especially in its stark desert scenes) blend and overlap into *In the Distance*'s disorientating hybridity. It begins, unsettlingly, west of the West, in Alaska, "the New World's 'new world'" (Kollin 2001, 29), as a "head emerged" from the ice, like a local force from *below*, as if being born into this white world with all its interlinked connotations of race and unending possibility. Yet this figure emerges into an "even, *horizonless* expanse," interrupting the horizontal with a vertical presence from under the ice and earth. Without bearings and direction, as readers, we are simultaneously born into a world of difference and surreality as Diaz, like most of the authors in this book, repurposes the western, deliberately toying with and interrupting tropes, assumptions, and frames of reference so often associated with colonial expansion and racial and gendered hierarchy.[7] Ultimately, in so doing, he interrupts its generic politics, for, as Diaz has commented, "I saw in the Western a slightly derelict genre that was ready to be taken over. And because of its ideological connotations, it seemed like hijacking the Western was a perfect way to say something new about the United States and its history. I wanted to write a book that relies on the Western tradition but ultimately subverts it" (Pinckney 2017). Initially, this icy emergence echoes Native American creation stories, yet this possibility is itself soon interrupted as the rising figure is a "naked," "colossal" white man, "like an old, strong Christ" (Diaz 2017c, 4), a sailor, we are told, caught up in global trading routes from San Francisco to the Sandwich Islands, to China and Japan. As we soon discover, the subject of fascination is the legendary Håkan Söderström, or "Hawk," a migrant, born in Sweden, who has traveled across the world and across America, becoming a vehicle for others' "tales multiplied" (8), embodying myth itself, a myth constructed, as the novel will testify, from the endless retelling of his past adventures as killer, Indian chief, hunter, and leader. When challenged as "lies" by one man on the ship, whose "hand hovered over his holster" (9), Håkan, rather than conforming to the genre's gunfighter trope, simply bangs two half logs together like a "Titan," scaring the man to the ground like a cowering beast.

Diaz has spoken of the western "as stubbornly provincial and parochial…proud of its regionalism," leading to its marginalization as an American genre, failing to "fulfil its promise or its potential" (Bady 2017). As with all the novels considered in this book, *In the Distance* reimagines and enlarges the western, unleashing its potential, mixing the local and global to address complex questions about personal and national identity, belonging and ecology, while boldly rethinking the West as nonexceptionalist and "worlded," bound into a global system of coloniality, capitalism, trade, and migration. Consequently, Diaz conjures what he calls a "highly ideological narrative" of America (Bady 2017) through his surreal examination of the West as a space of coloniality or "the logical structure of colonial domination" in the modern world system (Mignolo 2005, 7). To this extent Diaz *worlds* the western, placing it within this structure, to reveal "injustices" committed "in the name of justice" (8). Echoing both Glissant and Latour, Rob Wilson argues that *worlding* is "shifting the taken-for-granted and normal life-forms [that is, the western's ideology]…into the to-be-generated and remade," until the forces of globalization, with their air of generality and distance, are recast through a process of "de-distancing," "making the world-horizon come near and become local and informed, situated, instantiated as an uneven/incomplete material process of *world-becoming*" (Wilson and Connery 2007, 212). To achieve this, the novel *interrupts* and *disrupts* the underlying apparatus of the western and its long-established ideological framings following Håkan's "uneven" and "incomplete" local/global journey toward the Terrestrial.

A REVERSE MANIFEST DESTINY

Beginning in Sweden, the novel seems initially a conventional tale of Old World poverty and the possibility of New World "wonders" (Diaz 2017c, 17); from Gothenburg to Portsmouth to New York, two brothers migrate in search of their fortune and to escape the persecutions and poverty of Europe. However, soon parted, Håkan must find his own way to America, hoping his brother Linus is headed in the same direction. Speaking no English, Håkan is thrust into a strange, disarming whirl where Irish emigrants, the Brennans, take him in, explaining through a "rough map of the world" that they are not going to New York at all, but heading to San Francisco via Buenos Aires. Thus, traveling south and then north to arrive in the West disorientates Håkan, with San Francisco particularly perplexing: "either just sprung up or just partially collapsed" (21). These geographic shifts enhance Diaz's manipulation of genre expectations, since the typical image of American migration is linear and horizontal, simply east to west. Nevertheless, faced with the hysterical clamor for gold on arrival, Håkan's response is to turn inland, eastward, "traversing a whole continent," countering the typical migrant journey westward, in search of his brother in New York (22). His "tedious journey," initially working for the Brennans to survive, is far from the mythic tales Linus had told him of a "dreamlike, outlandish world" and instead defined only by "interminable sagebrush" and "monotony" (25, 24). Even the few towns along the way are "precarious, as if decrepitude had been built into them, the houses seemed eager to become ruins.... [T]he plains began where the thresholds ended" (32).

This West is on the edge of collapse even at the moment of its emergence, tottering between the promise of dreams and gold and the precarious reality of poverty, exploitation, and violence that so often confronts Håkan on his journey. So, when he asks himself, "What would he become?" (178), he reiterates the classic western theme of knowledge through experience, or the generic pattern of a bildungsroman. However, as Diaz's novel demonstrates, his lines of discovery are far from straight or clear, since the central protagonist or "hero" unfolds on a strangely circular but epic journey of "interrupted" motion, refusing to follow the well-trodden paths of western narratives, becoming instead discontinuous, frictional, confused, and irregular, full of fits and starts, with none of the supposed certainty of horizons West, or what historian Frederick Jackson Turner called "a continually advancing frontier line" (1961, 38).[8] Turner, like many before him, saw modernity as a distinct horizon, a triumphal historical process whose linearity Diaz interrupts by suspending time and space until Håkan felt "he had journeyed only from one now to another" (2017c, 239).[9] *In the Distance* tracks a discrepant path, interrogating and contrasting distant horizons with the close at hand, immanent, and material details of life through its central character's sojourn.

Håkan is a migrant from Sweden drawn to America and its promise of a good life, only to find himself adrift, alone, and desperately trying to find his brother whom he imagines in New York. His journey contradicts the linearity of typical frontier stories, moving "against the current of settlers" (121), heading east, not west, and simultaneously reversing assumptions of the western genre. Despite Håkan's fierce masculinity and immense size, he is captured, tortured, sexually exploited, victimized, and haunted by the terrible violence he both witnesses and commits. His travels are anti-Turnerian, "following a reverse Manifest Destiny" (Pinckney 2017), "away from the past but not into the future…in a constant present…but never heading towards a more or less certain destination that he could foresee" (Diaz 2017c, 239). The novel's very direction is unsettled, for rather than simply moving *across* and *over* the landscape like Turner's progressive horizontality, it circles around, returns, and digs down into the land itself, thus interfering with human time and history, engaging with something closer to geologic or, what Macfarlane called, deep time. As Robin Wall Kimmerer explains, in Native traditions such as the Anishinaabe, people "know time as a circle. Time is not the river running inexorably to the sea, but the sea itself—its tides that appear and disappear, the fog that rises to become rain in a different river. All things that were will come again" (2013, 207).

Contradicting the linear assumptions of progressive modernity and so traveling against "the all-consuming business of moving forward" (Diaz 2017c, 141), Håkan *circles* repeatedly around in time and space, undoing through his travails and painful education the myths that had led him, and others, westward in the first place. On a reiterative and worldly journey, he "walked in circles wider than nations," feeling like he had "circled the globe," when, in truth, "it's just a big country" through whose little local histories he experiences the global close at hand and sees the consequences on its landscape (269, 240). As readers we too are "circling the globe," seeing the world through Håkan's eyes, witnessing brutal coloniality strip away the exceptionalist glamour associated with westward expansion, and leaving instead an alternative "reality that no longer ended at the horizon" (239). The horizontal dream of westward expansionism is an exploitation of resources, people, and the earth itself, a conquering territorialism, moving like a "thin crawling line" (143) across the landscape, embodying what Glissant called "invading nomadism…whose goal was to conquer lands by exterminating their occupants," "an absolute forward projection: an arrowlike nomadism…a devastating desire for settlement," associated with colonialism and "an expansion of territory" (1997, 12, 19).[10]

Framed by the dark, brutal realities of Manifest Destiny, Håkan's discontinuous bildungsroman relentlessly exposes a surreal landscape of exploitation and rabid grasping of both space and humanity under the cover of opportunity and aspiration. Abandoned objects symbolically materialize the devastation of "arrowlike nomadism," like "a massive wardrobe" abandoned on the emigrant trail, conjuring a sense of "something profoundly intimate…something conjugal" while being a "concrete embodiment" of the "civilized comforts" Håkan had never known (Diaz 2017c, 134). Shortly after, he sees a rocking chair "swaying back and forth in the open wilderness" and thinks of it as a "word on a page made up by those signs that would forever remain a cipher for him" (136). Such moments of "perverse contrariness" are the "visual embodiment of a world constitutively out of joint, whose surreal dimensions have the effect of traducing the standing world and refracting it through a sinister, dissociative prism" (Giles 2013, 28). In trying to comprehend their meaning, however, Håkan feels strangely "out of place…lonelier than ever—smaller, frailer" (Diaz 2017c, 136), for they signify a West out of joint, turned upside down as expectations are shifted and its underlying imperial, expansionist values exposed and unsettled. The supposed certainties of a frontier mythology based on inevitable, "arrowlike" progress, dominant individualism, and precisely defined racial and gendered power relations—Giles's "standing world"—are loosened by such surreal, disruptive interventions.

Håkan is the accidental witness to these surreal brutalities of the "standing world" exposed by Diaz's "rhetoric of dislocation and transposition, where the sauntering westward narratives of manifest destiny are always liable to find themselves violently reversed" (Giles 2013, 164). In the town of Clangston, for example, Håkan becomes the sexual captive of a mysterious, predatory woman of immense wealth whose wagon is decorated with "painted scenes of men suffering the cruellest torments and of women forced in unspeakable ways" (Diaz 2017c, 38). Her rooms are "beclouded" with the trappings of ostentatious wealth: "Gleams of gold and hints of crimson…silver-framed mirrors, knickknacks, and gilded books with brass clasps…Diptychs, cameos, enamel eggs encrusted with jewels" (47). Yet despite these outward trappings of capitalist gloss and finery, the woman is rotten both physically, with "black, gleaming toothless gums, streaked with bulging veins of pus" (49), and morally, as she exploits and brutalizes migrants, like the Brennans whom she kills for their gold claim. Dressing Håkan up in fine clothes, she sexually assaults him, ushering him "into a new, lonelier region," a West of captivity, exploitation, and colonial power emphasized through the "bending and moulding [of] his body" in a manner traditionally associated with the patriarchal abuse of women in the western genre (49, 50). Reversing

gender as generic norms, he is dressed up for her pleasure, "modelled...
into some ordinary yet precise position," signaling her desire to control
both the gaze and his body, enslaving Håkan within the precise geography
of her claustrophobic world (50). Consequently, the "horizon" that signifies the journey east to his brother becomes "rippling mirages" in which
"he pictured himself out there, running, insect-like, in the distance" (51).
Giving the novel its title, this image shows the extent of Håkan's plight:
the manly "giant" becoming an insect, escaping a West of captivity, not
freedom, a terrible static cage, "an elastic present" (52), where time and
space are dictated not by seasons or his own mobility, but by the absolute
control of his keeper's reductive worldview.[11]

ONE PLACE WHICH IS NOT ONE

Eventually escaping Clangston, Håkan's journey resembles Latour's
notion of "walking on foot inside a flattened landscape," interacting
with humans and nonhumans at close quarters, amid the intensities of
the local landscape, challenging the domineering "Big Picture" or sweeping global context (2007, 192, 186). Håkan's affective journey is cotutored
now by the evolutionary naturalist John Lorimer, who rejects a simple
notion of God as the origin of life, and by an anonymous Native man
who understands how to heal using nature's medicines. Both teach versions of the "Great Chain of Being" as a series of interactions and relations between all things, for if nature is "frozen under the magnifying
glass," it becomes a "barren enterprise," whereas one should "look at the
world with warm affection, if not ardent love," thinking "us all one" (Diaz
2017c, 80–81).[12] Like Latour's Terrestrial rejecting the distanced view, both
men enable a *worlding process* that Lorimer explains: "Each minuscule
being has spokes radiating out to all of creation" (81). It is a view stressing relationality and entanglement as strands of existence, which, rather
than a one-way process from the small (local) to the large (global), is a
series of interrelations, interdependencies, and "correspondences"—or,
put simply, "warm affection, if not ardent love." According to the two
mentors, it is as if in the West, "the whole world gathered to one place
which is not One" (Drabinski 2019, 168). Their shared ecological vision
teaches Håkan that "man can no longer examine his surroundings merely
as a surface scattered with alien objects and creatures related to him only
by their usefulness," for to do so is to imagine the world as something to
be "grasped," "debasing nature by turning it into a storehouse, a symbol,
or a fact" (Diaz 2017c, 81–82). Without such affective relations with the

environment, Håkan realizes we are simply "intruders" (108), like the endless lines of settlers he witnesses crossing the American plains.

After dissecting a hare, Lorimer teaches Håkan that any notion of the "Whole-World" and "the chain that links all things together" relies on multiple "correspondences": "The guts of the anatomised hare faithfully render the picture of the entire world." As he explains, "The hare, like a blade of grass or a piece of coal, is not simply a small fraction of the whole but contains the whole within itself. This makes us all one." Quite simply, "because that hare is everything, it is also us" (81). As in Glissant's philosophy, oneness here is not about reduction or the desire to limit the intense variety of things, but rather a means "to appreciate the multiplicity of roots and the entanglements of relationality against compulsions to unify in the one and the single" (Drabinski 2019, 168). The mentors share a sense of worlding that echoes my discussion at the opening of this chapter, since viewing our environment "merely as a surface," a "storehouse, a symbol, or a fact," reduces the world's diversity to a detached and distant object. What matters is to "listen to the constant sermon of things" because "everything is in everything" (Diaz 2017c, 82, 83). Across time, each flows *processually* into each like "a net of tributary veins, rivulets, and torrents rushing away from the headwaters," yet "nothing in nature is ever final—all ends are ephemeral because they are pregnant with new beginnings" (83).[13] Ultimately, these men teach Håkan a version of what Donna Haraway calls "response-ability" (2016, 36), that is, the ability to respond to and entangle with the world as it is rather than as you might wish it to be—in other words, *worlding*.

Lorimer and the unnamed Indian teach care, responsibility, and an acute attentiveness to life, articulating through Håkan a worlding vision of the West that Diaz's novel returns to repeatedly, whereby the smallest and the largest thing correspond along chains of connection and relation, each intertwined and interdependent.[14] Life, under these terms, is "still in motion," rhizomatically evolving through difference and connection, like the tribal song Håkan later hears: "It had no refrain. No part of the melody…was ever repeated. It flowed forward in an ever-changing rivulet.… When one shift concluded, another group would take over without the slightest interruption or transition" (Diaz 2017c, 87, 113–14). When observing the postmortem practices of the Native man, Lorimer explains to Hawk his admiration for the connectedness he witnesses: "This is true religion—knowing there is a bond among all living things…because even though nothing can be retained, nothing is ever lost" (117). In the words of Jean-Luc Nancy, "This is the meaning of the world as being-with, the simultaneity of all presences that are with regard to one another, where no one is for oneself without being for others" (2000, 84–85).

Thus, through what Glissant would call the "poetics of relation," "the whole is not the finality of its parts" (1997, 192). As a result, therefore, the global is not *at* a *distance* from the local or its context but made "to sit *beside* the 'local'" as a "composition," not imposition, because "things have to be put together…while retaining their heterogeneity," creating a "common world…built from utterly heterogeneous parts that will never make a whole, but at best a fragile, revisable, and diverse composite material" (Latour 2007, 174; 2010, 473–74). Glissant's concept of "Whole-World" is similarly described as "our universe as it changes and lives on through its exchanges, and, at the same time, the 'vision' we have of it" (2020c, 108).[15] But crucially, his sense of "place" (the local in Latour's version) is inseparable from the world, since "the place that we live in, that we speak from, can no longer be separated from the mass of energy that calls to us *in the distance*…in the totality of the world" (73; emphasis added). Rather than resorting to a wider global explanatory metanarrative "in the distance," Håkan, through his relationship with his mentors, composes the world from its local heterogeneous elements, while developing it physically through the circular journey he undertakes throughout the novel. This composition is most evident in the analogy of Håkan's clothing, "mended and adjusted" by Indian women: "keeping the original fabric and structure of the garments and *grafting in* additional material—offcuts from their tents, snippets from old quilts, patches they had woven whenever the scraps were too small" (Diaz 2017c, 123; emphasis added).[16] This "grafting in" reflects a Latourian vision of the West as "fragile, revisable, and diverse," which, like the garment Håkan wears, has a "provenance… impossible to determine," juxtaposing "the European peasant, the Californian trapper, and the itinerant Indian…on an equal footing," presenting an alternative, if idealistic, vision of the *worlded* West as not homogenous or essentialist, but a "universe made of universes" (123, 111). In this image of hybridity, Diaz echoes Glissant's notion of "creolization": "In creolization, you can change, you can be with the other, you can change with the other while being yourself, you are not one, you are multiple, and you are yourself. You are not lost, because you are multiple. You are not broken apart, because you are multiple" (Diawara 2011, 7).[17]

Armed with this new knowledge gleaned from Lorimer and the short-haired Native, Håkan returns to his ongoing quest to find his brother,

Linus, somewhere in the East, traveling against the emigrant trail and the mythic flow of American history. Once more, this reminds us of the novel's rhythm consistently unsettling spatiality, disturbing established linearity to emphasize the impossibility of clear direction, enunciating a journey punctuated by circularity, recrossings, and uncertainty. This is a rhythm Håkan expresses as "cause and consequence, past and future… overturned and scrambled in the reverberations" (Diaz 2017c, 260), where even the emigrant trail is portrayed as "the stench of civilization," with its "swelling reek," a "long, low, creeping line…[a] massive city stretched out into one thin crawling line" (140, 143). It is here that he falls in with the colonist Jarvis Pickett, a Trump-like huckster "elected" as the leader of the wagon train because he promised "a fertile valley, rivalled only by the Garden of Eden," with land for all loyal travelers at the end of their journey. Through Pickett, Håkan is further exposed to the pyramidal brutality of capitalism that "pitched people against each other and had them compete, with presents and favours, for the best plots" in his mythical Eden (161). Håkan commits acts of violence to protect the colonists from what turn out to be "fake Indians" or self-styled "soldiers of Jehu," whose goal is to plunder from those on the westward journey.[18] Håkan's violence is not heroic or redemptive, for it brings only a "feeling of sorrow and senselessness" (174) and therefore, in keeping with Diaz's repurposing of the western, employs "fossilized moments of the Western genre…to disappoint and go against them" (Pinckney 2017). By "disappointing" the reader's expectations, Diaz breaks open these fossilized tropes to reveal their underlying problematic ideological assumptions. In this case, violence is the culmination of coloniality, deceit, and greed, and it leads not to redemption or communal salvation, as so often in the classical western, but to isolation, fear, and further violence. Håkan's ferocity acts "against the sanctity of the human body" and so breaks the chain of being learned earlier from Lorimer and the Native, and in reacting to these violations, he felt an "all-consuming hollowness—a corrosive shadow wiping out the world in its progress…an infectious nothingness colonising everything" (Diaz 2017c, 178, 179). Appropriately, Lorimer and the Native's sense of the world is overwhelmed by an "unworlding," colonizing process, spreading uncontrollably like an infection. This is Håkan's entrapping West that Diaz's novel unveils.

Despite his horror at his actions and his intuitive sense of the "colonizing" process he has inadvertently been party to, Håkan discovers that his acts of violence have grown into a legend, becoming a wider lesson in the distortion of history into myth. Ironically, he has become a mythic figure—"The terrible, the famous Hawk"—because of the savage killings for which he is ashamed: "The truth was awful enough, but who knew how the narrative had been distorted along the way?" (216, 183). Now moving out of the relative shelter of the wilderness and closer to the "civilized" world of cities, under the flag of the new United States, Håkan witnesses a cruel, judgmental place where "the laws of the United States" are driven by retribution and violence (217). This is exemplified by the sheriff who takes him captive and stitches a "coarse, irregular cross" into his chest to "save" him from the "dross of depravity," naming him a "beast from the underworld," an "Amorite," "son of Belial" (219, 222–23). Invoking such biblical references embellishes the sheriff's own mythic status as the conqueror and purifier of Hawk, comparing himself to the "valiant Benaiah, who struck down both a giant and a lion" and to the "king of Israel against the giant Philistine" (225). Yet, like so many of the characters Håkan meets in this supposedly new world of America, religion functions only as a screen for darker actions, for empire building, and, in this case, for making money by parading him in the towns as he takes him back to the Jehu brethren for reward and punishment.

Håkan is freed from captivity by the kindly and sensitive Asa, who continues to tutor him, like Lorimer and the Native, with lessons on foraging, cookery, and, above all, intimate friendship, which together are sufficient to bring back the sense of the world "brimming with hope and purpose" (251).[19] However, following Asa's murder at the hands of the sons of Jehu, Håkan is once again plunged into his unremitting reversal of Manifest Destiny, in which "invading" or "arrowlike nomadism" becomes closer to what Glissant calls "circular nomadism" or "errantry" (1997, 12). As Glissant explains, "In this context uprooting can work toward identity, and exile can be seen as beneficial, when these are experienced as a search for the Other (through circular nomadism) rather than as an expansion of territory (an arrowlike nomadism). Totality's imaginary allows the detours that lead away from anything totalitarian."[20] In simple terms, errantry brings one into relations with the world as human and nonhuman, just as Håkan discovers through his many "detours," learning that in "taking up the problems of the Other, it is possible to find oneself" (1997, 18). He has learned through Lorimer, Asa, the Native, and numerous other encounters that the world is not "something obvious and transparent, claiming for it one presupposed sense and one destiny…one set of ideas, which it sets apart from the others and tries to impose by exporting as a model"

(20), for that is closer to the darker forces of violence and control that assail him on his journey. Håkan's worlding in the course of the novel, like Glissant's errantry, "renounces any claims to sum it up [the world] or to possess it" (20, 21).

Gradually, he uncovers astounding *worldly* knowledge, like Lorimer's notion of "the earth…round like a ball," while recognizing that "reality no longer ended at the horizon" (Diaz 2017c, 239). In so doing, he "strives to know the totality of the world yet already knows he will never accomplish this—and knows that is precisely where the threatened beauty of the world resides" (Glissant 1997, 20). The horizon, once the symbol of migration and opportunity, has now shifted in Håkan's vision of things, offering instead a reminder of a world beyond the mythic, wherein he questions the "vain constructions" of Linus's migrant stories (Diaz 2017c, 249). Simultaneously, the reader is immersed in mythic constructions of Manifest Destiny and empire building, as if we too are "circling the globe," experiencing the world through Håkan's errant eyes, witnessing traits of greed, envy, violence, and coloniality that slowly strip away the West's exceptionalism.

In this "being with," unfolded throughout his journey, Håkan's *creolized* patchwork self challenges the expectations of Turner's frontier identity of immigrants "Americanized, liberated, and fused into a mixed race" (1961, 51). Instead, despite his physical size, Håkan is beaten, starved, and generally diminished, as though Turner's supposed civilized progress, "the evolution of each into a higher stage" (44), is inverted and undone as his acquired Native knowledge, errant thought, and geohistorical awareness transform him. In rejecting the tainted surface of the West, Håkan instead burrows down into the land, becoming like "one of the fossils encrusted in the rock face" (Diaz 2017c, 266). Having stopped moving, he becomes, in Latour's terms, "Terrestrial," digging into the earth "with its thousand folds" (2018, 81), eschewing the myth of relentless forward motion and the goal of the endless horizon for a static but productive return with every action "some sort of pattern…[that] repeated itself," with "simply no goals or destinations" (Diaz 2017c, 271, 273). Diaz even repeats passages in the text to imitate this recurrence and circularity within which Håkan exists, drawing us, as readers, into his strange echo-world of timelessness.[21]

At a key moment in this section, amid the Anasazi-like maze of passages he has built underground, Håkan notices an "upside down" image projected by the sun on the cave wall, commenting, "It felt like someone else's hallucination; as if someone, far away, were dreaming up that place (wrong side up), and Håkan, for some reason, were able to look into that dream" (279). Uncannily, this epitomizes the novel's surreal "upside down" image of the dream of the West hallucinated and projected into the world as myth. Indeed, Håkan, following his circular nomadism across America, understands the West as "place (wrong side up)," preferring to burrow into the earth until "land—its beasts and plants—had fed him for such a long time that it had become…in a strict sense, part of his body…the vastness around him now his flesh" (297).

For Håkan, the "distant" dream of the West as opportunity, wealth, and exploitation means nothing, and, most significantly, despite this closeness to the land, his existence within it, and his endless journeying across and below it, "nothing…had made it his" (297). He has become in this sense Terrestrial or "Down to Earth," as Latour would define it, participating in the rhythms of the world, but never grasping or claiming the landscape. Instead, his life becomes one of strangely calming, repetitive chores and creativity, filling a world of vibrant matter in which "everything took more time, and there was a full awareness of each action as it was being performed," until even a tin cup placed on a table with "utmost care" takes on a powerful resonance, a "miraculous feel…a gentle yet momentous meeting of alien worlds" (277). In this "thick present," as Haraway calls it, the local opens into and exists entangled with the global; the seemingly insignificant resonates as worldly (2016, 1).

QUIET, HESITANT BEING

Of course, Håkan's bodily connection to place and the local make him out of step with the modernizing West, and so, once again, he leaves his underground existence, moving closer to the "civilized" world and further from Native knowledge. He senses the only way to survive is via "performance," perfecting his role to ensure his safety: "Falsehood was a new experience for him" (Diaz 2017c, 300). Amid the lines of civilization (fences, telegraph wires, and railings), the unnatural "nightlessness" of artificial lights, and the "commercial frenzy" (306) of the ever-capitalized West, Håkan witnesses the wider duplicity of this new nation at close hand, epitomized by the confidence man peddling his tonics and cure-alls in the street. Clearly, as Håkan realizes, the man is "a fool and a liar" whose mock science is nothing compared to his own two mentors, Lorimer and the Native, yet his performance echoes the ghastly world of exploitation, depravity, and "fake stuff": "miners with faces ravaged by dust and defeat; Chinese labourers smoking from thin, sweet pipes; broken women, sad in their seduction; black men trying to remain unseen while enjoying their modest pleasures; a little boy bent over a box, blowing on a pair of dice in his cupped hand; drunks reduced to heaps on stoops, under wagons, in the filth" (309, 310). In a moment of dark irony, Håkan even stumbles across a man on stilts performing Hawk's legend in an elaborate tableau, dressed in a "fake" lion skin, enacting fantastic scenes from the myth of his own life, which, he notes, "rather than muting his story, time had amplified" (312). Without comprehending fully what he sees, once more Håkan's description alerts the reader to the novel's concerns about myth creation and how it "amplifies" particular ideologies. As Glissant points out, "The sole purpose of founding myths is to consecrate the presence of a community on a territory, by establishing this presence, this present, in a legitimate line of descent…[and] authorizes the community it addresses to consider its territory as being absolutely its own" (2002, 289).[22] As Håkan and the reader witness this tableau, it brings the novel into even sharper focus, demonstrating how myth making is central to the dominant logic of coloniality, stifling human diversity, narrowing the range of stories and voices. Consequently, its effect, as Roland Barthes would have it, "depoliticizes" the world, creating "a realm which has purged itself of ambiguity and alternative possibility" (1976, 143). Similarly, as Glissant wrote, "Myth disguises while conferring meaning…obscures and brings to light, mystifies as well as clarifies and intensifies that which emerges, fixed in time and space, between men and their world. It explores the known-unknown" (1996a, 71). In other words, myth functions to *de-world* the world, turning the hope and possibility of dreaming settlers into the stark capitalist exploitation and eco-damage of hellish mining camps, like those experienced by Håkan: "This inhuman place, with its filthy pits, abrupt walls, and tiered plateaus descending into the broken earth" (Diaz 2017c, 314).

Håkan's journey around the West takes him finally to the immaculate castle and landscape of "perfectly groomed" Captain Altenbaum (319), a fellow Scandinavian, whose estate epitomizes Manifest Destiny's dream of human achievement and control. It exemplifies "the triumph of man over nature," with "every plant…forced into some artificial shape; every animal…domesticated; every body of water…contained and redirected." However, haunted by coloniality, this pristinely ordered world betrays its origins, where "Indians in white made sure that each blade of grass stayed in place" (321). Even his name carries echoes of colonialism, seeming to refer to the work of Friedrich Ratzel (1844–1904) who wrote of colonies as seedlings grown and spreading westward toward the sun from ancient trees (or *alten Baum*).[23] Nonetheless, despite Altenbaum's kindness amid an ever-gridded environment of towns, streets, fences, railway tracks, and vineyards, Håkan turns his back on this California dreamscape and its manifest promise of the West, preferring "to end this journey as it had started—with nothing" (316). In Diaz's hands, Håkan's bildungsroman has questioned the control of history fashioned by myth through dramatizing its contradictions and complexity, questioned the assumed freedom of mobility, and unsettled the ideologies bound up in such simplistic narratives.

When Turner wrote that America was "another name for opportunity," taking its national "tone from the incessant expansionism," he paralleled settlers with Greek empire builders carrying their social customs across the Mediterranean, but *In the Distance*, while exposing "unrestraint," dominant individualism, and "restless, nervous energy" (1961, 61), most importantly, interrupts and alters the *rhythm* of coloniality. Diaz has spoken of the influence of Morton Feldman's "indeterminate" music on the novel's form and structure, with its quiet, slowly evolving, and recurring asymmetric patterns that often explore extremes of duration and create "temporal disorientation" (Diaz 2017b).[24] The music is full of repetition yet with a difference, altering time and bending sound like refracting light through a prism. Similarly, Diaz "questions the idea of development" with a "slow and repetitious" form, redirecting us away from inevitable linearity and progression toward an alternative interrupted perspective, permitting a break in its logic and an interrogation of its implicit values (Diaz 2017b). Following Mignolo, Diaz advocates "An-other thinking," demanding "a change in the terms, content and questions," thus "delinking" how we think, write, and live from taken-for-granted systems of logic and power while underlining in a contemporary sense that "the best solutions are not necessarily found in the actual order of things under neoliberal globalization" (Mignolo 2005, 114, 117). Just as Håkan's epic journey uncovers different worlds that make up the Whole-World, it reminds us that such diversity, however awkward and painful, is a "field of energies": "Burst open, winding, its colours shimmering, its subject matter dispersed, and at the same time full and compact" (Glissant 2020c, 125). In a phrase Diaz once used to comment on the music of LCD Soundsystem, the novel has conveyed, like others considered in this book, an "epic intimacy [that] is overwhelming" (Diaz 2017a).

Finally, *In the Distance*'s great white giant is not the conventional colonial western hero on a migrant quest for power or redemption, but a "quiet, hesitant being" (Diaz 2017c, 322) whose traumatic experiences teach him different values: to heal, to sow, to cook, and to empathize with others (Indians, women, insects, animals, and the earth itself), so often exploited or overlooked in the rush to conquest, modernization, and globalization. As John Drabinski wrote of Glissant's work, "The painful past…becomes the condition for the possibility of being," and the same is true of Håkan's lifelong trek around the West in which "the fecundity of the pain of history and memory…underscores the chaotic swirl of relationality across time and geography" (2019, 161, 163). Out of the abyss of exile faced within the supposed promise of the New World emerge moments of care and responsibility for and by others, which "is also world-making," forging "another kind of totality, another kind of world, another kind of thinking about the wholeness of the whole" (163, 170).

CONCLUSION—AN AGITATED HISTORY

At the end of the novel, when gazing at a globe in the house of the wealthy wine grower Altenbaum, Håkan traces his journey with his fingers, noticing "how all those lands came together in a circle" (Diaz 2017c, 328), as if his experiences have brought him to a position akin to Lorimer's vision of connectedness in nature. Rather than an exceptionalist vision of the West, or what Glissant calls "closed uniqueness" (2020c, 52), Håkan's errantry suggests a world constructed from local/global relations whereby, in Lorimer's words, "each minuscule thing has spokes radiating out to all of creation" along complex entanglements of repetition and difference like "an endless [Indian] song" (Diaz 2017c, 81, 114). Even the supposedly straight-lined trail west curves back on itself, as in the novel, into a surreal circularity, or a process of *worlding* in which "we come from other bodies and are destined to become other bodies. In a universe made of universes" (111). It is a vision of the Whole-World, as Glissant called it, a totality that is not total or finished, but one that, born in relations, "changes and lives on through its exchanges" (2020c, 108).

As the novel closes, where it began, on the icebound sea of Alaska, we recall the "broken star" of that opening paragraph and cannot help but think of the course of empire described as a "star" in the infamous misquoting of George Berkeley's "Verses on the Prospect of Planting Arts and Learning in America." Håkan's inadvertent journey questions and breaks the "star of empire": reversing, interrogating, and exposing Manifest Destiny as a dark betrayal of dreams and a terrible "grasping" exploitation of land and people. Thus, as Latour asserts, echoing both Glissant and Diaz's novel, the world is not *in the distance* from the local, not its context, but composed from heterogeneous elements that refute a wider global explanatory metanarrative. Håkan's relationships with Lorimer, the Native man, and Asa underscore this most tellingly, as does his circular and vertical journey undertaken in the West. Recalling Latour's point from the beginning that space must become "an agitated history in which we are *participants among others*" (2018, 42), one can comprehend Håkan's journey to ecological understanding, as imperfect, errant, unfinished, yet always challenging, always "opening itself up" (54) to worlds as other values and multiple ways of being.

Following the reiterative pattern of the novel itself, it seems right to return to the opening of this chapter and see how Macfarlane's words, "Ice breathes. Rock has tides. Mountains ebb and flow. Stone pulses. We live on a restless Earth," foresee Håkan's overland and underland journey through the West. The *worlded* West is, in Macfarlane's words, "an assemblage of entanglements of which we are messily part" (2019, 103), an earth alive with our participation and responsibility to others. So Håkan, having been immersed in this restless, messy world, lights out once more, not like Huckleberry Finn for the territory of the American West, but due west from Alaska to Russia and beyond that, to where his journey commenced, Sweden. This Terrestrial, *worlding* story loops around, unsettling settler-colonial narratives of adventure, linearity, opportunism, and conquest, turning back time and challenging the relentless spatial flow of westward, colonial expansion, or what Macfarlane calls "the onwards-driving version of history" (104). Consequently, when Håkan tells a young boy he is going "West," the boy looks "confused," asking, "What west?" And perhaps, ultimately, this is the novel's final interruption; what indeed is this thing that myth and history have called the American West? Where is it? Moreover, what does it ultimately reveal about our sense of the world?

◀ 3 ▶

"What World We Making?"

Sebastian Barry's *Days Without End*

<blockquote>
There is not only need for tenderness, there is also need to be
tender for the other: we shut ourselves up in a mutual kindness,
we mother each other reciprocally; we return to the root
of all relations, where need and desire join.
—Roland Barthes, *A Lover's Discourse: Fragments*
</blockquote>

THE WORLD STRANGE AND LOST

At the end of *A Thousand Moons*, the sequel to Sebastian Barry's prize-winning novel *Days Without End* (2016), the Native girl, Winona, reflects on her condition: "That the world was strange and lost was not in argument. That there was no place to stand on earth that was not perilous was just the news of every moment" (2020, 251). Her words reiterate the precarious worlds Barry dramatizes in both novels and remind us of the instability his characters must endure in their multiple journeys West. Accordingly, early on in *Days Without End,* its Irish narrator, Thomas McNulty, thinks, "It's a dark thing when the world sets no value on you or your kin, and then Death comes stalking in, in his bloody boots" (2016a, 36). The meaning of "value" is central to a novel concerned with political and social judgments of sexuality, race, class, and national identity, or what Judith Butler terms "the reproduction of bodily norms" (2010, 52). *Days Without End* asks, above all, who is valued and who is not? As the comment suggests, *the world*, governed by dominant and powerful voices, judges people based upon prejudice, myth, and ideology shaping and framing the accepted order of things. As Butler explains, "Those whose lives are not 'regarded' as potentially grievable, and hence *valuable*, are made to bear the burden of starvation, underemployment, legal disenfranchisement, and differential exposure to violence and death" (25; emphasis added). She could, of course, be referring to the precarity of a poor Irish immigrant like McNulty, escaping the hunger of his homeland for nineteenth-century America, and willing to take any work to survive,

65

including joining the army in the Indian Wars. America is an uncaring space for McNulty, remote from any dream of the promised, mythical "sweet country": "The world don't care much, it just don't mind much. That's what I notice about it" (Barry 2016a, 80, 44).

"What world we making?" asks McNulty's partner, John Cole, at a key point in the novel, as if concisely setting its thematic tone (167). In many ways, Barry's novel of the American West seeks to *revalue* lives through engendering a sense of worlding generated by "communities not quite recognized as such" managing to form "new coalitions" based on a shared understanding of their precarity and vulnerability (Butler 2009, 32). As we shall examine, *Days Without End* ultimately "makes" a world through unlikely coalitions, a world in which, according to Jean-Luc Nancy, "there is room for everyone…a genuine place, one in which things can genuinely *take place* (in this world)…. To take place is to properly arrive and happen…it is not to almost arrive and happen" (Nancy 2007a, 42). In this respect, it is only at the end of the novel that its central immigrant characters finally "arrive and happen," for it is then they make a world for themselves, having, ironically, inverted the westward dream and moved east to Tennessee.[1]

Sebastian Barry has referred to himself as a "placeless listener" (2017a), gathering stories from the genealogy of his family and those scattered, diasporic histories of Irish people spread across the globe. The narrative seed for *Days Without End* was "a scrap, a tiny tiny echo" (Evans 2017) Barry heard from his grandfather Jack O'Hara about his great-uncle who emigrated to America to escape the famine and ended up fighting in the Indian Wars. Alongside this personal history, Barry grew up at a time when "the true mythology of [his] generation would be John Ford's films or 'B' movies or even 'Z' movie westerns" (Barry 2017b), creating a fertile blend of familial and cultural myths from which the novel's environment emerged.

Central to the novel is the irony of the Irish involvement in the Indian Wars or, as Barry defines his main protagonist, McNulty's role, "dispossessing people like his own people" (Barry 2017b). Equally important is McNulty's homosexual relationship with his fellow part-Indian wanderer, "the vulnerable soul John Cole," like "two wood-shavings of humanity in a rough world" (Barry 2016a, 4, 5).[2] Such ironies and twists in the history and myth of the West are critically important to the novel's extraordinarily lyrical exploration of racial, sexual, and gendered identity, alongside survival and loss, while ultimately looking toward the hopeful possibility of tenderness, love, and community. Through his repurposing of the western, like all of the authors in *Worlding the Western*, Barry interrogates the genre's assumptions and, in so doing, revalues it as a productive, creative, and political form for the twenty-first century.

A LAWLESS INTERVAL

The West of McNulty and Cole in *Days Without End* is closer to that described in Washington Irving's *Astoria* (1836) as "a lawless interval between the abodes of civilized man," for, "here may spring up new and mongrel races, like new formations in geology, the amalgamation of the 'debris' and 'abrasions' of former races, civilized and savage, the remains of broken and almost extinguished tribes; the descendants of wandering hunters and trappers; of fugitives from the Spanish and American frontiers; of adventurers and desperadoes of every class and country, yearly ejected from the bosom of society into the wilderness" (Le Menager 2003, 687–88). This "lawless interval" is described by Stephanie Le Menager as "a space of radical mobility, aggressive self-interest, and ethnic amalgamation" (687), producing horrendous acts of brutal violence and depredation, yet, simultaneously, within Barry's novel, giving rise to a more positive "shadow" world of presence.[3] Barry's alternative history, "like new formations in geology," conjures up a fugitive community from human "abrasions" and "remains" existing precariously at the very edge of the official dream of the frontier West. Thus, the novel imagines and performs the West and America *differently*, offering up from this "lawless interval" the "nascent possibility" of a "seam of something else unnamed" (Barry 2017b; 2016a, 90), with its "debris" of unclaimed and hidden histories amid "sites of definitional creation, violence, and rupture" (Sedgwick 1990, 3).

At its heart is Thomas McNulty's story, a poor Irish immigrant thrown into America after escaping the "famishing" in 1840s Ireland and quickly discovering, as Noel Ignatiev puts it, "while the white skin made the Irish eligible for membership in the white race, it did not guarantee their admission; they had to earn it" (1995, 59). McNulty's is the tale of a "jettisoned life" (Butler and Spivak 2010, 40) trying to "earn" some place in America, and, at one level, as the narrator thinks at the novel's end, it is truly a migrant's story of "how he came to be an American and of everything put against him that he pushed aside" (Barry 2016a, 244). Central to what he "pushed aside" is his struggle to survive at all costs in this New World as poor, Irish, and homosexual in a fiercely heterosexual, racist country, where performing onstage as a woman and being a soldier fighting Indians were contrasting ways to feed oneself in such an unforgiving place. In taking this approach, Barry renders the West *differently*, adding to it the complicated histories that result when one "turns backgrounds into foregrounds," as Susan Lee Johnson writes, "producing countermemories…doing battle with dominant narratives that reinscribe social inequities" (2000, 343). It is my contention here that, as Geoffrey W. Bateman has it, Barry contributes significantly to fiction that "queers the directional norms of the US frontier" (2016, 136) and, in so doing, critically "reinscribes" gender, sexuality, and race as intersecting and complex formations of worlding identity. As Donna Haraway puts it, "Queering has the job of undoing 'normal' categories" (2008, xxiv).

In a key scene about halfway through the novel, its central group of characters prepares for a performance at Titus Noone's "fine hall on Grab Corners" in Grand Rapids, Michigan (Barry 2016a, 105). It is a minstrel blackface variety show including "little plays" proposed by McNulty's "beau," John Cole, in which the former would cross-dress, while their ward, Winona, a Native child, would "black up" and sing for the crowd.[4] As elsewhere in the novel, this theatrical space of confused and unfixed identities focuses the reader's attention not on America's obsessive desire for a settled national identity, so crucial to the cohesive move westward, nor on any accompanying presumed, coherent "terrain of signification" (Butler 1990, 148), but rather on a more complex and fluid performativity that problematizes all forms of gendered and racial identity. Significantly, Winona, the adopted Lakota girl, highlights this when she looks upon herself in a mirror in full blackface and asks, "Who am I now?" reminding us of the book's wider interest in "queer states" of identity falling outside the singular mythology of "one nation–one people" implied by the ideological drive of Manifest Destiny in the West (110).[5] For example, William Gilpin, the evangelist of American identity formation and the West's assimilative powers, told an audience of Irish in Colorado in 1868 that their westering would create a "single people…identical in manners, language, customs and impulses: preserving the same civilization the same religion, imbued with the same opinions" (quoted in Emmons 2010, 179). In contrast, however, the reflective theatricality of Noone's (signifying *no one*) "sparkling tribe" (Barry 2016a, 173), with their richly diverse, inclusive, yet troubling performance, suggests anything is possible and nothing is as it might be assumed. Any sense of national uniformity is subverted by a performative tribe of Irish, Indian, "Africans," and Americans whose various worlds, "between Timbuctoo and Kalamazoo" (105), unsettle any fashioning of a nation-state. In the spirit of Judith Butler's interest in drag as a performative and "subversive enactment," Barry utilizes scenes of gender and racial disruption to question the wider hierarchies at work in the nineteenth-century American West where in many respects "politics itself is shaped" (Butler 1990, 125, 128). The "problematic dualisms" (129) that lock down power relations—for example, gender as male/female, sexuality as straight/gay, and race as white/other—come under scrutiny and critique within the sweeping national drama and intimate everyday moments of *Days Without End* that constantly "queers" these supposed stable points of reference. "Queers," in one of the senses conveyed by Eve Sedgwick, means "a person's undertaking particular, performative acts of experimental self-perception and filiation" that might create "the open mesh of possibilities, gaps, overlaps, dissonances and resonances, lapses and excesses of meaning when the constituent elements of anyone's gender, of anyone's sexuality aren't made (or *can't be* made) to signify monolithically" (1994, 9, 8).

Hence, in the emblematic minstrel/drag show outlined above, rugged gypsum miners, whose lives supposedly conform to the West's "monolithic" expectations of masculinity and its associated hierarchies of power and authority, experience some of this "dissonance," becoming transformed into romantic fools desiring McNulty's "Thomasina" in a world of "creatures not ourselves, wonders of people" (Barry 2016a, 110). Suddenly, the presupposed, fixed rules of everyday life on the western frontier where "men are men" and society is structured by simple goals based on repetition of norms and behaviors regimented into the "assured future" ideology of Manifest Destiny (Emmons 2010, 78) are turned upside down in the stage's carnival "fog" or "open mesh of possibilities," until even the hard-nosed miners "don't know what they are seeing" (Barry 2016a, 110). Following the implications of Sedgwick and Butler, it is as if "the firm foundation" of America's assumed identity or "suspect generality" (Butler 1990, 129) is being undone through the exaggerated repetition onstage of recurring gendered and racial "acts" in society and their subsequent acknowledgment and appreciation by the audience. Following the initial reaction of "riotous" uproar, the room turns to a "silence more speaking than any sound" (Barry 2016a, 111), as if in this moment the fragility of society's "regulatory fiction" and its illusory coherence are being exposed and questioned (Butler 1990, 137). Crucially, this "fragility" is not about gender and sexuality alone, for the "quick Negro lingo" (Barry 2016a, 110–11) and Winona's Indian-blackface act visualize the West's investment in norms of racism and prejudice, reducing complex cultures to simplistic vaudeville entertainment. As the performers and audience freeze momentarily in this eerie silence, Barry dramatizes what Zeese Papanikolas senses under the din of dominant cultural noise in the West, an "American silence" or "palpable absence or sense of loss," which he expresses as "a kind of longing, a sense of something lost, lost perhaps even at the moment of gaining it, and possibly irretrievable" (2007, 19). Barry has expressed this loss in an interview as follows: "All that [was] removed, the people, the landscapes and the spirit of the place, the rapture of the landscape, both in the sense of 'beauty' and 'being seized.' Something immense was lost, not quite in our lifetime but in the lifetime of our grandparents. It's terrifying, but also so fascinating that human groups have these impulses" (Page 2016). Here at the carnivalesque Grab Corners, the silence reflects precisely this sense of loss, of men detached from the mythic dream that drove them across America and, perhaps even, the realization of its human costs and consequences. Suddenly, it is as if they recognize in the playful tableau their loss, mingled with "memories of elsewhere" (Barry 2016a, 11): settlement, wealth, family, and hope, now existing only in these surreal fabrications of desire and identity played out as a drag act and minstrel show onstage.

Butler makes the argument that drag acts in fact reveal how "all gender acts are an imitation of an unreachable ideal" (Loxley 2007, 126), and in this silent moment, it is as if the miners understand the limits of their own illusions of a westward American dream. As Barry puts it through McNulty's narrative voice, "We have reached the very borderland of our act, the strange frontier," where dream and reality blur and all recognized lines of demarcation have been unsettled and disrupted. It is this "cultural mechanism of their fabricated unity" that determines gender and racial hierarchy and the social norms that are exposed here, which in so doing simultaneously indicates the wider organization of society and region as regulated and defined by the powerful myths of Manifest Destiny and nation building. "They have seen something," admits McNulty presciently, "they don't understand and partly do, in the same breath." Ironically, in this moment where foundational myths of the masculine white West are turned inside out and men desire women they know to be men and play along with the conceit of "blackface minstrelsy," there erupts some partial knowledge, a "craziness in it all that betokens a kind of delicious freedom" and "a flickering picture of beauty" (Barry 2016a, 112). It is not in the regimented order of the given, framed world of the West, with its gendered and racial controls and hierarchical power structures, that this audience feels "delicious" freedom (the great promise of Turner's frontier forming its "composite nationality" [1961, 51]), but rather subversively in this "queer," carnivalesque arena where all such "notions are cast off. If only for a moment" (Barry 2016a, 112).

What these hardworking, death-shadowed miners feel, "for a crazy, foggy moment," amid the commonality of affect engendered by this performance of "delicious freedom" where fixed gendered and racial identities are "cast off" is, above all, "love imperishable" (112). Here, it is as if the endless cycles of time and events that structure the novel and those lives who are caught up in the onslaught of the frontier suddenly freeze "only for a moment," "for a minute," to experience a different unscripted utopia, born of freedom, love, and common purpose rather than the "foundational illusions of identity" (Butler 1990, 34). Any stable category of presumed coherent identity and its foundation within a unified notion of region or nation is unsettled or "dispossessed" here. Performativity shows all such categories to be illusory and serves to describe a "turning of power against itself to produce alternative modalities of power, to establish a kind of political contestation that is not a 'pure' opposition, a 'transcendence' of contemporary relations of power, but a difficult labor of forging a future from resources inevitably impure" (Butler 1993, 184).

SURVIVAL AND LOVE

Although the course of American history runs like a bloody and dangerous thread through the novel, with Time and Nature often appearing like coconspirators in the relentless and pitiless passage of events, nonetheless, there is a countercurrent of human goodness and love acting to slow down and dispossess this apparent remorselessness. Referring back to Butler's words above, this countercurrent is "forging a future from resources inevitably impure" and, in so doing, rejecting "the alleged interests that belong to a set of ready-made subjects" in favor of "a new configuration of politics" emerging from McNulty's journey West (1990, 149). Commenting, for example, on the unlikely marriage of a soldier and an Oglala Sioux woman, McNulty says, "I guess love laughs at history a little" (Barry 2016a, 77), or in the aftermath of a particularly bloody battle he asks, "Why should a man help another man?" At a time when the "world is just a passing parade of cruel moments and long drear stretches," Barry's novel turns away from unremitting darkness to find glimmers of light in simple acts of kindness and care, or what McNulty terms "that strange love between us" (150). Love, as Butler and Athanasiou argue, can indeed be a force for dispossession, pushing us beyond the individual body, "exposed, dismembered, given over to others," and toward "thick and intense social processes of relatedness and interdependency" (2013, 55).[6] Love in the context of the novel reaches beyond the individual body toward the shared and intimate everydayness of life across boundary lines, across races and genders, nationalities and geographies, classes and religions, finding within this process untold but unrealized "riches": "All that stint of daily life we sometimes spit on like it was something waste. But it all there is and in it is enough [*sic*]" (Barry 2016a, 248). As James Baldwin wrote in *The Fire Next Time*, "Love takes off the masks that we fear we cannot live without and know we cannot live within. I use the word 'love' here not merely in the personal sense but as a state of being, or a state of grace—not in the infantile American sense of being happy but in the tough and universal sense of quest and daring and growth" (1981, 82). A phrase from the latter part of the novel suggests this "state of being" perfectly and succinctly as a "down payment of hope against…despair" (Barry 2016a, 251).

In such "flickering" moments, another America is glimpsed, perhaps the one Papanikolas writes of as "lost perhaps even at the moment of gaining it," where the genuine hopes of some new society of care and love were first sketched out and imagined in the West. However, as Barry's novel so often demonstrates, the region is a brutal and unforgiving place of racial violence, genocide, gender inequality, and cruel disappointment, a "country ill at ease" (178). Papanikolas traces loss and "silence" through white Americans whose "melancholy…is not rooted in the deep past and the inevitability of suffering, but in some sense of a utopian possibility that we just missed, and of an unspoiled nature that was almost within living memory" (2007, 22). Barry's West is similarly drawn, with McNulty, an Irish immigrant from Sligo, escaping the famine to an America defined for him not by any high-flown dream, but by a different and ironic "*enterprise* of continuing survival" (Barry 2016a, 4; emphasis added). For McNulty, schooled in the famished world of Irish poverty under the tyranny of British colonial rule, and then on the "coffin ships" across the Atlantic, survival is initially his greatest hope. Rejecting any nostalgic or romanticized version of America for the Irish, Barry has called it a "country for nobody" (2017a). As Emmons puts it, "If the legacy of the West was of conquest, then the Irish clearly had a limited role: they could be the blunt instruments of conquest, the foot soldiers of the American conquistadores, but not themselves conquerors" (2010, 10). McNulty is one such "blunt instrument" whose life unfurls on these edges of empire, giving him a surprisingly sharp critical insight on his adopted land through a lens of necessary skepticism: "Pictures of those fine American scenes of grandeur that are more comfortable to gaze on than to be in" (Barry 2016a, 6). McNulty's words spell out this awareness of a duplicitous country of racial and gendered power even more clearly: "The bottom was always falling out of something in America far as I could see. So it was with the world, restless, kind of brutal. Always going on. Not waiting for no man" (59). What the novel explores is the differences between the repeated mythic rhetoric and acts constituting those "fine American scenes of grandeur" in the West and the relentless lived experience of immigrants, Native peoples, and slaves who suffered or barely survived there. The American West in Barry's lacerating vision, therefore, exists as "an ideal that no one *can* embody" (Butler 1990, 139).

Initially, McNulty's decision to "make a few bucks…the great American way" in drag is a part of his will to survive in a world whose "bottom was always falling out," realizing that men "need only the illusion, only the illusion of the gentler sex" (Barry 2016a, 8), just as they similarly needed the grander illusion of the promise of the West itself as "another name for opportunity" (Turner 1961, 69). Gradually, McNulty's "down payment of hope" toward a different vision of a world becomes inextricably bound to his loving relationship with John Cole, a handsome boy from New Hampshire with Indian ancestors whom he meets early on his westering journey. Concealing their relationship seems almost second nature within a country brokered on an illusion and structured around a mythology of supposed equality and fraternity. In the performance of drag, however, McNulty feels a strange freedom that takes him beyond the compulsory expectations of the national dream of masculinity, conquest, and white power, until he feels ironically more akin to the slaves freed by the Civil War or the Natives he kills in battle: "I was a new man now, a new girl. I was freed, like those slaves were freed in the coming war" (Barry 2016a, 10). Once again, Barry utilizes McNulty's position (as homosexual, immigrant Irish, *and* poor soldier) to provide a different and more complicated perspective on American events: "The agents of dispossession had themselves been dispossessed" (Emmons 2010, 10). *Dispossessed* in this sense, McNulty becomes dispossessed in another way as well, undone through contact with others and by the secret life he is forced to lead. This "double valence" of dispossession (Butler and Athanasiou 2013, 3) develops within him the capacity to recognize "the story in our story" (Barry 2016a, 12), seeing the curious kinships with "others," between the Irish and the Native peoples he is paid to kill, or the slaves he fights to free in the Civil War. As discussed earlier, relationality dispossesses because it surprises, disconcerts, and displaces until we "no longer know precisely who we are" (Butler and Athanasiou 2013, 3). Because McNulty must be eternally vigilant of society's judgment of his relationship, he brings a unique perspective to bear as narrator upon a world that holds on to its mythical story without such self-awareness or critical insight. Indeed, as we follow the epic journey of McNulty and Cole across the West, we are inevitably conscious of these multiple intersecting narratives of self and nation, race and gender, class and power, illusion and reality, best expressed as "stories that tell another story just the whole while they are being told" (Barry 2016a, 71).[7] Consequently, McNulty and Cole are an uncanny presence in a West of invariant narratives: "We knew we was just fragments of legend and had never really existed in that town. There is no better feeling" (13). Their relationship and the "love" and "freedom" are a ghostly trace written across the West, bringing to others new, challenging forms of kinship, like a haunting and "silent" reminder of some possibility of a different and more hopeful community.[8]

McNulty's ability to live this double life is, he argues, not just about his homosexuality, but also about his Irishness, since being from Ireland means you are born double, capable of being angel and devil "both the same": "you're talking to two when you talk to one Irishman" (23), he says. Under the British colonial system in Ireland, Catholics had become a subjugated people, since, as Ignatiev explains, "the Penal Laws regulated every aspect of Irish life, civil, domestic, and spiritual. In effect they established Ireland as a country in which Irish Catholics formed an oppressed race" (1995, 35). Coming through the experience of the famine, the horrific death of his family, followed by the hellish journey to America, McNulty is transformed to "nothing," with everything he once was or might be turned to waste: "Talk, music, Sligo, stories, future, past…all turned to something very like the shit of animals," turned to "Silence" (Barry 2016a, 25). As Emmons puts it, the Irish were "the refuse of an empire" (2010, 1), citing Edward Everett Hale who saw them as "nothing": "Their inferiority as a race compels them to go to the bottom; and the consequence is that we are all, all of us, the higher lifted because they are here" (66). As a colonial "other," it is only meeting John Cole that provides the abject McNulty with the possibility of a new beginning, yet it is ultimately his experience of being *nothing*, of being an oppressed race, a precarious life, and a subjugated sexuality, that gives him this vital perspective on America: "We knew what to do with nothing, we were at home there." If *nothing* was his new home once evicted and exiled from Ireland, then the myths and "grandeur" of American life had none of the allure they promised for someone so cut adrift from his roots. Instead, McNulty experiences an austere and brutal program of survival, ameliorated only by the possibility of love: "Then nothing. Then America. Then John Cole. John Cole was my love, all my love" (Barry 2016a, 25).

QUEER WORLDING

This oft-repeated sense of nothingness and precarity links McNulty and Cole to a fundamental struggle to "become" something and to leave their ghostly abjection behind. Having committed terrible acts of violence during the Indian Wars, McNulty describes their feelings: "There didn't seem to be anything alive, including ourselves. We were dislocated, we were not there, now we were ghosts" (33). In Judith Butler's later work, her questioning of gender norms widened into a concern for political ethics in times of racism, terrorism, and state violence, and this work illuminates McNulty's perspective in the novel. As he recognizes his ghostliness in the scene above, he does it *in relation to* others who have suffered too, with lives made precarious by war and racism, mirroring something of his own Irish experience. As Butler puts it, "Precariousness implies living socially, that is, the fact that one's life is always in some sense in the hands of the other" (2010, 14). The novel's violent scenes remind us of these relations and how characters are "impinged upon by the exposure and dependency of others" in the terrible intimacy of war. Despite its brutality, McNulty understands what Butler calls "grievability" as "a condition of life's emergence and sustenance…[because w]ithout grievability, there is no life, or, rather, there is something living that is other than life" (14). He constantly remembers and grieves for his family back in Ireland, for his sister and mother "who perished like stray cats, no one caring much," or how "for a violent moment in my inner eye I see my father lying dead in Ireland" (Barry 2016a, 24, 111). In his empathetic kinship with the dead, McNulty grieves for their loss, and in so doing he begins to understand more fully the value of life—both his and theirs—and from within loss and mourning begins to experience some hopeful sense of intersectionality. McNulty recognizes a troubling "interdependency" that runs counter to the rhetoric of racial violence prevalent in the Indian Wars and later in the hideous sectionalism of the Civil War that spoke only of linear divisions and unbreakable "frames of war" (Butler 2010, xiii). This divisive rhetoric chooses some lives as "ungrievable" (Indians, slaves, Irish, for example) and their "precariousness" a weakness to be exploited and targeted rather than understood as interdependency. They are "framed as being already lost and forfeited" to the broader claims of nation building because in its "twisted logic…the loss of such populations is deemed necessary to protect the lives of 'the living'" (31).

Of course, as a famished Irishman, McNulty is, according to Barry, "himself essentially a native person, an aboriginal person" (Barry in Gross 2017), feeling an empathy for those others oppressed in the New World, reduced like him by colonial power to a ghostly "nothing people" (Barry 2016a, 125). Dehumanized by poverty, hunger, and then by the violence of war, his struggle is simply *to be* and to locate some sense of self, of materiality, in the world surrounded by the ever more persuasive and demanding rhetoric of national identity (of both Ireland and America), personal identity (sexuality, gender, race, and class), and the sweeping metanarratives of myth and exceptionalism in the West. What McNulty and Cole increasingly express is an uncanny kinship with the Indians they fight, themselves reduced to nothing by the genocidal policies of American settler-colonialism, just as in Ireland British policy since Oliver Cromwell had been to exterminate the "vermin" Catholics and drive them from their land. As historian Patrick O'Farrell has put it, "The bloody colonization of Ireland provided the 'template for English understanding of North American savages'" (quoted in Emmons 2010, 139). Similarly, as Ignatiev explains, the Irish were frequently referred to as "niggers turned inside out" and "the Negroes, for their part, were sometimes called 'smoked Irish,' an appellation they must have found no more flattering than it was intended to be" (1995, 42). Let us recall the quotation with which this chapter began, "It's a dark thing when the world sets no value on you or your kin," to comprehend McNulty's sense of uncanny kinship with others oppressed in America. Once more, the struggle within the novel is clear: How does one move from *nothing, not there*, and *no value* to *something, being with*, and *value*, without simply succumbing to the conventional settler-colonial metanarratives of conquest, war, and acquisition? Perhaps part of the answer is contained in Donna Haraway's thought that "we become—with each other or not at all" (2016, 4).

McNulty's productive "doubleness" as cross-dressing homosexual and poor Irish soldier forces him into seeing the world differently, like the "wondrous kind" he witnessed among Native peoples, the "winkte" or "berdache": "braves dressed in the finery of squaws" who still fought in men's garb only to return afterward to "the bright dress" (Barry 2016a, 58).[9] This notion of what has become known as "Two Spirit" described people who were thought to embody both the feminine and the masculine spirits and, therefore, existed as a troubling "third gender" with an alternative perspective on the world. Told through the eyes of McNulty, traces of his version of "Two Spirit" wisdom, or what we might in this book's context also think of as "queer worlding," permeate the novel, permitting "value" to emerge from desolation and interdependency to question division (Haraway 2008, xxiii).

Hence, the novel does not dwell exclusively on dominant metanarratives of masculinist westward expansion and nation building but instead charts a troubling "becoming-with" or an alternative "queer" course toward love and its counternarratives of hopeful community, social acceptance, and resilient endeavor. For all the suffering and callousness within the novel, there is always this powerful undercurrent at work, perhaps best expressed as the troops trudge across the landscape after a massacre and McNulty describes them thus: "Desolate, and decimated though we were, there was *something* good there. *Something* that couldn't be extinguished by flood and hunger. That human will. You got to give homage to it. I seen it many times. It ain't so rare. But it is the best of us" (Barry 2016a, 44; emphasis added). The repetition of "something" here underlines once again the novel's movement toward "communities not quite recognized as such" (Butler 2010, 32), asserting human will to goodness as still possible despite the seeming indifference of Nature and Time. As Jean-Luc Nancy explained in chapter 1, community does not have to be a fusion of people into one like the great American myth would have it, but instead can be singular beings coexisting in mobile, unfixed, and shared relations. Throughout the novel, however, the individual journeys of McNulty, Cole, and Winona contrast with the nation's tumultuous development through the Indian Wars, the Civil War, and then Reconstruction. This is apparent, using the same tension between *nothing* and *something*, as they witness settlers struggling back and forth on the Oregon Trail: "Guess the Promised Land is draped in hues of grey in the upshot. It's hard to make something out of nothing as even God might attest" (Barry 2016a, 71).

Too often, for these poor immigrant soldiers, former slaves, and Indian scouts, their experience of the mythic Promised Land is banal, harsh, or even delirious, since "oftentimes in America you could go stark mad from the ugliness of things." Riding on the endlessly flat, featureless plains makes them "feel clear loco…as if the stern and relentless monotony makes you die, come back to life, and die again," confronted by "atrocious wonders," and bitten to hallucination by swarms of mosquitoes with "your brain molten in its bowl of bones" (79). Their violence too stakes out a terrible reality in the West running counter to its popular mythology of promise: "The knives opened the flesh like they were painting paintings of a new country" (22). However, occasionally, the novel's grim rendition of human cruelty and the absence of promise contrast with the indifferent sublime of Nature functioning as a wondrous backdrop to the horrors of war and genocide. For example, as the soldiers experience Yellowstone, "a strange country we often hear stories of," for the first time, it is described "as if maybe a man was out there painting it with a huge brush" in rich, lustrous colour, not the "hues of grey" that too often define the landscape of their journey (79, 80). "He is choosing a blue as bright as falling water for the hills and there is green for the forests so green you think it might be used for to make ten million gems. Rivers burn through it with a enamelled blue. The huge fiery sun is working at burning off all this splendid colour and for ten thousand acres of sky it is mighty successful.... God's work!" Faced with the sublimity of "God's work," the "vicious ruined class of man" feels humbled, as the scene seems to tell McNulty "his life is not approved," yet it simultaneously reminds him that there is a "remnant of innocence" burning "in his breast like an ember of the very sun" (80). Once again, Barry's novel draws attention to contrasts, to "stories that tell another story" of untapped possibility, or "something" etched in the human will but too often hidden or subsumed behind the veil of survival and necessity or the persuasive myths of frontier. The ember-like "innocence" glimmers behind the terrible realities of war, poverty, and racism that haunt the novel but do, nonetheless, find moments of emergence even in the most unlikely places, such as at the death of Sergeant Wellington: "He was a queer sort of man alright. Mostly cruel and thoughtless but there was the seam of something else unnamed" (90). The notion of the "queer...seam of something else unnamed" once more invokes the novel's interest in the "something" to be uncovered from the "nothing," and that behind the frames of war and the screens of myth, duty, survival, prejudice, and necessity, there still exist "queer" energies of potential, "just as the Black Hills were said to be speckled with gold...man was likewise" (91). From the precarious "nothing" of being Irish, according to McNulty, or of being homosexual in a world defined by masculine pursuits and western myth, or of simply being poor and uneducated, the novel touches repeatedly on the possibilities implied by the notion of the "unnamed," running like a rich seam through its unforgiving landscape.

MAKING KIN AND MAKING KIND

McNulty is, of course, caught in between these stories with his lover, John Cole, and Native "daughter," Winona ("the child of nothing" [Barry 2020, 32]), trying to navigate some path through and toward a space where these unnamed seams might find some visibility and permanence. But as with Winona's confusion of racial identities that emerges in the minstrel show, McNulty too comments as he travels farther from Sligo and deeper into the conflicts of the Civil War, "I couldn't say who in that while I was myself" (Barry 2016a, 134). Following the violent ravages of Civil War and imprisonment in the notoriously brutal Andersonville military prison in Georgia, McNulty returns to the nagging thread of the novel, "What world we making? We don't know" (167). To him, barely living amid the ghosts of terrible war and once more trapped in a "famishing" like the one he thought he had escaped in Ireland, "whatever world it is is ending. We come to the end time and here it is. Just like the goddam Bible says, says John Cole." The cyclical returning to hunger, violence, and loss punctuates any progress in the novel and reminds the reader of the extraordinary distance between the dreams of a new life and the reality of survival, whether in terms of immigration, the journey West, the Indian Wars, or the Civil War. McNulty and Cole exist along a terrible rhetorical borderline constructed to both define and contain them: "They could tell us any damn history and we wouldn't know the truth of it. They seem to believe all the words in their mouths. It hurts us to hear of such things" (169).

Yet despite this massing of "damn history" riddled with its contradictory horrors, these two men persist: "We set to go on. Why not" (172), even marrying after the war and settling down as a queer, worlded "family" with Winona in Tennessee at their friend Lige Magan's farm. Like the once "sparkling tribe" of Noone's company, Lige's rural community is equally diverse, with free slaves Rosalee and Tennyson, Winona, Lige, McNulty, and Cole living with the rhythms of nature and the cycle of the seasons. It is here that McNulty carves out an alternative community, or *muintir* in Gaelic ("people of the place"), built not on American values of "individual rights, private property, and the moral duty to guard both," as Emmons puts it, but on something closer to more traditional Irish beliefs in the system of "rundale" (or open-field system). This is a community operating as a "silent economy of friends," with "land held jointly…based on cooperation and community obligation…among interrelated kin groups and on the exchange of favors among them" (2010, 110).[10] Based not on competition, but on reciprocity and cooperation, rundale rejected what Haraway calls "bounded individualism" for a different sense of kin community, "making kin and making kind (as a category of care, relatives without ties by birth, lateral relatives, lots of other echoes) [that] stretch the imagination and can change the story" (2016, 5, 103). Such a vision comes close to Nancy's coexisting community of "indefinite intertwining," with its "proximity and its spacing, the strange familiarity of *all the worlds in the world*" (2007, 111; emphasis added).

But, as always in the novel, stable settlement is short-lived, and the past will return like a terrible and inevitable specter to claim the present for itself. It is as if conventional lines of kinship and race reassert themselves, since following the murder of Major Neale's wife as revenge for the earlier killing of Caught-His-Horse-First's child, the Indian chief demands Winona back in exchange for the major's surviving daughter. The ghostly echoes of the past gather around McNulty, recalling his own family's deaths in the potato famine, as well as the harrowing times he has lived through with John Cole, and once again he feels powerless in the face of a duplicitous world where "we blunder through and call it wisdom, but it ain't. They say we be Christians and suchlike but we ain't. They say we are creatures raised by God above the animals but any man that has lived known that's damned lies" (Barry 2016a, 213). Stripped down to such fundamentals, the world is once again redrawn along lines of "they" and "we," with power held by the former as they constantly set and reset its terms of reference until moral perspective is lost by the twists and turns of exigency. Under such tumultuous circumstances of universal doubt, McNulty sees the reality of his and Cole's own actions, having stolen a child from her home and tribe, renaming her "Winona," and assuming control over her life and history. Returning to the novel's interest in identity and belonging, McNulty asks of Winona, "What is she now?" (214), and recognizes in her something of the colonized nation itself, torn in many directions with split loyalties and complex relations of love, race, fear, and duty. In the novel's sequel, *A Thousand Moons*, Winona describes her experience "as a child of sorrow…[who] could hear the under-songs in what they spoke of. The fall of things that had been precious, the rise of trouble and the taking away of joys" (Barry 2020, 86). Ultimately, in *Days Without End*, Winona is an Indian girl "dressed as a drummer boy," willing to return to her tribe to save Neale's daughter because "the major's wife once showed her kindness" (Barry 2016a, 214). With a strange echo back to the muddled identities of the minstrel show discussed earlier, in this moment it is as if there was a "sudden breeze of sense and you see things clear a moment like a clearing country," and it is Winona, above all, despite her liminal state, who seems "the queen of this o'erwhelming country" (213, 214). With her multiple puzzled identities, flexible sense of belonging, and intense loving faithfulness, it is as if she is living with the ghosts of past, present, and future, yet remains tied to people and place not by sovereign loyalty, mythic destiny, or ethnic identity but by different bonds of kindness, kinship, and powerful feelings of love.[11] As the exchange takes place of child for child, Native for white, such visions of "a clearing country," where new and different identities might be forged, with hope and "the tincture of possibility" (Barry 2017b), defined earlier as "a sense of something lost, lost perhaps even at the moment of gaining it," dissolve into something "like a performance…in Mr. Noone's hall" (Barry 2016a, 214–15). Nonetheless, without any of the earlier liberation of performance, this one is based upon strict "scriptures of manifest manners," regulatory orders, and "colonial enactment" (Vizenor 1994, 11) in which the Native Americans, whose "fathers owned everything here and we was never heard of," are confronted by a changed nation where "Now a hundred thousand Irish roam this land" along with "Chinese…Dutch and Germans…[who] Poured across the trails like a herd without end" (Barry 2016a, 215).

When Major Neale betrays the nature of the exchange and takes full revenge on the Indians, the terrible performance is complete with all slaughtered in a scene McNulty compares once more to Ireland and Cromwell's promise to "clean out the country for good people to step in to." Cromwell's claim was to "make a paradise" in Ireland, and McNulty sees the irony of the once-colonized Irish, its "dispossessed," doing the same in America, since "now we make this American paradise I guess." Nevertheless, who is this paradise for? Perhaps Winona provides the answer, since although McNulty saves her from Neale's destruction, she reacts to the brutality she witnesses by retreating into silence, "so silent the silence of winter is like a clattering" (226). Perhaps, as Papanikolas termed it, it is *the* American Silence.

Faced with the inevitable consequences of colonization anew, McNulty refutes Major Neale's madness and escapes from military law with Winona, dressed once more as a woman and "shown my path" by the liberating lessons of the "winkte" and "berdache," alongside the gentle spirit of his long-dead sister who "crept into me and made a nest" (233, 234). Recalling Noone's show discussed at length earlier, he defines his drag act as "no subterfuge," but rather as "strange magic changing things" within which he was empowered by "thinking along some lines and… becom[ing] that new thing" (234). As he dons Major Neale's wife's clothes, it is as if McNulty becomes a "new thing" beyond the control of military rules and conventional kinship, but without any clear sense of what this might mean. "Am I American?" he asks (235), as if to remind us of his own ambivalence about his gendered self, the immigrant dream, and the supposed role of the frontier in molding national identity. In his precarious, uncertain state, "the easily torn spider's web of who we were" (Barry 2020, 89), McNulty finds no resolved sense of Americanness, no regeneration in violence, and no clear path to prosperity and individualism, embracing instead a different reality formed not by national myths but in the uncertain and "strange magic changing things." Simultaneously, Winona breaks her traumatized silence and "blossoms back to talk" while "her hands like two maps of home" lead McNulty toward a reunion with John Cole at Magan's farm in Tennessee (Barry 2016a, 235, 236). As if recalling Sedgwick's notion of "experimental filiation" (1994, 9) and Haraway's empathetic kinship of "making kin and making kind" (2016, 103), with this "shard of love" prompting him, McNulty expresses the moment perfectly, capturing the peculiar ambivalence of their alternative queer, worlded community: "A daughter not a daughter but who I mother best I can. Ain't that the task in this wilderness of furious death" (Barry 2016a, 236). Set against this landscape of "furious death," it is this vital, life-enhancing task of love, kindness, and care that carries them forward to "Home. Our riches. All I owned. Enough" (248).

CONCLUSION—LEARNING TO LIVE

So, McNulty's America of *Days Without End* is not a neat story of entrepreneurial progress and settler-colonial authority, like that promised in the myths and "static time" (Le Menager 2004, 222) of Manifest Destiny, but is instead a process in which people, communities, and worlds are made and remade through their experiences and struggles along the way. His actions and practices are not expressions of some prior identity laid down in a predefined script of masculinity and nationhood, but the very means by which he comes to be what he is. McNulty and Cole refuse to express a given identity and instead through the course of the novel perform different and often contradictory acts that refute any fixed or stable notion of identity within the American West. Unlike the supposed foundational status of the West as the crucible of American nationhood and selfhood, Barry's novel proposes instead an alternative ghost or shadow world in which these two men compose themselves performatively from "nothing" to "something." But ultimately the "something" they become refuses to conform to the supposed Turnerian formula of the "masterful grasp of material things…that restless, nervous energy; that dominant individualism" (1961, 61), for they opt instead for an open, communitarian culture of kindness and love based around their revised notion of gender relations, kinship, home, and community. As McNulty says, amid a violent attack on Winona's tribal camp, "What chokes my throat is love. I ain't saying love for them but for her. I don't care if she ain't my daughter but all I know is the fiery feeling" (Barry 2016a, 222).

How appropriate it is that McNulty, in the last of his many journeys *away from* and *back to* that home in Tennessee, stands alone, penniless, and in tattered clothes, as if reduced once more to *nothing*. In this moment, he mirrors his entry point into the novel, representing the antithesis to the dream of westward hope and its potent mythologies of plenty and promise. Yet typical of the novel's errant, contrary movements, McNulty, at this very same moment of apparent emptiness, feels *something*: "free like a mourning dove," with "such joy of heart…such pure charge and fire of joy," knowing that he can "rely on the kindness of folk along the way. The ones that don't rob me will feed me. That is how it is in America" (258). As Winona comments of McNulty in *A Thousand Moons*, "He knew the absolute menace of the world. He knew it was a place so knotted with evil that good could only hope to unknot a tiny few threads of it. But he was a man that believed in the great freeing possibility of the untoward good outcome of matters" (Barry 2020, 194).

Ultimately, this is an impure and critical tale of love and hope in which Thomas McNulty, on the edge of his return home, is finally "let loose from…his own discomfited self" (Barry 2016a, 258), not to become a dominant individual in the spirit of the traditional frontier myth of the West, but in order to assert and share his life with others and forge something of a new community, as if, in Butler's words, "one is beside oneself, not at one with oneself…already given over, beyond ourselves, implicated in lives that are not our own" (2004, 28). In laconic John Cole's words, they *make a world* in which "Two is better together" (Barry 2016a, 4). It is as if McNulty slowly "unknot[s] a tiny few threads" of pain to become radically *dispossessed* of the hauntedness that has been with him from his days in Sligo, through "the absolute menace of the world," the trauma of war, and the deep wounds of suffering and survival encountered moving across the West. Coming through slaughter, as he has, through the terrible violence he has committed and has been committed on him, he stands in recognition of his and others' vulnerability before death, like a "sudden address from elsewhere" (Butler 2004, 29). If one denies this vulnerability and refuses to see the bodily and social harm it can do, then war, violence, and terror are perpetuated, yet if one embraces it, to "stay with the sense of loss" (30), it will remind and warn us of the pain we inflict on others that is always also our pain too. In this moment, *Days Without End* projects "the great freeing possibility," as it edges us through love and care toward Baldwin's "state of being" and "a new configuration of politics," as Butler called it earlier, as if "to make trouble, to stir up potent response to devastating events, as well as to settle troubled waters and rebuild quiet places" (Haraway 2016, 1).[12] Through McNulty's confrontation with such "affective dispositions" (Butler and Athanasiou 2013, 71), his dispossessed, revalued self at the novel's end turns toward interdependency and collective responsibility, toward the lives of others to which he is bound communally "to solicit a becoming, to instigate a transformation, to petition the future always in relation to the Other" (Butler 2004, 44). As the novel closes, as if reminding us of the long road home to this new possibility of a "discomfited self" *dispossessed*, McNulty tells us in wonderful understatement, "soon I would be there" (Barry 2016a, 259). He is moving back once more to those "others" who help define him, back to his unconventional but vital "queer sociality" (Wander 2016, 163) with its potential "silent economy of friends." Perhaps, in this final moment, the novel achieves something of the goal suggested earlier in this chapter, of "doing battle with dominant narratives that reinscribe social inequities" to produce both troubling and settling stories that "people and plot the past anew," and thereby remembering it differently, more fully, as a resource for hope with new and engaging political visions for the future (Johnson 2000, 343). This tentative new community recalls Roland Barthes in the chapter's epigraph, calling for a "need to be tender for the other," find "a mutual kindness," and "return to the root of all relations, where need and desire join" (2002, 224) and in so doing answers the question "What world we making?" As Winona says at the beginning of the novel's sequel, *A Thousand Moons*, "Even when you come out of bloodshed and disaster in the end you have got to learn to live" (Barry 2020, 2).

"The World in All Its Workings"

Téa Obreht's *Inland*

I thought I was writing a book set in the west in the 1890s
and I didn't realise how much of it was going to align with
this particular cycle that we've fallen into now.
—Téa Obreht interviewed by Joanna Scutts, "Téa Obreht: 'In America,
We Make Progress, Then Revert in Horrific Ways'"

The dead don't stay where they are buried.
—John Berger, *Here Is Where We Meet*

A STEREOSCOPIC WEST

Like Diaz's *In the Distance* and Barry's *Days Without End*, Téa Obreht's *Inland*, as the epigraph states, although set in the nineteenth-century American West, has deep resonance with contemporary US history and politics. This is further endorsed by the novel's epigraph from James Galvin's "Belief":

Time doesn't change
Nor do times.
Only things inside time change,
Things you will believe, and things you won't.

There are cycles and patterns in history that, rather than reassuring us, return like the repressed, haunting time's myths of progress or "gilded talk," confronting us repeatedly with questions that refuse to disappear. At the heart of the novel is the "want" (as Obreht terms it) associated with the West and its nagging sense of possibility and opportunity, driving land surveys, military incursions, mining camps, and railroad crews deep into its hinterland, as well as luring migrants from foreign lands to seek new lives there. One such is the appropriately named immigrant drifter Lurie Mattie who cannot escape this feeling of "want" and promise: "Don't we all got a thing makes us get that look in our eyes? All of us who ever said let's go, let's go on, who starved for the sight of something new?" (Obreht 2019a, 343). This double-edged drama of opportunity and risk drives the novel forward, giving its action, as Obreht pointed out, a Trump-era resonance.

Born in Belgrade and raised in Cyprus, Cairo, Georgia, and California, Obreht brings to the novel, like Diaz and Barry, a "worlded" sensibility of dreaming "something new," alongside deeper considerations of home, settlement, and belonging, building these themes into the dual narratives that structure *Inland*: Nora Lark's family tale of survival on the Arizona frontier and Lurie Mattie's immigrant tale of wayfaring around the West. Although different stories, they shadow each other in interesting ways. For example, Lurie's errantry across the West is balanced by the settled, if hardscrabble, homesteading of Nora, yet their dissimilar perspectives nonetheless act to destabilize our expectations and assumptions about the western genre's values and ideologies. Both stories are also driven by undercurrents of unspoken, unfulfilled desire, voiced by the living characters of Lurie and Nora, and through the restless, haunting presence of the perpetually wanting dead providing another linking thread between them. Nora's desire for water and her desperate thirst, quenched only at the finale, symbolize this want throughout the novel.

Toward the end of *Inland*, Nora's son Toby receives a stereoscope through which he views strange and exotic "pictures…from all over the world": "the zoological gardens of Paris…the Palace of Horticulture…the great train station of Philadelphia" (295). This suggests both the method and the structure of the novel itself, presenting through Nora and Lurie, like any stereoscope, "two offset images" combining in the brain (of the reader in this example), giving cultural depth to this story of the American West. Late in the novel, Nora's ward, Josie, expresses this relationship as a form of haunting: "He's got his hand on your shoulder" (332).

Indeed, in 1838 the stereoscope's inventor, Charles Wheatstone, wrote of "the simultaneous perception of the two monocular projections," suggesting the novel's structure as Nora's and Lurie's worlds gradually overlap, providing a fuller and different perception of the West to the reader. In the words of Oliver Wendell Holmes, the stereoscope, having provided "two different views of an object, the mind, as it were, *feels round it* and gets an idea of its solidity" (Holmes 1859; emphasis added). Of course, part of this fuller perception—*feeling round it*—is that a stereoscope creates an illusion, producing an appearance of solid reality that cheats the senses with its seeming truth. This is evident too in Obreht's novel as its narrative constantly reminds us of the fakery, delusion, lies, and mythmaking circulating within the histories of the West. Therefore, while *Inland* offers a varied and often surreal portrait of the West, it does so, like *In the Distance* and *Days Without End*, with an acute, critical awareness of its persistent mythologies. Out of these real, surreal, and imagined Wests, Obreht fashions a historical novel with contemporary resonance, but one that, like the stereoscope, is focused on what we might term "ways of seeing." It is perhaps no surprise that there is a minor character in the novel called John Berger, reminding us of the art critic whose most renowned work had this precise title.[1]

Obreht's novel employs multiple perspectives through Nora, Lurie, and Merrion Crace (a wealthy and ruthless landowner), dramatizing *ways of seeing* the West in the context of colliding worlds. In the words of critic John Berger, "It is seeing which establishes our place in the surrounding world…[but] the relation between what we see and what we know is never settled…[because] the way we see things is affected by what we know or what we believe.…[W]e are always looking at the relation between things and ourselves. Our vision is continually active, continually moving" (1972, 7–9). As this chapter will examine, what we might call these *relations of seeing and knowing* are vital to *Inland*'s structure and thematic content as it dramatizes a "continually active, continually moving" West.

Even though Lurie is an immigrant outsider and an outlaw who sees the dead and has visions of "what was, or what might, or what never could be" (Obreht 2019a, 103), he shares something significant with Nora: resilience. She is a tough, independent "woman of action," an "opinionated, rangy, sweating mule of a thing" in a world ruled by men (196, 199). She is also "half-habited by the apparition" of her dead daughter, Evelyn, and has conversations with her throughout the book (199). Obreht's "stereoscopic" (or "doubleeyed," as Holmes called it) narrative functions to unsettle accepted notions of US western history while reminding us too of its tireless mythologies—of "things you will believe, and things you won't"—both from within the stories themselves and through the form she adopts to construct them. For example, Nora's story unfolds on a single day, spiraling in and out of others' lives and drilling down into the histories that construct their present and that of the Arizona Territory in 1893, while Lurie's story spans a period from the mid-1850s to 1893, moving across Asia, Europe, and America, before their stories collide at the novel's climax. Thus, the local and the global are crucial to the novel's converging elements, mirroring two narratives of isolated, traditionally marginalized outsiders: an immigrant's story, on the one hand, and a woman's story of settling, on the other.[2] Through Obreht's stereoscopic structure, we see the uncanny similarities between their very different lives, struggling to make a life in America against backdrops of violence, prejudice, stereotyping, and social limitations, and consequently gain a fuller perception of the West itself. Through this collision and interaction of worlds, the novel dramatizes what Pheng Cheah terms "a web of meaningful relations," wherein place, in this case, the American West, is not viewed as simply "quantified spatial location," but rather seen as dynamic and active "multiple temporalities" (2016, 101, 200).

AT THE EDGE OF THE WORLD

Crucial to its worlding process, *Inland* is a novel steeped in many nations, cultures, and religions, with its setting, the American West from the 1850s onward, described as "at the edge of the world" (Obreht 2019a, 200). Of course, consistent with the stereoscopic nature of the novel, this phrase has a double meaning, suggesting both the wild remoteness of the landscape of Arizona Territory and its relation nonetheless, through trade, migration, and culture, to the wider world beyond. As suggested throughout, this is a novel of relations "that overlap and flow into each other…because each force, as part of a world, is necessarily opened up to what lies outside" (Cheah 2016, 211). Its characters' lives are "caught between worlds" (Obreht 2019a, 2), *edging* between inside and outside, life and death, material and spiritual, past, present, and future. Consequently, people in transition populate *Inland*: arriving, wandering, searching, conquering, struggling, raging and dreaming, engaging in what we might define as a process of worlding. In this sense, the novel maps what Kathleen Stewart calls "a series of worldings" between Nora and Lurie, their lives "unfolding, pausing and setting off again…[with] Registers, spaces thrown together into something to be in, or to be next to, or to be wary of" (2013, 42).

Obreht explores what she calls "communities at the periphery of legend" (2019b) and finds within them a West full of the world as multiplicity, as if once more corresponding to Nancy's view that "the unity of the world is not one: it is made of a diversity, including disparity and opposition.… [A] world is a multiplicity of worlds" (2007a, 109). As such, Lurie is the Mostar-born son of Hadziosman Djurić, an immigrant from the

Ottoman Empire, whose journey across the West brings him into contact with Hadji Ali, a Syrian Turk, the Greek Yiorgios, and Mico Tedro from Smyrna, all cameleers working for Edward Fitzgerald Beale, "staking a wagon road to California" (Obreht 2019a, 100).[3] In addition, their cook is a freed slave, Absalom Reading, who becomes a Buffalo soldier in the Civil War, and while crossing the West they encounter Native tribes—Sioux, Mojave, and Cheyenne—as well as stumbling across the great Anasazi dwellings cut into the desert rock. Nora Volk is an emigrant from Laibach, Slovenia, settling in Arizona, while her husband, Emmett Lark, has "far-flung Scots kin" (27–28). They work in Amargo alongside Mexican, Castilian, and Anglo neighbors, surrounded by their fear and guilt over Native American dispossession (with "Indian fires…fewer now and always more distant" [228]). Even Merrion Crace is described by Nora's son Toby as a "limey carpetbagger" (292), an epithet learned from his father. After all, as Obreht has said, Arizona was "a community filled with immigrants from all over" (Barenbaum 2019), marking a West in formation, less a finished, exceptional, or single region, and more a complex entangled series of negotiated identities and communities, truly Nancy's "multiplicity of worlds." As the ghostly mother tells her son in Berger's *Here Is Where We Meet*, "It's not any place, John, it's a meeting place" (2005, 7), and ultimately the same is true of Obreht's West, imagined as a meeting place of nations and peoples, of different lives with differing relations, of competing ways of seeing and knowing like an imperfect space of worlding. In the words of Iain Chambers, it is a worlding that "sets an inherited way of seeing into movement, deprives it of a privileged viewpoint, renders its linearity vulnerable to other gazes that cross, deviate and interrupt its path" (2018, 10).

As discussed earlier, Obreht presents a worlded West exceeding its mythic status as foundational of the nation-state reinforced by all "the facile cowboy myths I was fed growing up" (2019b). Her misconceptions of the West and the western were often challenged in significant ways while researching the novel: "My lens opened up completely. People came to the territories from all over, places totally unaffiliated with what we romanticize or mythologize. The way the communities grew and combined was really interesting to me. There was a lot of language mixing, a lot of culinary and cultural mixing" (Chapman 2019). As if referring to her image of the stereoscope discussed earlier, this opened lens allows Obreht the possibilities of multiple worlds coming back into her *reworlded* West.

THE OTHER LIVING

The novel's "opening lens" materializes through the dual narratives' backstories, contributing to a rich worldliness, digressing into the multiple worlds of its characters, places, animals, and even beyond these, to spirit worlds of the "other living." As Nora ponders at one point, "Might the dead truly inhabit the world alongside the living…invisible merely because the mechanism of seeing them had yet to be invented?" (Obreht 2019a, 254). In keeping with the novel's interest in ways of seeing, this sense of hauntedness establishes an alternative temporality wherein the past is never lost or irrelevant, but rather circles around, reemerging in lives as echoes and hauntings. Obreht has commented, "It's like that, America. Its ghosts seem to haunt from both the past and the future" (2019b), and this supernatural presence provides another "mechanism of seeing," contributing to the novel's worlding weave. As Obreht has asked, "Is the world made up of only what we see? Or is it made up of the things we believe? And I think to explore that on the page is a great pleasure and a great need for me" (Neary 2019). After all, as Josie, with her "intermediary powers," puts it, "[T]he 'other living' were apparently everywhere" and, like the lost histories the novel is concerned with, cannot be dismissed or consigned to the past (Obreht 2019a, 51, 41). As Jacques Derrida explains, "To learn to live with ghosts, in the upkeep, the conversation, the company, or the companionship…[is] [t]o live otherwise, and better. No not better, but more justly." Both parts of Obreht's stereoscopic narrative converse with the dead, "being-with specters," in order to learn to live "more justly," acknowledging the presence of those "no longer present" in the West, but whose stories nonetheless demand to be heard (1994, xviii).

Derrida refers in this process of finding justice to "the principle of *responsibility*, beyond all living present" (xviii), to those dead or yet to be born (the past and the future), and not simply to be fixated upon the "living present in general." In other words, a linear notion of the historical "arrow of time," moving from past to future, like Turner's frontier history or the methodical progress of Manifest Destiny, is interrupted by these "spectral moment[s]" that function as "not docile to time," "furtive and untimely" (xix). As discussed in chapter 1 and explored in Diaz's *In the Distance*, interruption is a method in worlding westerns, as they break open the fixed assumptions of the genre and the national unanimity it often maintains. As Derrida reminds us, behind this process is the focal desire for justice, "be they victims of wars, political or other kinds of violence, nationalist, racist, colonialist, sexist, or other kinds of exterminations, victims of the oppressed of capitalist imperialism or any of the forms of totalitarianism" (xviii). Fundamental to Obreht's experimentation with narrative time is the dawning awareness that one of the narrators, Lurie, is in fact dead and telling his tale from his position among the other living. Thus, as we read *Inland*, the narrative circles and eddies, as we learn to live with ghosts and their stories, plunging us back and forth in time, entering minds and dreams, hopes and fears, that collectively assemble a different, worlded, and perhaps more just West.

This worldliness contributes to the novel's rich layering of time and space, expressed by Obreht in an interview:

> The history of the West is a deeply turbulent, unstable, and violent one. Bloodshed and colonialism and repurposing and renaming. Everything about that kept the living population, from various walks of life, in a constant state of unrest. I thought this constant state of unrest must be true for the dead as well. That was baked in from the beginning: *nobody in this book is going to catch a break for a long time, or at all.* It's a cauldron of increasing instability run by malicious, impervious powers. That's just empire, right?" (Chapman 2019; emphasis in the original).

Thus, the West of the novel *worlds* because it refuses a linear, one-dimensional, romanticized, or mythological nationalist viewpoint, promulgating instead this atmosphere of turbulence, instability, and violence alongside Lurie's often Adamic sense of wonder. Hence, from the very opening of the novel, as Lurie arrives in America with his father, his story is steeped in death, from the "dead…outlaid in their white shrouds side by side along the stern" of the ship (Obreht 2019a, 1), to his soon-dead father buried incorrectly as "Hodge Lurie" because his real name was too difficult to pronounce. Lurie's first job in America is as a collector of the dead "round the dens and fleahouses on Bleecker Street" (3) and then as a grave robber. Yet there are still moments when Lurie, addressing his companion, the camel Burke, is struck by the awe and wonder of the West, "the old emptiness of this place: the blue of distant mountains" (229). "You have stood on the shores of the mighty Platte, where Red Cloud's Sioux, gathered for the parley that would wright their ruin.… You have stood on bluffs planted up with scorched saplings where the ground was pocked with exhalations, with ruts belching white gobs of mud as if the earth were breathing" (220). The "wayfarer" Lurie reveals himself a troubled man unable to settle into such a landscape, since he is tormented by the "occasional dead" and "all who'd come before me" (103, 95, 103), like historical reminders of pain and loss inscribed in the deep history of western places, not as paradisal, but as spaces of terrible violence, suffering, and hurt. It is the "wants" of the dead that Lurie senses, "in pursuit of whatever it was they could not see," their desires, losses, and unfulfilled lives that reshape the established and progressive narrative of settler colonialism, until "the skin prickles like a dreaming limb…. It blows you open" (102). In the West, as he later understands, "I found the sadness just beneath my want, like frozen soil" (222).

Thus, the novel becomes a type of critical "ghost western," wherein the dead rehearse an alternative history of the West, acknowledging and questioning simultaneously the optimism and boosterism of Manifest Destiny. As Derrida puts it, "Haunting belongs to the structure of every hegemony" (1994, 46). Lurie's identification with the dead also links his immigrant story to the Native peoples who had once occupied its landscapes but, by the time of his wandering, are being removed into smaller areas of land or annihilated altogether.[4] In the novel, Natives, though "righteous and unafraid" (Obreht 2019a, 226), become an absent presence, ghostly western traces reminding us of the price paid for settler-colonialism and the perpetual expansion of capitalism across the West. Their "want" and their absence, "distilled generation by generation" (229), is a reminder of what Gerald Vizenor called "centuries of separation, proscription, removal by treaties, and *disappearance*" (1998, 21) that, nonetheless, haunt hegemony still (see chapter 6).

Thus, in the West's "great theatre of belonging" (Luiselli 2017, 99), Lurie's phantoms of "thinning souls" haunt the landscape, underlining the terrible isolation he feels wandering across the desert: "They could see the living, but not one another. Nameless and unburied, turned out suddenly into the bewildering dark, they rose to find themselves entirely alone" (Obreht 2019a, 229, 158). In his restless search for a new life in the West, Lurie's "want" is echoed by the generations of dead he senses all around him "dotting the horizon in their loneliness, the unburied dead of battle upon battle" (228). It is the worlds of the "nameless and unburied," therefore, that matter to Obreht, for they are the forgotten and marginalized who, nonetheless, contribute to the formations of history.

WOMEN, WESTERNS, WORLDS

Obreht's comment that *Inland* should illuminate "the story of the woman scowling in the corner of the Western" (McCarthy 2019) further reflects her concern for marginalized worlds. Nora Lark's centrality clearly articulates this, alongside a variety of strong, singular female characters who populate the novel. Rather than the "scowling" minor character associated with the conventional western, Obreht moves women into the light as active, expressive characters with significant roles, achieving what Victoria Lamont argues is crucial for women in westerns, that they "play an active and independent role in the narrative," shifting the "account of the western" so that it is shown as "a complex cultural field in which both men and women participated" (2016, 4). Initially painted as the archetypal "woman in distress" abandoned by her husband, Emmett, and two of her sons, Dolan and Rob, Nora ultimately refutes the tendency of so many westerns that relegated female characters to an "ephemeral or subgeneric status or simply erased them" (158).

In Nora's sections of the novel, the family settler narrative of the West is pivotal, with the Larks building a life for themselves in Amargo, Arizona Territory, in 1893, ironically at the exact time Frederick Jackson Turner is pronouncing the frontier closed in his essay "The Significance of the Frontier in American History." As I have noted, Nora is no conventional stereotype of frontier femininity, since she is strong, independent, and willing to take on local seats of power, such as the booster newspaper the *Ash River Clarion* and its wealthy, ruthless supporter, Merrion Crace. She holds the family together despite the absence of her husband and sons, yet seems to have had at some point in the past some affection for, and possible relationship with, the local sheriff, Harlan Bell. Therefore, Nora's life may appear to be a small, local story of the "less than Edenic" Amargo existing at "the northernmost habitation for miles. The last known point before the page went blank," yet layered within it are worlds revealed as not blank at all, but richly textured with the details and struggles of a complex everyday existence (Obreht 2019a, 58, 37). Nora's guilt over a dead child, her strained relationship with her husband, her unrequited love for the local sheriff, and the "hardening" (198) necessary to survive in the harsh landscape of drought-stricken Amargo all contribute to her complexity. Above all, Nora is a strong-minded survivor managing the homestead as well as her family and helping run the *Amargo Sentinel* newspaper, while engaging in the politics of the town that is at risk from the encroaching presence of Crace's capitalist machine.

However, Nora is flawed too by the guilt for the death of her daughter, Evelyn, left out in the blazing sun because she thought Indians were raiding her homestead. Marked by the racism of her times, "growing in her like an illness all her life," Nora has a deep fear of Indians and the violence associated with them. For her, every story she had ever heard of "guts pulled out in streamers" is contained in the word "Apache" and imagined in the illusory figure of the "dark rider" threatening her farm and family (325). In exploring Nora's and Lurie's outsider identities as uncannily linked, Obreht reaches into the tradition of the western to draw out new and different patterns of worldliness. As she has said, "Having both grown up with westerns and relished the twists and turns of the genre in literature and film over the past decade, I was very keen to get a chance to play with some of its tropes—chiefly the idea of the hardened wanderer and the woman waiting by the hearth, both of which, funnily enough, were elements baked into the historical framework on which *Inland* is based" (Greengrass 2019).

Safe to say, the novel employs many other well-rehearsed tropes of the western: outlaws and lawmen, power-crazed cattle barons, ambushes, and double-crosses, "balcony girls," prospectors, and Indian killers. However, within these "baked-in" parameters, like all the novels in *Worlding the Western*, Obreht unsettles the received narrative of westward expansion, not to deny the terrible colonialism of Manifest Destiny, the violent destruction of indigenous populations, the exploitation of environment, or its gender bias, but rather, in revealing them, to provide new and challenging perspectives. Indeed, Ryan Chapman goes as far as calling the novel "like a full reset of the American Western" (2019). As we have seen, it does this by taking the reader *outside* the broadly comforting and familiar world of the traditional western in order to, according to Francisco Cantú, ensure that "the future resonance of the Western is rooted in a continuing revision of its terms, and in an expanding notion of who might occupy its center" (2019). With this in mind, the novel goes metaphorically "Inland," digging *into* the land of the West and its multiple stories, for us to appreciate and understand its relationships with and debt to the wider world—to "the world in all its workings," as the novel would have it (Obreht 2019a, 80). As Lurie comments about the soldier Shaw's notebooks, "whole worlds could be found on those pages" (93), and in the same way, Obreht's novel delves into the "workings" of many different worlds rather than simply describing and endorsing a single and overrepresented familiar one that has helped define and fix our perception of "Westness." In "revising the terms" of the western, Obreht exceeds its assumed tropes, stretching and redirecting the generic framework until it becomes a more open, magical, sometimes dreamlike story, mixing gothic visions and realism in equal measure, until its many worlds are seen as interlocking and layered, existing as if uncannily suspended in time.

GOING INLAND

The title, *Inland*, refers, according to the author, to all the land away from the railroad tracks marking the distance between developed places and those that wither in isolation (Scutts 2019, 23). Alongside the "want" of those in the West, the sense of loss and change permeates the novel, marking the shift from "the old emptiness of this place" to "yellow lights, once so sparse, [that] have brightened more and more our black nights" as settlements encroach on wilderness (Obreht 2019a, 229, 355). Like John Berger, another innovator with forms of fiction, W. G. Sebald has his narrator, Austerlitz, describe a sense of time that mirrors *Inland*'s swirling worldliness: "an unquantifiable dimension which disregards linear regularity, does not progress constantly forward but moves in eddies, is marked by episodes of congestion and irruption, recurs in ever-changing form, and evolves in no one knows what direction" (2001, 101).

Inland's eddying, magical irregularity takes many forms, but most noticeably through the relationship of Lurie to his camel, Burke, who becomes central to the narrative, indeed confided in as he travels alone through the West like an "absurd centaur" (Obreht 2019a, 91). The camel's mythical quality, with its "snake neck and frowsy mane…huge periscope head…tent-peg underbite," for whom "the enraptured came to marvel and stare" (83, 91), further defamiliarizes the western genre, unsettling its frames of reference. We soon discover that the nearest thing to "cowboys" in the story are the Muslim camel drivers working for the US Army Camel Corps whose religious and moral code is constantly at odds with the hard-living image of the westerner: "No pig, no tanglefoot, no gambling nor whoring around—all of which accrued distrust from the infantry entire" (92–93). Coming from other places and cultures to the West, these men allow Obreht to tell an alternative story about the frontier, with the myth of promise and exceptionalism countered by comparisons to the worlds they have left behind. A conversation between Lurie and Mico as they survey Fort Green, Texas, dramatically underlines this: "'I am from Smyrna, misafir. Smyrna. Do you know it?…It's a magnificent city by the sea. The port is full of ships and the hills shine with lighted windows. This. With a disdainful wave of his hand he took in the whole barrens below. 'Where *is* everything?'" "This" is the West they have come to rather than the West portrayed in the alluring myths and stories of opportunity and promise: "Around us were ragged trails and oases greened by underground creeks, the occasional dead flitting across the plains, always searching, always moving on in pursuit of whatever it was they could not see" (95). Rather like the western towns Hawk encounters in Diaz's *In the Distance*, these foreigners see mostly disappointment, not promise, and ghostly wandering, rather than civilization. Alongside this critical view, as Susan Kollin has examined at length, there are "traces of a Moorish presence" in much western American literature, with many of its archetypes, including the cowboy, owing much to the Arab world (2015a, 65). As she goes on to say, these Eastern influences on the West are substantial, "questioning the bounded and quintessential U.S. Americanness of the American West itself" (86).

Of course, Mico's critical view of westering is in contrast to other narratives within the novel, most noticeably that of Merrion Crace, who, coming from England around the exact time that Lurie arrives from farther east, longs to fulfill his mother's gypsy fortune teller's prophecy that "if I didn't die by ten, I'd be a king" (Obreht 2019a, 302).[5] Crace's description of arriving in Galveston in 1858 is full of a romantic yearning and possibility, more closely associated with western mythology: "Whole swaths of nothing, and a smell of horses and rain, and green-gray sky, and all the young blood of the world riled with talk of slavery and statehood and secession. I set my boot on that beach and knew I weren't going back across the water not ever again" (305). Ignited by this moment of colonial desire, Crace's life follows an almost Turnerian mythic path from prospecting and riding the Pony Express to buffalo hunting and, finally, cattle ranching in Arizona. Yet alongside his vision of the West emerges another trace, his sinister and threatening will to power: "I got the sense that everybody had found out what I had known for years: the West was too fine a promise to waste. They were heading here with wagons and sheep and their trampling feet to make life that just bit harder and more crowded for folks like me who had known and kept this secret for years" (307).

Obreht presents Crace as a man obsessed by power and control for whom the West was the "harshest test a soul could face" through which one might become "The Cattle King of Carter County" (310, 311). The West "was where I renewed myself," he claims, amid a landscape "designated for his own, solitary soul," since, as he told himself, "the sublime lives here, and I am the only one who sees it" (309, 307). Sounding increasingly like the judge in Cormac McCarthy's *Blood Meridian*, for Crace the mythic promise of the West is not available to all and certainly not to men like Lurie, but rather for the few godlike, powerful ones who keep its secrets for their own advantage.[6] Crace exemplifies what Richard Slotkin called the "protean qualities of the self-transcendent westerner" for whom "progress is equated with the remaking of one's individual fortune and one's individual spirit" (1973, 430–31). In Crace's worldview, the West is his personal fiefdom, outdoing Moses in a search for the Promised Land, "baptized in sweat and blood," so that *before him* nothing of merit existed, only wilderness: "Before me, we were all the way inland," he says (Obreht 2019a, 310, 309). With such a monomaniacal vision, the one thing Crace cannot tolerate is "dissent," like that encountered in his battle with the stubborn Larks who oppose and challenge his dominance in the region: "It's my work that raised this place up. And I'll be damned if I'll sit here and let you say that I don't belong to it" (310).

Crace's position, like so much in the novel, has a resonance with contemporary politics and in particular with debates about rights over land, citizenship, and resources in a time of rapid globalization. Crace's accumulative worldview wants to quash difference and enforce uniformity, as if, in Jean-Luc Nancy's words, "circumscribing the earth more and more in a horizon without opening or exit" (2007a, 47). Lurie amplifies this circumscription when talking to his Muslim friend Hadji Ali, who expresses his doubts about belonging in the United States:

> All my life some fool has promised me this or that. My father promised me manhood, but all I got was capture. The French promised me gold, but all I got was a couple of camels. Beale promised me pay, but you know he never had me enlisted?… He never even put the papers in to make me an American. That's why Lilo left. He said: 'If it couldn't be achieved by the kind of journey we took, well then, what will it take? Shall we have to fly to the moon? Ten years I worked for that man, and learned only that I might as well never have existed. (Obreht 2019a, 348)

Ali articulates the immigrant's sense of promise alongside the almost inevitable experience of disappointment and loss as the reality of life within Crace's colonized West hits home. What does one have to do in order to be accepted? Resonating forward, this moment interlinks with the contemporary immigrant stories of Valeria Luiselli's *Tell Me How It Ends*, in which she expresses the frustrations of those seeking citizenship in Trump's United States: "And once you're here, you're ready to give everything, or almost everything, to stay and play a part in the great theatre of belonging. In the United States to stay is an end in itself and not a means: to stay is the founding myth of this society" (2017, 99).

In such ways, *Inland* circles forward and back, as if shadowing contemporary politics and most obviously the anti-immigrant rhetoric of President Donald Trump: What is an American? Who qualifies as an American? The timeliness of this novel's discussion of immigration and settler culture arrived at the very point Trump accused Alexandria Ocasio-Cortez, Ilhan Omar, Ayanna Pressley, and Rashida Tlaib of not being "capable of loving our Country" and that they should, consequently, "go back" to their "countries whose governments are a complete and total catastrophe" (Rogers and Fandos 2019).[7] For so long, the western genre constructed a unanimous sense of nationhood, whereas *Inland* uses this supposedly most American of genres *differently*, interrogating notions of belonging and home, identity and nation. It understands and concludes that, above all, the West was always already multiple and multicultural, a place "haunted by the spectre of loss, by the eventual and seemingly inevitable demise of those very forms of freedom frequently promised by the form" (Kollin 2015b, 28). In his review of the novel, Alex Preston wrote, "If the western is the tale that America tells about itself, then this is an attempt to write a new chapter in that story" (2019).

THE TRUTH ELSEWHERE—

"ONLY FLESH AND BLOOD REMEMBERING"

In telling the western story differently, as we have seen, *Inland worlds* through both its characters' histories and their subsequent experiences in America. However, it also worlds in other ways too, becoming a novel of secrets, lies, fake news, myths, hidden stories, campfire tales, and disappearing histories. For this reason, it is both a powerful rethinking of history and an astute commentary on the persistence of such issues in contemporary US politics. Late in the novel, Nora explains how she has covered up the truth of her daughter Evelyn's death for years by inventing an Indian attack on her homestead. The lie she created takes on the life of a myth, and her discussion of it seems crucial to Obreht's concerns in the novel as a whole: "And the lie, so easy in its time, a kind of evening in and of itself, was carried forward. Out it went, in the mouths and minds of women and freighters and soldiers, to some unknown amalgam of harm, a greater evening, so vast, so abundant, that every now and again, when she thought about it, she could convince herself it must be something else. How could there be so much of something so evidently poisonous?" (Obreht 2019a, 327). The "amalgam of harm" created by such personal myths spreading beyond the control of the individual, "carried forward" by others, out into the world corresponds with how public myths, like Manifest Destiny or racial hierarchy, function. On many levels, *Inland* examines how stories are "carried forward," with both positive and negative consequences, ultimately presenting the West as a complex web of relations and histories, some strangely lost and some overly dominant. Ultimately, as we have shown, these competing ways of seeing and knowing structure the novel.

Lurie's task, for example, is to record, often in conversations with his camel, Burke, the "vast and immutable want" (230) and loss of the dead he carries within him and, in so doing, to recall voices and lives themselves lost to history, like the "always more distant" Natives he describes: "But we remembered, you and I. It saddened me. Who would speak of these things when we were gone? So, too, must the makers of those distant fires have asked themselves as they fought the fading of their world. I began to wish that I could pour our memories into the water we carried, so that anyone drinking might see how it had been" (229). Clearly, Obreht's purpose in writing of the West was to capture such memories from history's footnotes and margins, from "the silence and secrets of wild living" (351), from Native disappearance, through the immigrant wanderings of Lurie, to Nora Lark's homesteading tales. Echoing Berger's comments on ways of seeing discussed earlier, Sebald writes in *Austerlitz* how "our concern with history…is a concern with preformed images already imprinted on our brains, images at which we keep staring while the truth lies elsewhere, away from it all, somewhere as yet undiscovered" (2001, 72). As we have seen already, Obreht's sense of history mirrors this interest in the "elsewhere," countering the "preformed" and dominant notions defining both history and its mythologies. Her attention to the "undiscovered" narratives of people like Nora and Lurie creates an entangled West of complexity and contradiction, strangely poised between magic and realism, myth and fact, the living and the dead: not *a single* world, but *many* worlds.[8]

For Obreht, the West is anything but a single world, like the one Crace desires, for it is instead a whirl of living and dead voices, a complex space of interlocking histories, myths, and secrets, manifested throughout the novel as Native stories, travelers' tales, immigrant pasts, spiritualist séances, ghostly presences, and dramatic visions, as much a magical realist landscape as it is the rational frontier of economic and cultural change. As Sebald puts it, "The world is, as it were, draining itself, in that the history of countless places and objects which themselves have no power of memory is never heard, never described or passed on" (24). Under such terms, the history of the West becomes in Obreht's hands a multifaceted convergence of strange beasts, droughts, spirits, Muslims, Natives, Mexicans, and Anglos sitting alongside "Cattle Kings" and "the latest scientific advancements: anatomical marvels and the wonders of automation" (Obreht 2019a, 254). Her challenge in the novel is to "pass on" these atypical lost stories in order to, as Sebald would have it, replenish a world drained of its fullest possibilities.

This aspect of the novel relates also to the West as a place of change, on the cusp of modernity, already transforming the land through what one character, Sandy Freed, calls "Information" (67). Of course, as we have already seen, information *in* and *about* the West takes on many forms, and this is a significant aspect of Obreht's exploration of history and myth. In *Inland* myth's ways of seeing "necessarily feed on wilful delusion" (61), promoting particular versions of reality, ranging from the Old World stories told to Nora by her father, Gus Volk, that "teemed with vengeful hags—woodland witches shoving pretty children into ovens, or else fencing their houses with the bones of men who had aggrieved them," to the New World tales of the writer Lurie meets, "who'd come to the West to make something of its stories," only to die violently along with all his words (191, 231). The West is being mythicized as it develops, through the dime novels read by Nora's boys, the photograph Crace displays of him with Wyatt Earp, or Indian tall tales retold by prospectors of "a mountain…fallen in a burning arc from the sky…two hundred years ago, and in its heart sat the richest veins of gold and quartz anyone had ever seen" (269, 342). All these strands "carried forward" create the multiple and often contradictory worlds of "Westness" that Obreht conjures up in the novel.

However, there remain prominent and dominant versions of "information" that drained the world of its multiplicity, representing a narrative that best suited a drive to unanimity and what Turner called "composite nationality" (1961, 51). In relation to the Native experience, Gerald Vizenor famously termed this settler mythmaking process as "the scriptures of manifest manners…the simulations of dominance" (1994, 5). In contemporary politics, the debates over "fake news," the power of social media to control public opinion, and the accusations that the media are the "enemy of the people" (as Donald Trump tweeted) suggest a similar process.[9] Obreht's comment in the epigraph to this chapter, referring to "this particular cycle," suggests the resonance she found between such recent battles over information and those prevalent on the frontier in the 1890s.[10]

An example of the power of information "carried forward" is via the world of "News, debate!" (Obreht 2019a, 67), conveyed through the *Amargo Sentinel* newspaper that Emmett Lark sets up in Arizona and through its rival, the *Ash River Clarion*, controlled by Merrion Crace, both claiming their versions of the truth. Torn between committing her thoughts in letters to the paper and holding back, as her husband wants, Nora thinks at one point, "She had better not write any of it" (72). Nora, despite her self-censorship, understands the power of language, commenting on the authority of the printed word in letters published in the *Clarion*, "That it was raised will make it true for half our citizenry" (78).

In fact, there are letters everywhere in the novel, becoming the battleground over the status of Amargo versus Ash River, but also those carried by Crace for the Pony Express, which he secretly opens and reads, providing an early lesson in the power of language and information. As he says, "A man who knows your secrets is a man who knows you whole," and through the acquiring of such illicit knowledge, he "knew more of the world than was ever meant for one man" (306). Information ("secrets") represents power for Crace, and, as he says later when taunting Nora and Harlan over their hidden desire, untold secrets are just like an "unopened letter…waiting for the right reader" (320).

Throughout the novel, modes of information distort language and spread contributory myths, from the pulpit, where a sermon is "dedicated to outlaying the desecrations…good men had suffered" fighting the Dakota (62), to the telegraph lines spreading across the country from east to west, which, as Bruce Cumings writes, were "momentous for expansionism" (2009, 78). As Harlan explains in the novel, "Wood and wire, and suddenly the whole horizon of human thought was altered" (Obreht 2019a, 253). Later it is Crace who sets up the "first telephonic transmitter" (252) between his ranch and the local hotel. Cumulatively, these modes of communication and information represent a rapidly changing West with "the effect of drawing things closer to one another, of illuminating that grainy twilight beyond which lay the landscape of a new and truer world" (254). This is the recognition of an unavoidable global, technological West acknowledging its relationship to the "world" through formal lines of communication—*drawing things closer to one another*—creating a space for increased trade and capital expansion. However, this modernization process carries with it another consequence, an inevitable uniformity, which, as the novel dramatizes, excludes and diminishes difference and alterity. It is the onset of what we now call globalization, heralded by new forms of information that standardize multiple worlds into a single manageable and disciplined one. The very histories Obreht articulates through Lurie's journey and Nora's struggle are the exact same marginal lives lost in the great sweep of western history toward "unworlding," imminent globalization.

As we have seen, countering this pull to uniformity and "unworlding," the novel continually asserts that multiple worlds have been always already present in the development of the West through conquest, immigration, and settlement and that, despite its headlong rush toward the future, the region was actually built upon its many pasts, layered amid the living and the dead. Obreht's rhythmic narrative moves back and forth, in and out, spiraling through history and story, imagination and reality, landscape and psychic space, actively producing a West that is more than dry, narrow information. She replaces the cause-effect linearity of history with a more spatial sense akin to that described by Jessica Dubow in her discussion of Sebald: "where the world and life of things are parachuted into the activity of presentness, into the immoderate moment of the now, to awaken a very different understanding of historical and temporal process" (2007, 822). *Inland*'s "presentness" is rather more like Sebald's sense of Europe as a complex network of spectral and material spaces brought to life through writing itself: "a long lineage of grey, ancestral faces, rendered unto ash but still there, as ghostly presences, on the harried paper" (2002, 162). On the "harried paper" of *Inland*, Obreht's West, as in Sebald's Europe, according to Lewis and Tatum, is a "site that despite the traces of evidence left behind might forever remain, at least at the margins, inassimilable" (2017, 15). Thus, western history cannot simply explain the nation's development through an explication of the past, for it is revealed as "unsettling and uncanny, but so too is the present" (16). Rather than the clarity of myth, as an explanatory tool Lewis and Tatum assert the "mystery or problem" of the West that they claim, following Sebald, "is not narrowly localized but is expansively dislocated" (17), bound up in a process of what this book terms "worlding."

So, returning to *Inland*, one notes that as much as the book appears to be "narrowly localized," it is, in fact, "expansively dislocated," pulling the West, as we have seen, into *relations* with other cultures, other religions, and even with the "other living" (the dead). Working together, these uncanny relations produce Obreht's West as troublingly nonlinear, stubbornly opaque, refusing to conform to the supposed unanimity and transparency of national mythology, since, as we stated earlier, it "disregards linear regularity, does not progress constantly forward but moves in eddies, is marked by episodes of congestion and irruption, recurs in ever-changing form, and evolves in no one knows what direction" (Sebald 2001, 101). As Glissant explains, what matters is diversity in relations: "We see this as radiant—replacing the absorbing concept of unity: it is the opacity of the diverse animating the imagined transparency of Relation" (1997, 192).

CONCLUSION—"THE FULLNESS OF HEART"

To return to the idea of the stereoscope with which I opened this chapter, it is noticeable that the gift to Toby is from Merrion Crace, a man whose purpose, as we have seen, is to control and order the world to his particular worldview. As he tells Nora, "It's mine.... It's my work that raised this place up" (Obreht 2019a, 310), and, like Turner's archetypal frontiersman, he is the ideal of the "self-made man…that all men might become," who "dreamed dreams and beheld visions" (1961, 69, 70). As Crace says, "I knew more of the world than was ever meant for one man" (Obreht 2019a, 306), and the wondrous pictures in the stereoscope he gives to Toby depict a world contained, measured, and available to the imperial gaze. Of course, the stereoscope was a device that gained particular popularity during a period marked by globalization and colonialism, functioning to make "the forms of the whole world available" (Plunkett 2013, 396) to its viewers. In fact, Oliver Wendell Holmes, writing in 1859 (a few years after the opening of *Inland*), compared the stereoscope to a hunting trip: "Men will hunt all curious, beautiful, grand objects, as they hunt the cattle in South America, for their skins, and leave the carcasses as of little worth." As Plunkett comments, "Holmes's domineering trope suggests the onto-logical violence inflicted upon materiality by the pursuit of stereographs for the comfortable drawing rooms of America and Europe" (2013, 396).

In the context of Obreht's novel, Toby, already partially blind, is "lost in the world of its pictures" (Obreht 2019a, 333), distracted by the stereo-scope's images of that "pale half-world across the sea," which included "a stone beast in the desert" and "a grim, dark-faced man, shawled head to toe" (362, 295). Ironically, as Toby views this "foggy interior" (295) of exotic, distant images, a real, material world close at hand comes crashing toward him and his mother, who raises her gun to shoot the approaching camel and rider. It is as if in this moment, the disavowed world of Merrion Crace, the world of others he would contain and control through his worldview, returns with all its messy diversity. To shield her son from the oncoming beast, Nora cries out, "Keep on looking at your pictures," and even after Burke is dead the boy refuses to look upon the scene except from the safety of the house, "behind the glass" (362, 364), as if still using the distancing of the stereoscope to frame the world. As he finally looks down upon the scene, Toby's remarks seem a strangely acute commentary on the novel's efforts to counter perceptions of the West and its "one-eyed" mythology: "It don't look anything like they do in the books" (364). What books record or what stereoscopes reveal are always already versions of the real and reductions of the truth, belonging alongside *Inland*'s interest in newspapers, dime novels, and other forms of communication, as discursive formations of partiality. They constitute only part of the relations of seeing and knowing the West that Obreht engages with throughout her novel. As John Berger put it, "It is seeing which establishes our place in the surrounding world…[but] The relation between what we see and what we know is never settled…[because] The way we see things is affected by what we know or what we believe.…[W]e are always looking at the relation between things and ourselves. Our vision is continually active, continually moving" (1972, 7–9).

In its final pages, however, *Inland* proposes a "vision" reaching beyond the divisions of the stereoscope discussed earlier. Borrowing Berger's words once again, something "reciprocal" emerges, a "dialogue" that attempts "to explain how, either metaphorically or literally, 'you see things,' and an attempt to discover how 'he sees things'" (9). This dialogue between "you" and "he" translates to the communication in the relations of Nora and Lurie, meeting, as they do, for the first time in this bizarre moment of violence and redemption at the novel's finale. In this final scene, Nora undergoes a series of redemptive epiphanies, shifting her toward a "fullness of heart" that she claims to have "lacked" earlier in the novel (Obreht 2019a, 325). Thus, in killing the camel, Nora saves Toby's life, something in the past she could not do for her daughter, Evelyn. Long plagued by her fear of the native "Other" blamed for Evelyn's death, in this moment she also reaches out across the racial divide to the "dark rider" figure of Lurie tied to his camel. In Nora's act of "cutting the ropes away," binding Lurie's fragile corpse to the now dead beast, something is released into the living world, an alternative lost archive of Lurie's life and history joining with her own: "the contents of his life—who was he? To whom did he belong?" Yet the inevitable answer to the questions would "necessarily" be "to somebody unknown. Might as well be nobody" (365), since Lurie belongs to the margins of western history, to its forgotten or erased elements, overwritten by the dominant stories of people like Merrion Crace. However, Nora's attention to the dead man's body as she "marked the tips of his fingers" and delicately "unbuttoned his coat" suggests a care and devotion approaching a salvific holy act (365, 366). Yet it is a worldly action born of a calm reciprocity and sharing. It is as if Lurie symbolically embodies her absent sons and husband, a body she will later return to, "to gather him up" (365), like the relics of a saint restored to a religious shrine.

This secular, worldly imagery of redemption, care, and new communion culminates in Nora drinking from the canteen Lurie has carried throughout his journey and into which he had told Burke he would "pour our memories into the water" (229). As the ever-thirsty Nora drinks, she hears and senses "the singing tumble of water…singing in the darkness. Rain and river. Iron and salt" (366), experiencing an intense revelation. Once again, though, it is an epiphany of *this* world, not of any other transcendent one, in which Nora feels what Jean-Luc Nancy calls "coexistence," that is, when existence is "exposed" and "expulsed from its simple self-identity…exposed…to creation, thus to the outside, to exteriority, to multiplicity, to alterity, and to alteration" (2007a, 110). It is as if she absorbs Lurie's existence alongside her own. She "put the canteen to her mouth *and saw*" (Obreht 2019a, 366; emphasis added) the memories stored in the precious vessel, mingling Lurie's life with her own, the settled with the wanderer, the past with the present and the future, amalgamating their singular worlds in a form of coexistent vision, like "the reciprocal action of parts of the world" (Nancy 2007a, 110). "The number of lives that enter our own is incalculable," wrote John Berger (2005, 161), and as Nora sips Lurie's water, it is as if she opens to these worlds in all their intricate patterns. It is a worldly *communion* of sorts, a ceremony commemorating a different West, a different America based on "no ground," as Nancy terms it, no essential and fixed unanimity, but rather one in which "there is only the 'with'…the strange familiarity of all the worlds in the world" (2007a, 111).

At this moment, Nora appreciates *all the worlds in the world*, seeing in a cascading vision the pasts and futures of Lurie and her family, "coins, buttons, buckles, dizzy blue beads," and even a mythic "coyote in his winter coat," and then "no town at all," as Amargo disappears in an ever-changing West (Obreht 2019a, 366, 367). She grasps all her possible futures in Wyoming with Toby; her ghostly daughter, Evelyn; and her spectral husband, Emmett; as well as Rob, Josie, and Dolan alive and living elsewhere in the rapidly modernizing West of trains, motorcars, and expanding towns. Beyond the closed and exclusive vision embodied in Merrion Crace and all those boosters of the West that produced its subsequent "one-eyed" and mythic history, Nora's redemptive survival "opens a world and lets [her] be *with* others" (Cheah 2016, 330). She draws into her (and our) purview new ways of seeing, worlds lost and forgotten, until, as the last words of the novel tell us, "she saw everything, she saw it all" (Obreht 2019a, 368). Nora is called out and beyond herself when confronted by the othered presence of the dead Lurie and his camel and in this strange encounter feels a powerful mix of mortality and love.[11]

In these final scenes of the opening and sharing of worlds, Obreht suggests we must, in Derrida's words, "learn to live with ghosts… To live otherwise and better… more justly. But *with them*… [as] a politics of memory, of inheritance, and of generations." This is to understand that the past and its haunting of the present and future are essential to the worlding western and its responsibility to all those "beyond… the living present," that is, "those who *are not there*, of those no longer or who are not yet *present and living*" (Derrida 1994, xvii–xviii; emphasis in the original). The divisions of short-term contemporary politics denying this responsibility for the past and for others are never far away from the historic echoes of *Inland*, and through Nora's ultimate revelatory vision one is, finally, reminded of the potent, ghostly conversation between John and his mother in Berger's *Here Is Where We Meet* about the possibility of repairing a broken world:

> *Yet you are not really here, are you?*
>
> *How stupid can you get! We—us—we are all here. Just like you and the living are here. You and us, we are here to repair a little of what is broken. This is why we occurred.*
>
> *Occurred?*
>
> *Came to be.* (2005, 51)

"A Land of Missing Things"

C Pam Zhang's
How Much of These Hills Is Gold

In our culture it's easy to absorb Western
tropes passively, through osmosis.
—C Pam Zhang quoted in Alice Cary, "Interview with C Pam Zhang"

Philia begins with the possibility of survival. Surviving—
that is the other name of a mourning whose possibility is never to
be awaited. For one does not survive without mourning.
—Jacques Derrida, *The Politics of Friendship*

A life that counts is a life that is valued,
and a life that is valued is a life we grieve.
—Pamela Sue Anderson, Sabina Lovibond, and A. W. Moore,
"Towards a New Philosophical Imaginary"

C Pam Zhang's epic novel *How Much of These Hills Is Gold* (2020) numbers each section in an unusual and intriguing manner—for example, as "xx62" or "xx67"—and when asked about this in an interview, she explained: "I borrowed that idea from the Haruki Murakami book, *1Q84*…[where] he uses it to depict a slightly alternate, twisted version of the world. I like that idea because my book is labelled as historical fiction, which it is; but it also has surreal elements. It has fantastical elements, for one: having tigers roaming the landscape of the American West" (A. Watson 2020). Zhang's comment draws attention to the novel's "slightly alternate, twisted version of the world" in which the "world" of the West around the time of the California gold rush is retold through diverse perspectives, often fantastical and surreal, that "would gnaw you down like… buffalo bones" (Zhang 2020b, 161). Myths of the West are ever present in the novel, but juxtaposed and interrupted, "gnawed down," by other stories, languages, and histories, producing a rich, heteroglossic, and critical topography. As two comments by Zhang suggest, with both historical and contemporary perspectives in view, being "the naturalized citizen of a country that tries to kick dirt over its bloody history" (Zhang 2020c) she is fully aware that "the desire to cling to a bucolic (very white) myth of America is toxic" (Zhang in Cary 2020). To disturb these positions, "alternate, twisted" worlds enter the established world of the mythic and historic West from elsewhere, like those incongruous "tigers roaming the landscape" mentioned above. Tigers are recurrent in folktales carried by Ma, a Chinese migrant, and retold in stories and songs to her husband, Ba, and children, Lucy, and Sam. In the Chinese tradition, "The tiger occupies and embodies the spaces in between the human and the beast, between conquering and venerating nature, between mountains and villages: tigers…'were transitional creatures, spiritual in-betweens who variously cautioned, cajoled and assisted humans in relating to the life-world'" (Kim 2017, 2). Thus, tigers function in the novel as reminders of an alien culture while disrupting the expected landscape of a western novel, or, as Zhang put it, "to fuck up the fabric of reality" (Cary 2020). This is evident, for example, when Ma "put her hand in the tiger's print" (Zhang 2020b, 174), or when drawing a tiger character in the doorway of each new house they occupy "as protection against what might come" while singing a nursery rhyme, "Lao hu, lao hu" (42).[1] Consequently, the novel becomes like the tiger, "transitional," moving the reader between traditions, voices, temporalities, and emotions, creating an unsettling liminality so that, as Zhang put it, "the story floats in a place that's outside of time" (Etter 2020). So, the world of the West we might expect, created as either immigrant or frontier story, is undone by the friction of Zhang's material, its "awkward engagement" across "encounters and interactions," between traditions, races, classes, and genders (Tsing 2005, xi). As Anna Tsing argues, "Cultures are continually co-produced in the interactions I call 'friction,'" like that constantly sparked by the "awkward, unequal, unstable" encounters of the novel, reminding "us that heterogeneous and unequal encounters can lead to new arrangements of culture and power" (2005, 4, 5), or even to a changed appreciation of what our sense of "world" might be.

As China grates against the American West, this "frictional" perspective, with its echoes of Obreht's *Inland*, relentlessly shifts time, offering multiple living and dead narrative voices, variant geographies, and fragmented language. Zhang assembles a history countering the linear and progressive while moving toward something collage-like in which elements overlap and collide. Collage, as Zhang has commented, is "a great way to explain the texture of the book, and also how lineage feels to the two children in the novel" (Etter 2020), suggesting both a narrative technique and a thematic device. As Susan Stanford Friedman explains, "In collages, fragments set side by side lead the eye to move across the surface and to discover or invent some patterns of relation in color, shape, form, and meaning" (2018, 217). In Zhang's fiction this collagist style "invites relational thinking" as the reader shifts between sections, times, voices, and places within the novel, as if we are "reading separate things together" (218, 278). As Friedman argues, one rarely "reads" a collage in a linear fashion, from left to right, but rather through "circulations back and forth," encouraging the tracing of connections and relations through the "identification of different networks of meaning" (278). Rubbing against each other, the elements of any collage produce friction yet, nonetheless, from this very action generate surprising energy through the intensity of unexpected associations.

Thus, in *How Much of These Hills Is Gold*, a space of three pages in a section called "Mud" (Zhang 2020b, 47–50) creates a collage in which Lucy and Sam awake having finally buried their father's remains. In a series of fragmented, collagist actions, Lucy smears Sam's face with mud like "two tiger stripes," addresses the skull placed on the grave, and simultaneously begins to feel "something inside has changed, laid to rest with Ba's body" (47–48). It is as if something of the past buried with her father allows Lucy to "squint" toward an image of the future: "Onward. To hot meals. White bread. Meat. A nice long bath…Once we get past the mountains, we've plenty of time to find a new home" (48). Set against Lucy's desire for a new home in her "civilized" vision of America, Sam sees "home" as the wilderness yet still connected to their Chinese heritage: "There's tigers here. Buffalo. Freedom" (49). When Lucy sees Sam, "a foot on the tiger's skull," with "one foot raised, head thrown back, hands on hips," she sees her with her assimilationist eyes, like a figure from one of her "history books…filled with conquering men who stood this way. Flags waved behind them in land emptied of buffalo and Indians" (48). The edging together of these moments suggests the differences between Lucy and Sam and, as Zhang put it, "makes their lives feel very much like a collage" (Etter 2020). The section ends with Sam retelling one of Ba's magical stories on the fate of the buffalo, one Lucy has heard many times before and of which she accepts Teacher Leigh's disparaging view, *"Pure sentiment…A pretty little folktale"* (Zhang 2020b, 50; emphasis in the original). Whereas Lucy wants to integrate and belong in America, Sam is as uncertain about her place in this world as she is about her own gender and sexuality.

Hence, in these few pages of Zhang's collage, the novel's cultural dynamics collide through its characters' differences, their "patterns of relation" made apparent, and the tensions evident through the "back-and-forth" methods of its narrative structure. Such collagism is indicative of the novel's complication of narrative construction, shifting readers away from the "unidirectional" (Friedman 2018, 278), linear tradition and toward a more relational, juxtapositional form. Zhang admires a similar approach in Michael Ondaatje's *Divisadero*, which she calls a "lyrical collage of a book about identity and family and fracture" (Winnette 2020). Ondaatje "completely puts aside the need for a linear chronological plot," opting instead for what Zhang terms an "extreme structure…an emotional arc rather than a plot arc" (Chang 2020).[2] Similarly shifting perspectives, Zhang's novel redirects assumptions about immigration as an assimilative, one-way process moving from periphery to center, poverty to possibility, and past to future. Such routes of migration, like those supposedly followed by the Chinese coming to America, cannot remain unquestioned, since, as Zhang demonstrates, they can be reversed and undone by the "friction" of experience.

Therefore, as the novel unfolds, we learn of frictions in characters' lives, like Ba, who, orphaned on arrival in America and found alongside his dead parents with "saltwater stains on their clothes," embodies an archetypal immigrant dream, moving "always toward the newer. The wilder. The promise of sudden wealth and shine. For years, it was gold he pursued" (Zhang 2020b, 163, 20). He feels innately at home in the California West, having known no other place, and is skeptical of the concept of westering, asking, "West of where? It was just our land, and we were just people" (162). In contrast, although Ma "had come seeking fortune" from China, following the myth of "*Golden mountain*," the story she "carried inside her is bigger…than the West, bigger than the whole of the world Lucy was born to," because, "accented with longing," she still yearns for home, for China, "like a fairy-tale" of "wide cobbled streets and low red walls, mists and rocky gardens," a "place…unknowable" (171, 127).[3] "This will never be *our* land," Ma asserts, insisting her sense of belonging is tied not to the West but to a vision of return, a *reverse migration* to China, and so to "somewhere much better" (127, 126). At one point, Ma is described as "like the story of a serving girl raised from cinders—only the wrong way round" (51), because her desire is not one of rags to riches like Cinderella, but rather to earn enough money in America to return home to a better, more civilized life in China.

Consequently, Zhang deliberately contradicts and interrogates accepted notions of migration, articulating instead its ambiguities, complexities, and multiple circuits, suggesting migrants' sense of belonging is rarely simple or straightforward. Fundamental to this process is Ma's suspicion of the fragile promise of linear history tied to the West and her preference for her own worlded, ancestral past, "years and centuries… swallowed with those bones… Something enormous, ungentle," close to what Lucy names "history" (82–83).

"WEST OF WHERE?"—HISTORY AND FAMILY HISTORY

In a different context, Iain Chambers writes, "History gives way to histories, as the West gives way to the world" (1994, 5), suggesting the trajectory of *How Much of These Hills Is Gold* wherein the promise and "truth" of migration, both as history and as experience, are scrutinized constantly. Ba is particularly aware of the dangers of what people claim as truth, telling Lucy, "That history in your books is plain lie," because "too often truth ain't what's right.…[S]ometimes it's in who speaks it. Or writes it" (Zhang 2020b, 162, 176). This writing of history, as Michel de Certeau explains, is about power and authority, "basing its mastery of expression upon what the other keeps silent," meaning that in the suppression of certain voices, "the power that writing's expansionism leaves intact is colonial in principle" (1988, 3, 216). In this warning, Ba intuitively understands what he calls "paper law" with its "assumed…truth" (Zhang 2020b, 178), equating it to the colonial expansionism of writing history, "which invades space and capitalizes on time," as it defines, delimits, and approves what can be said and archived (de Certeau 1988, 216). Nonetheless, with her love of books and learning, this written world entices Lucy, setting her apart from Sam, who like her father prefers action and impetuosity.

Subsequently, history, in all its forms, is repeatedly debated in the novel, from that "set in ink" in books (Zhang 2020b, 94) to oral folktales from China, campfire stories, and the lived experience of Lucy and Sam as they travel westward. Teacher Leigh, Lucy's influential schoolteacher, is writing a "monograph on the Western territory" and immigrants from "the savage unknown," gathering information through informants, betraying a biased, colonialist, perspective: "What are your hygiene practices? How often do you bathe?" (33, 112).[4] His is a particular version of history with "those names and dates orderly as bricks, stacked to build a civilization" (122), in which otherness is never more than a source of ethnographic fascination and intellectual challenge. Such monographs inform the authorized archive, but, as Zhang has explained, "beneath that official history is this other history of people deemed unimportant at the time, whether that's women or people of color or queer folk or domestic help" (Chang 2020).[5] Appropriately, Teacher Leigh's motto is "He who writes the past writes the future too" (Zhang 2020b, 93), asserting a direct relationship between language and power through which "he orders her [Lucy's] family's story with words neatened as the schoolhouse is neatened" (112). His colonialist *neatening* of history is also, of course, a *whitening* through which other cultures are controlled, diminished, and erased in favor of dominant white patriarchal culture. When Lucy tells Teacher Leigh of her plan to leave and so discontinue her interviews, his response reveals the true nature of this colonial authority: "All the work we've done is useless now....You understand *I'll be removing you from the history*—there's no value in a half-finished chapter" (135; emphasis added). Years later, when Lucy uncovers the published monograph, she appears in only a "few lines, herself reduced to something crude and unrecognisable" (270), as if confirming the ways by which written history selects and diminishes the rich variety of worlds. Teacher Leigh reveals here what James Clifford means by an ethnography that "enacts power relations" in the way it organizes material for distribution and approval (1986, 9).

Nonetheless, Zhang situates all their lives within the wider history of anti-Chinese racism in a West already guilty of multiple crimes against the other, crimes revealed through both personal and institutional cruelty and abuse. As Zhang has explained, "That's one of the great tensions at the heart of the book—how can you feel so deeply about a place and then be told at every turn that it is not yours to inhabit?" (Chang 2020). As with Teacher Leigh, racism is systemic: "Run on, you filthy Little. Chink," the bank manager tells Lucy early in their journey. Later, they remember a drunk shouting at the family from the roadside, "about the land, and claims to it, and who belonged by law, and what should be buried," or written into a "new law" that "takes away the family's future" by stripping "all rights to gold from any man not born in this territory" (Zhang 2020b, 9, 82–83, 151).

Although Lucy's "fondest dream" is to be "unnoticed in the crowd" (41) and to assimilate invisibly into American society, she finds herself nonetheless suspended between the promise of Teacher Leigh's history, the "rememory" offered by her parents' lives and stories, and her own experience with Sam (178). The novel refutes, therefore, a history that wraps "all of the complexity and problematic history of America in a tidy bow" or replicates Teacher Leigh's order, preferring instead "to really embrace…uncertainty and ambiguity," contributing to a "dialogue [that] would be a little bit healthier and more open" because it wasn't "pushing hard for a clean ending" (A. Watson 2020). Echoing Luiselli in chapter 7, Zhang asks readers to contemplate "what happens when a country or countries don't really take the time to think about reparations, to come to terms with the political violence of their past, to try to heal those wounds.…I think when you ignore violence that way…it just comes up again and again and again. When you don't address historical trauma properly, it always returns" (Floyd 2019).

In chapter 1, I discussed Glissant's term "filiation" as a linear genealogical descent, a family order of belonging in which a patriarchal hierarchy is inscribed, with time and history flowing from past (father) to future (child). However, Zhang's novel opens with trauma, "Ba dies in the night," prompting his daughters to action and, in Lucy's case, to language, as she "feels a need to speak" (Zhang 2020b, 3). Action and speech are inextricably linked to the death of the father and the sudden gap this opens in their lives, as if "the water's long gone, the world after the flood left somehow thirstier." Nevertheless, as this first section closes, Zhang adds, "And long gone, Ma" (5), reminding the reader that Lucy and Sam are doubly wounded both by Ba's sudden death and by the supposed death of their mother. As the novel opens, the flow of linear time and filiation is disturbed with the children's line of inheritance interrupted by the traumatic loss of parental guidance, which, in turn, is intimately linked to their experience of the West itself. For example, when their family "first arrived," we are told, there was "long yellow grass…and poppies after rain," but the floods came and "rooted up…oaks, drowned or chased away half the people," challenging the immigrant life, with Ba left "dead down the center, roots still gripping on" (4).

From this point forward, Lucy and Sam struggle, consciously and unconsciously, with the ghosts of their past, the psychic and material inheritance of Ma and Ba, their presence and histories struggling to be introjected and mourned in the course of the novel. In the work of Nicolas Abraham and Maria Torok, introjection is "a constant process of acquisition, involving the active expansion of our potential to open our own emerging desires and feelings as well as the external world" (Rand 1994,

100). In the novel, such an idealized process of introjection, sometimes referred to as "successful" mourning, is interrupted or blocked by "silence and its varied forms—the untold or unsayable secret, the feeling unfelt, the pain denied, the unspeakable and concealed shame of families, the cover-up of political crimes, the collective disregard for painful historical realities" (21).[6] Accordingly, introjection is the "psychic equivalent of growth…conceiving of life as a series of transitions that are far from automatic and not necessarily harmonious or pleasurable" precisely because of such blockages (9–10). As in the case of Lucy and Sam, introjection involves revealing and, to a degree, working through "underlying individual traumas," loss, and pain that test and disrupt their development and place in the world (11). From within this "thicket of formative experiences and influences," there needs to emerge ideally "the continuous activity of self-creation" through which "we open and fashion and enrich ourselves, transcend trauma, adjust to internal and external upheaval and change, create forms of coherence in the face of emotional panic and chaos" (10–11, 14). For Lucy and Sam, it is the possibility of any "continuity of psychic life," having inherited these "silences" that form the substance and drama of the novel as they attempt "harmonious progression…emotional development and self-expansion" while dealing with the trauma of migration, ethnic prejudice, and gender discrimination (21–22). Lisa Lowe makes the point that Chinese Americans felt at a "distance" from the "national culture" of America in their struggle to belong and, as a result, preserved "an alternative site where the palimpsest of lost memories is reinvented, histories are fractured and retraced, and the unlike varieties of silence emerge into articulacy" (1997, 6). Zhang's novel plays out this struggle between silence and articulacy, the past and the future, China and the West, all within the troubled and turbulent western landscape.

Initially, the trauma and loss experienced by Lucy and Sam come through the death of Ba, whose decomposing corpse they transport across the West, hidden within Ma's wooden trunk brought from China. Symbolically, the father is *within* the mother, and both are now being carried by their daughters, like "inassimilable life experiences" and "inexpressible mourning," "encrypted" in a "psychic tomb," as Abraham and Torok might explain it, their family secrets sealed away, "entombed" in the lives of their children (Rand 1994, 22; Abraham and Torok 1994, 130, 156). What is contained within the crypt (the entombing wooden trunk) is the father/mother haunting their children, because, as Abraham and Torok explain, "what haunts are not the dead, but the gaps left within us by the secrets of others" (1994, 171). Both Lucy and Sam "refuse to mourn" or rather cannot *successfully* mourn the losses they both feel because they cannot "reclaim" as their own "the part of" themselves "placed in what [they] lost" and so instead "incorporate" this loss and carry these "gaps" within their lives (127). They struggle to undergo "the painful process of reorganization," as Abraham and Torok term it, to *introject* (to *cast inside*) these losses and emptinesses (their parents' absence, their heritage, traditions, language, and so forth), finding ways to unfold these secrets and integrate them into "the gradual, assimilative work of mourning" (127, 141). What they carry inside, as "carrier[s] of a shared secret," is the trauma "reconstituted from the memories of words, scenes, and affects" (131, 130), specifically Ba's death, alongside "a jumble of myth. Half-truths not found in Teacher Leigh's histories, mixed with longing that made Ma's words fly up and apart" (Zhang 2020b, 56). Sam and Lucy's collagist journey takes them through the West, travels out and back, circling around this crypt of "undisclosed grief," in pursuit of a problematic sense of what home might mean (Abraham and Torok 1994, 131).

Abraham and Torok refer to these encryptions as "phantoms" that pass from the parent to the child's unconscious, working "like a ventriloquist, like a stranger within the subject's own mental topography" (173). The phantom is restless within the crypt, doomed to endlessly repeat the trauma and the loss, and so "obstructs" successful introjection by pursuing "its work of disarray in silence," to "wreak havoc…on logical progression" (174, 175). Phantoms are like "foreign bodies lodged within the subject" (174), which through successful mourning would be absorbed (introjected).[7] In this way, Ba and Ma *reappear* as "foreign" voices and stories *ventriloquized* into the narrative through Lucy and Sam, who recount, remember, recall, reexperience, and even reenact them within the course of the novel. Early on, for example, Lucy's search for language results in exactly this form of spectral ventriloquism: "Ba's words tumble out the tunnel of her throat like a ghost clambering from the dark" (Zhang 2020b, 6). In a similar vein, Sam reveals "the little of me…in your blood and speech" when she too speaks "a shadow of Ba's voice," while also carrying and using his phallic pistol (174, 9). Lucy's intention is to bury her father's decomposing corpse piece by piece across the West, as if ridding them of his influence and power. At one point, she grinds his penis into the dirt: "It's as long as a finger but thicker. Softer, with wrinkled skin. No bone that she can see. It gives under her toes, like a dried plum" (30). When not directly manifested through Lucy's or Sam's speech or actions, Ba articulates his past via a ghostly narrative, revealing the unspoken secrets of their family history. Thus, just as the novel reassembles (or "worlds") American western history through the variant experiences of Chinese immigrants, it parallels this public unfolding with the specific and personal uncovering of the complex relations entangled within the family structure. As Lucy says of Ba, as if to underline his hold over her, and with a nod to the complexities of western history, he was a "man she couldn't solve" (21).

Appropriately, Zhang, echoing Abraham and Torok, explains the novel as a work of mourning: "The kernel at the heart of the novel is grief. It is really a novel about how grief deferred, as the children have to defer it in the beginning, always comes back and haunts you. I think that secrets—the secrets that we're forever cut off from as a result of death—came after the theme of grief" (Jurczyk 2020). This grief is personal, communal, and historical as the children live in the shadow of both their parents' "deaths," with the secret history of their parents' meeting, and the terrible violent act that shapes and haunts them thereafter.[8] The fire that their parents set, killing two hundred Chinese immigrants, stands as "an unspeakable secret suspended within the adult" (Rashkin 1992, 27), carried around from that point forward, because, as Ma says, "sometimes truth needs burying too" (Zhang 2020b, 105), ultimately becoming "lodged" within their children's "mental topography as an unmarked tomb" (Rashkin 1992, 27–28). Rashkin terms this secret between parent and child a "silent partnership…a mute pact" (28), which, when Ba remembers the fire, is like "a tiger that marked me…the truth of it in my bones" (Zhang 2020b, 186).

Critically, it is the parents' secret, "the 'unsayable' and 'unsaid' of *an other*," that is ever present in the child, like "a gap in the unconscious, an unknown, unrecognized knowledge" (Rashkin 1992, 28; Abraham and Torok quoted in Rashkin 1992, 27). This is Lucy's "sole inheritance" (Zhang 2020b, 65), forming a "transgenerational haunting" (Rashkin 1992, 165). As Zhang explained it: "I realized the novel wanted to explore how trauma and similar themes echo through this family across generations.…The chapter titles point to the repetitiveness of the tragedy and trauma the family experiences" (Etter 2020). These echoes and their *working through* drive the narrative.

For Zhang, fiction "is an act of imaginative empathy," allowing her "to resurrect the lost stories" (A. Watson 2020) to construct a complex fabric of competing personal, regional, and national histories around the characters of Lucy and Sam, who themselves are, in turn, marked by their inheritance. They both carry, unconsciously, the "wound" (Abraham and Torok 1994, 135) of their parents' cryptic secrets and must organize their own lives to survive accordingly. As noted, Lucy remains torn between the pull to her mother's Chinese ancestry and to her father's attachment to the American goal of a better, richer life: a dream of the past and a dream of the future. Sam's ambiguity, however, plays out in her gender identification and the challenges it brings into her life in the West. Drawn more to her father, she hides her own femininity, cross-dressing as a man, covering over her Adam's apple, and adopting a carrot as a false penis, stating early on her desire to be "a cowboy…an adventurer…a famous outlaw." Sam is "young enough to believe desire alone shapes the world," and, consequently, her world becomes one distinct from Lucy's, driven by a rejection of society and choosing instead a life of violence, sexuality, and banditry (Zhang 2020b, 7).

Once Ba's remains are buried, Lucy hopes they "don't need any history at all," as if she and Sam might step outside of time, but as their remaining journey demonstrates, "rememory can hurt" (63, 178). Therefore, both must undergo continued incorporation, introjection, and mourning, requiring a working through the very histories bound up with family, community, and the West itself. What Lucy uncovers is a diverse and complex history making its various claims upon her. "To cross over to the future" (64), it would be necessary to rationalize Ma's folktales, ignore her father's stories of the West's opportunities and wealth, and dismiss all such "unwritten history" in favor of the order and reason she had learned from Teacher Leigh's books. Yet her own travels through the West disclose not the mythic land of Ba's tales or the relentless reason of Teacher Leigh's, but rather an experiential reality of "a land of missing things… stripped of its gold, its rivers, its buffalo, its Indians, its tigers, its jackals, its birds and its green and its living" (122). Nevertheless, for all her experience and the written history she has been taught, she "never quite escapes that other [history]. The wild one. It prowls the edges of her vision," a history "that speaks not in words but in roar and beat and blood," for it is a part of who she is, the secret crypt of the Chinese past and her parents' lives within her. "It made Lucy as the lake made gold. Made Sam's wildness" (122). Indeed, this remains Lucy's dilemma, existing *in between* the past and the future, Ba and Ma, China and America, and from these diverse elements trying to fashion a self in the West.

GENDER AND THE "WORTH" OF FEMININITY

As Lucy and Sam journey through the West, "the world unfurled its hidden side" (Zhang 2020b, 19), confronting the consequences of their family secrets and how, in particular, they impinge upon their own survival. Above all, as Zhang has commented, gender was "always the central question to this book," and its "exploration of gender—what it means to be a man or a woman and how that impacts wealth and value—is certainly a crux of the book" (Etter 2020). Working through the haunting presence of their parents, "deep, deep down in that last layer" (Zhang 2020b, 178), is, as we have seen, critical to the possible process of introjection or growth. Sam is "prized by a father who wanted a son," grows up hiding her femininity, and "resisted Ma's manners" to appease Ba and fulfill his desire for a "false son" (13–14, 46). Following her father's death, as we have seen, Sam masks her birth gender, assuming a masculine identity, rejecting the social order, and adopting an outlaw lifestyle. With Sam gone, following her wild life in the territories, the novel focuses on Lucy's attempted assimilation in the town of Sweetwater, where she settles into a self-constructed life defined by an elaborately scripted performance: *An orphan. Left. Don't know. No one*" (199; emphasis in the original). To follow the script, Lucy "orphans" herself, refusing to identify with her past, and instead *writes* a version of her own history, "a blank story to suit this town," whereby "the words made a lacquer over the truth." The "truth," of course, is the crypt she carries within her, her Chinese past and the unspoken secrets of that history, whereas Sweetwater has "no danger, no adventure, no uncertainty," being "a place so bled of wildness" that people imagine a "false tiger" stalking its streets (201). Hollowing out her own history, Lucy creates a version of her self to fit Sweetwater, denying her cultural heritage and minimizing her racial difference. In secret and to survive, Lucy succumbs to prostitution and to the contradictory sense of power it gives her, "playing a game that thrilled and scared her both" (208).

Following this, Lucy becomes drawn to a wealthy prospector's daughter, Anna, whose life is an inversion of Lucy's own, defined by ostentation and social success, of "silver boxes of salt, velvet dresses." It is a world of entrepreneurial success, of the American dream writ large and symbolized in Anna's house by "a deed in a frame. The frame is solid gold. The deed is mere paper." This frame of gold signifies her father's "claim to his first prospecting site" and, therefore, his claim upon the very same land that Ba had prospected since 1842 (203).[9] However, the uneasiness between Anna and Lucy is evident, and the fragility of the relationship is built on class and racial division. Lucy's beauty and allure to men are her only power, "the only thing she has, and she won't give it away. Anna has everything else" (222).

This precarious gender performance is radically challenged by the reentry of Sam into Lucy's Sweetwater, appearing like Ba's ghost (a "haint" she calls her/him [209]), bringing the secrets and memories of her/his past, but also a jolting reawakening to the haunted worlds of the West she had chosen to "lacquer over." Sam's travels have brought her closer to the marginalized West and those excluded from the wealth and privilege enjoyed in Anna's world. As Sam explains to Lucy, "We weren't the only ones wronged. There's others, Indian and brown and black. None of us think it was right, what got took from us." Sam comprehends and reminds Lucy of the brutal cost of westward expansion, with exploitation by the few, like Anna's father, who "really think this land belongs to them" (215). Sam's stories "rememory" what Ba had experienced and understood about a West already ecologically ravaged and subjugated, since "they arrived to find the same ruined hills, dug up, the same streams choked with rubble," so that in time, the soil goes dry, "crumbles like left-out bread…and when the dry season comes, a spark can set it all aflame" (21, 172). In contrast, Sweetwater was an "orderly place where all the streets are mapped and known," where Sam's disturbing presence affords *disorderly* lessons in western history, epitomized by the deed on Anna's wall, "that diminishes the land even as it claims it," hanging "in a big frame, that, if melted down and sold, could feed a hundred families" (212, 213). Moreover, symbolically by the extravagant garden of their mansion, "far from the hills he'd emptied of riches," "For his daughter's sake, Anna's father ripped plants from their native soils. Vast territories were plundered to fill the garden. Some plants came with their own names, now discarded. Anna renamed them according to her fancies" (227, 203, 220). Tellingly, at the very heart of this created artifice is a bush "that drinks in one week what a whole family uses in the dry season" (221).

When Lucy reveals the advances of Anna's predatory fiancé, Charles, this world of privilege and power closes ranks to shut out the lower-class Chinese American girl. Anna is threatened by Lucy's sexuality and her racialized tigerlike quality, wanting "a domestic thing, a harmless thing," belonging to a "declawed" world where "tigers are pets." Anna's inheritance, unlike Lucy's, is power and the certainty determined by social rank, wealth, and class: "She's untouchable, protected by her hired man, her father's gold." At this moment Lucy comes to another point of transition in her journey of education, rejecting the influence of Anna's world, ripping away the pearl buttons on her "white linen dress" and stepping free, "no longer the same, no longer Anna's poor reflection," but returning to "herself, barefoot as the day she came to Sweetwater" (227). As if remembering her past and her "cryptic" inheritance, Sam comments appropriately, seeing her newly liberated sister, "You look like your old self" (228).

Sam's untamed wildness and phantomlike presence remind Lucy of their otherness, of the unassimilable past, like a foreign body within their bodies, becoming "the impossible tiger" "who doesn't bend to the world's rules but bends them" (228). Sam's influence empowers Lucy to change, to embody the spirit of the tiger she has rediscovered in her refusal to be domesticated by Anna's world and cowed by Charles's predatory masculinity. Lucy's hope is to join Sam on a new adventure, a journey across the ocean back to China and away from the settled but "lacquered over" West she had come to know in Sweetwater. Returning to the two images that defined that place, the deed and the frame, Lucy now feels "terribly exposed" yet also freed by her vulnerability: "This is a land free of its frame, loosened from a deed, and it is huge and whistling and uncontainable" (233). Having felt "buried" in Sweetwater, she now undergoes further transitions, enabling a new phase of her life to begin, casting a stone into her reflection, "breaking that image into fragments," then cutting off all her hair, as if overcoming obstacles to her introjection and permitting "the unhindered activity of perpetual self-creation" (Rand 1994, 101). For Lucy, this is a recognition of a new and different world, "almost a new kind of land," which is both familial and about the West itself: "There is, she is coming to see, a place that exists between the world Ba pursued and the world Ma wanted. His a lost world, doomed to make the present and future dim in comparison. Hers so narrow it could accommodate only one" (Zhang 2020b, 236). This imagined space is Lucy's vision of home, where both she and Sam can live "unhindered," drawing from both their parents' dreams in order to shape a future that is "not a place where we'll have to look over our shoulders, not stolen, not belonging to buffalo or Indians, not used-up" (239). It is an idealized future beyond the tainted world of the American West marked by the legacy of conquest, a world still farther west, across the ocean, to her fantasy of China. This is not a desire for the unproblematic Edenic West but, like many of the novels discussed in this book, for another journey to elsewhere, an "exit" from the West that seems to be marked only by violence, prejudice, and injustice.

Their journey, therefore, circles back on itself, across the West to the

Pacific Ocean from where their parents came. "West for the last time. The same mountains, the same pass…In reverse they chart their own course… Same and yet changed, as they are same and yet changed" (241). In this section of the novel (241–46), their journey is marked by repetition, creating a strange rhythmic pattern—with "Travel goes quicker than the last time," "Maybe on account of…," "crossroads," and "another" repeated several times.[10] It is as if the logic and order of Lucy's prized history books are being undone, with the "pages disordered, the colors melted by sun and years, the story misremembered" (241), and each crossroads they pass takes them back through their previous lives and histories. Like Håkan's "circular nomadism" in *In the Distance*, their journey West too is an uncanny, epic spiral through mines, saloons, "Indian travellers…searching too," an "ancient Indian city," "befriended men and women black and brown and red," with the "boom of dynamite," buffalo, and, finally, back to where it all began, to the originary moment (242, 243). Even the landscape underscores their condition: "The clouds begin to circle, them two at the center," for they are the "same and yet changed" by their experiences, as if finally learning to mourn the secrets they both carry (244–45). But the mourning they undergo is marked by melancholy, and so, according to Judith Butler, introjection cannot take place, for that interiorizes and assimilates loss and pain, whereas incorporation keeps it alive, "sustained 'in the body' in some way" (1990, 67–68). As Lucy stands amid the circling clouds and the dry yellow hills, she admits "feeling a sorrow kin to love" alongside "pain and sweat and misplaced hope." Only now can she process all she carries within her, recognizing "a part of her is buried in them, a part of her lost in them, a part of her found and born in them—so many parts belong to this land" (Zhang 2020b, 245).

Lucy is a product of this West, of "all these things that shape" her within, and together they form an "ache in her chest" that convinces her that the land beyond the ocean, the China of her mother, cannot ultimately be her home. For the first time, the word "mourning" is used (245) because Lucy feels "at a loss" yet, in some way, changed, recognizing the actively preserved "other" within her. Butler's discussion of mourning is helpful in understanding Lucy's situation: "Perhaps, rather, one mourns when one accepts that by the loss one undergoes one will be changed, possibly for ever. Perhaps mourning has to do with agreeing to undergo a transformation.…But maybe when we undergo what we do, something about who we are is revealed, something that delineates the ties we have to others, that shows us that these ties constitute what we are, ties or bonds that compose us" (2004, 21–22). These "ties" Lucy recognizes are a "relationality" that connects her to her family secrets and beyond her family, to something larger, "a sense of political community of a complex order" (22), and also to a sense perhaps, of an increasingly interdependent world. What Lucy learns are the ties she feels to her sister, Sam, whom she chooses to save at the end of the novel, taking up her debt as she once took on the burden of her parents' dreams. Lucy's choice is to give her newfound self over to the brutal "gold man" and the brothel owner Elske transforming her into one of her "girls in their pretty frames" (Zhang 2020b, 251), dressed as fantasies to appease the desires of men. In a further example of Zhang's symbolic framing in the novel, Elske "rewrites" Lucy once again as an exotic Oriental, "of poured tea and lilting speech, downcast eyes and sweetness," making her "blank" like all the other prostitutes, so "they remind me of pages" ready to be inscribed with someone else's story (267, 254).[11]

Ironically, Lucy's sacrifice for Sam is to slip backward into "a new tale" framed now by Elske's hand, like those she inhabited earlier, "written" by Teacher Leigh, Anna, and Charles. What transpires is "a story as unlike Lucy's as fool's gold is unlike true gold," yet this loss of self and of a "value" (267, 266) measured only by sexuality is the price she is willing to pay for her sister's survival. To borrow again from Butler, Lucy stays with her sense of loss, finding within it and within her vulnerability a greater "collective responsibility" for others, "a point of identification with suffering itself," and an awareness of her "unknowingness" (2006, 30). Lucy's acquired bookish knowledge and understanding of history learned from what Ba calls *Teacher talk* (Zhang 2020b, 26) are stripped away ("unknowingness") and revealed as another example of "fool's gold" in this sham world of appearances and performance. In the novel's final pages, Lucy must unlearn in order to relearn and see again from the "derealized" position Elske constructs for her how her race, gender, and sexuality have been artificially framed and consumed (Butler 2006, 33).

"But this can be a point of departure for a new understanding" (30), emerging through Lucy's incorporation of the dead and the past into her own survival. Death, as Derrida puts it, "continues to lodge there like something other and to ventrilocate through the 'living'" rather than "assimilate it, idealize it, and interiorize it" (1988, 57–58).[12] As Lucy puts it, recalling Ba's burial, "She dug a grave years ago; now she throws into it every Sam and every Lucy that came before. All her soft rotting parts." Just as she had once buried the decomposing body of her father, she now inters all the fragments of her and Sam's lives to focus on the future. "The parts she keeps are her weapons" (Zhang 2020b, 268), because these are her "new understandings" of the world, learned not through Teacher Leigh's skewed history books but through incorporation and introjection as "a process of acquisition and assimilation" of her desires and feelings and also, critically, "the events and influences of the external world" (Rand 1994, 9).

Lucy's "weapons" allow her to see through the blank performance of prostitution—of being "wife…daughter…mother…pet…a slave, a statue, a conquest, a hunt"—and to recognize her customers' "wants [as] a pattern as predictable as campfire tale" (Zhang 2020b, 268). The pattern she outlines is of the intersectional "frame" of patriarchy, racism, and sexism that has surrounded Lucy for all her life in the West.[13] Comprehending the world in this way, Lucy feels empowered, "erasing the last mark of her old self," stepping out from the frames of others, until she "writes the stories she wishes" (268–69). Discovering this power for self-fashioning, she connects it to a greater awareness of the wider world of male control and its distorted history. This is embodied in her comment on the famous photograph of the golden spike marking the joining of the transcontinental railroad: "A picture is drawn for the history books, a picture that shows none of the people who look like her, who built it."[14] For her now, such images wrestle with those from her own past, flickering "like mirage, gone the moment she gets close," yet in her process toward introjection, "she stares as long as she is able, *mourning* what she can before it slips away" (270; emphasis added).

As discussed earlier, the work of mourning for Lucy is closer to that explained by Derrida, whereby introjection and incorporation are "played out on the borderline that divides and opposes the two terms" (1986a, xvi). Abraham and Torok seek to return the ghost to the order of knowledge, while Derrida wants to "avoid any restoration and to encounter what is strange, unheard, other, about the ghost" (Davis quoted in O'Connor 2011, 112). Derrida preferred to keep the "other *as other*" or "to love the dead as a living part of me" (1986a, xvi).[15] Rather than sealed away in the crypt, this "ambiguity" was the "deciding factor" to "blur the very line" proposed between introjection and incorporation. Hence, when "introjection (gradual, slow, laborious, mediated, effective)" "fails," "the only choice" is incorporation, "fantasmatic, unmediated, instantaneous, magical, sometimes hallucinatory." Although Lucy's parents are dead or gone and her sister, Sam, left for a new life in China, these "losses" are, following

Derrida, incorporated into her, but never fully absorbed or forgotten. They remain like "a foreign body preserved as foreign" yet "excluded" from Lucy's self, a "commemorative monument" to her past, "barred from introjection: like so many tombs in the life of the Self" (xvi–xvii). This ambiguity, blur, or "semi-permeability" (xviii) *between* incorporation and introjection helps us to understand how Lucy's self manages her past experiences of the West alongside Ba, Ma, and Sam. Michael Naas, writing on Derrida's work on mourning, glosses its meaning as "I am who I am because of this relation to an other whom I can never simply make my own" (2014, 119). Lucy's "others," in her attempts at mourning, never fully "slip away," remaining both within and beyond her, constituting the self she has become by the end of the novel. After all, "we are who we are because of the memory of those we have loved and carry within us. We come into being in dialogue with the dead and can only think of ourselves in 'bereaved allegory'" (Kirkby 2006, 464). As Zhang has written, "Think of Bluebeard's castle: a girl can have all the easy riches, if only she promises not to seek the room that holds the bones" (2020c). In *How Much of These Hills Is Gold*, the bones live on.

THE END OF THE WEST

Ultimately, Lucy is learning to mourn for all her losses and, in so doing, to "come into being in dialogue with the dead," but as we have seen, the dead have been with her from the book's very first words—"Ba dies." Carrying the "crypt" of the past with her, including the losses of Ba, Ma, and Sam, Lucy is ultimately enlarged by this process of mourning, taking parts of others and of herself as resources for a new and different being. As Derrida explains, these are "lacunary fragments, detached and dispersed— only 'parts' of the departed other. In turn they are parts of us, included 'in us' in a memory which suddenly seems greater and older than us... sublimely greater *than* this other that the memory harbors and guards within it, but also greater *with* this other, greater than itself, inadequate to itself, pregnant with this other" (1986a, 37). Although not a term used by Derrida here, one senses that which is "greater and older than us... greater *with* this other, greater than itself" is pivotal to this book's notion of *worlding*, wherein a relationality of self, other, and their "beyond" signals the possibility for change.

Hence, when Lucy receives the gift of a mirror from her imprisoning "gold man," she "lets herself look at last—no, *see*" (Zhang 2020b, 271), *beyond* the bounded frame of her exoticized existence, *beyond* the restraints of western history defined by "teacher talk," and *beyond* the culturally imposed limits of her race, gender, and sexuality. For Lucy, the work of mourning learned throughout the novel is the processing of "deferred grief," as Zhang called it, forging a dialogue with the dead, who although wholly other are now within her, "constitutive of her interiority and self-relation," yet not as "a private, secret, phobic, guilty internalising memory, but…a thinking externalising memory that gives us over to writing and thought" (Kirkby 2006, 467). The ghosts that once possessed her, preventing her from defining her own existence, have undergone transformation through mourning, leaving Lucy "deframed" or *dispossessed* and, in this regard, more aware of her relations with others and with the world— "greater *with* this other, greater than itself, inadequate to itself, pregnant with this other." In contemplating loss, it "makes manifest the limits of a *me*," Derrida argues, because we "harbor something that is greater and other than them; something *outside of them within them*" (1986a, 34).

As Judith Butler puts it, in such moments of positive dispossession, "one is beside oneself," pushed beyond our limiting sense of self (the limits of a *me*) and, therefore, "implicated in lives that are not our own" (2006, 28). What emerges is a recognition of our "fundamental sociality" and our "vulnerability" that together might present a "collective responsibility for the physical lives of one another" (30). As discussed earlier, a changed Lucy "writes the stories she wishes," *sees* herself in the mirror, and sees "the white of her neck is *her own*. Her unblemished face, *her own*" (Zhang 2020b, 271; emphasis added), as if she is reclaiming her body from those who had, for so long, possessed it physically or psychically. "By writing her self," as Hélène Cixous has argued, "woman will return to the body which has been more than confiscated from her, which has been turned into the uncanny stranger on display—the ailing or dead figure" (1981, 250). As Lucy explains, it is as if her body "died so many deaths in so many men's stories" and as though part of her mourning process or deferred grief is, indeed, for her many "deaths" already lived. Yet in this moment of "dispossession" from the haunting past, "she is a ghost, inhabiting this body," but one vitalized and empowered, and, as a result, "she fears no longer" (Zhang 2020b, 271).

Now dispossessed and without fear, Lucy realizes any return to China and to Sam is impossible, since "that land no longer has a place for her" (271), and whatever her future might be, it is in the West where she was born. Having circled around the West within her physical journeys throughout the novel and circled through the psychic pull of Ma's China and Ba's immigrant dream of success, she now dwells on her own future. In Cixous's words, "she draws her story into history" for the first time (1981, 251). In a crucial paragraph Zhang repeats "She thinks" three times to emphasize this phase of Lucy's transition, toward Derrida's "thinking memory that impels us to writing and thought" (Kirkby 2006, 467, 470). What Lucy thinks (writes) is a West she both remembers and conjures as a future in the novel's collage-like final paragraphs. As discussed earlier, Zhang's use of collage creates a sense of shifting and bristling provocations that present place, life, and identity "not as a boundary to be maintained but as a nexus of relations and transactions actively engaging a subject" (Clifford 1988, 344). Indeed, the final page of the novel projects Lucy's identity, formed by ambiguous introjections and incorporations *in and of* the West, in the collage-like nexus of "thinking memory": "Horizon to horizon a shimmer. Who could truly grasp it, the huge and maddening glint, the ever-shifting mirage, the grass that refused to be owned or pinned but changed with every angle of light: what that land was, and to whom, death or life, good or bad, lucky or unlucky, countless lives birthed and destroyed by its terror and generosity." Through this spectral western collage with its contradictions, juxtapositions, and poetic politics, Lucy's West emerges anew, like herself, not as a space for ownership or defined by its value in gold, but rather as an unknowable space of *being-with* and as a reconfigured sense of home within the world. "There is the claiming of the land, which Ba wanted to do, which Sam refused," Lucy thinks, "and then there is being claimed by it. The quiet way. A kind of gift in never knowing how much of these hills might be gold" (Zhang 2020b, 272).

In her relationship with the *worlds* of the West, Lucy rejects the exploitative cultural narratives of Manifest Destiny, the curtailed history of Teacher Leigh, and the predatory sexism of Charles and the "gold man" to embrace a natural, "quiet," affective sense beyond these narrow patriarchal frames and chains of filiation, "because this land had gouged in you an animal's kind of claiming, senseless to words and laws" (272). In this "Terrestrial" worlding, to recall Bruno Latour, the "gift" Lucy receives makes her "part of a greater whole; [where] our words and worlds are larger with this trace, with these traces of the other, which in turn incline us to speech and writing. The voice of the other permeates us constituting, traversing, exceeding, defying all re-appropriation" (Kirkby 2006, 467–68). In her thoughtful and affective memory of the West, Lucy feels "something like and unlike an echo, coming from before or behind … calling [her] name" (Zhang 2020b, 272). It is as if, finally, she is hailed by these ambiguities into what is yet to come, beyond the trauma of what came before, and, therefore, tentatively "strain[ing] toward the future" (Derrida 1986a, 59). For Lucy, like Derrida, "the ghost's secret [*something like and unlike an echo*] is not a puzzle to be solved; it is the structural openness or address directed towards the living by the voices of the past or the not yet formulated possibilities of the future" (Colin Davis quoted in O'Connor 2011, 112). As Zhang has written, "Not all hauntings are bad ones. There are worse things than to invite the ghosts in" (2020c). With distinct echoes of the ending of Obreht's *Inland*, Lucy too learns to live with ghosts and waits on the very edge of the West, with the secret she holds hidden within her, "not unspeakable because it is taboo, but because it cannot not (yet) be articulated in the languages available to us" (Davis quoted in O'Connor 2011, 112). Lucy echoes Glissant's comments at the opening of *Poetics of Relation* about another terrible journey of slaves: "But their ordeal did not die; it quickened into this continuous/discontinuous thing: the panic of the new land, the haunting of the former land, finally the alliance with the imposed land, suffered and redeemed" (1997, 7).

At this moment of expectancy, Zhang anticipates a possible shift: "She opens her mouth. She wants" (Zhang 2020b, 272). With no full stop, only an open space on the page, it is as if Lucy reaches out beyond the frame of the novel where, finally, "the unlike varieties of silence emerge into articulacy" (Lowe 1997, 6).[16] In one sense, it is a curious type of "aporia," a word much used by Derrida and Paul de Man. Its literal meaning is "absence of a path…paralysis…immobilization of thinking, the impossibility of advancing, a barrier blocking the future," however, as Derrida interprets aporia, it instead "promises the thinking of the path, provokes the thinking of the very possibility of what still remains unthinkable or unthought, indeed, impossible…the future of another promise" (1986a, 132–33). As Glissant wrote of the haunting of the abyss, it "served as the alluvium for these metamorphoses," shaping the hope for an "alliance with the imposed land" (1997, 7). Thus, this aporia offered at the end of the novel provokes "a leap of memory and a displacement of thinking" for Lucy, which potentially, promisingly, "leads…toward a new thinking…whose structure is wholly other, forgotten or yet to come" (Derrida 1986a, 133). Indeed, we might here consider her aporiatic "want" or desire, a transformative new path, a tentative but promising "dialogue with the world" (Kirkby 2006, 470).

‹ 6 ›

TO REMEMBER OTHERWISE AND AGAINST

Tribalography, Robin Wall Kimmerer, LeAnne Howe, and Tommy Orange

What is the power of native stories? Did they create our people,
our tribes, ourselves? Are our stories "a living theater" that
connects everything to everything, as we say they do?
—LeAnne Howe, "Tribalography: The Power of Native Stories"

Let's enter our own world, which also means entering the world.
—Édouard Glissant, *Treatise on the Whole-World*

WORLDS THAT LOOK IN ALL DIRECTIONS

In the opening page of *The World, the Text, and the Indian*, Scott R. Lyons announces "tribal/national contexts are themselves always already 'global' in character, [with]…no real possibility of a separate textual or critical sphere divorced from global forces" (2017, 1). In 1847, for example, the Choctaw Nation, despite their own hardship, collected money in support of Irish people suffering during the famine, sending $170 ($5,000 today) for relief. As reported in *Time*, in remembrance of this earlier gift, Ireland sent funds to help with the fight against the rapidly spreading COVID-19 on the Navajo Reservation in 2020.[1] As Lyons underlines, "If you do not look at the native situated in a global context—a context that includes the tribe as well as the nation-state (among other things) but is not reducible to them—then you could miss out on a story that deserves to be told, and the story you do tell could very well be incomplete" (7). Native writing, Lyons concludes, and this historical exchange proves, "deals with the world, not simply the tribe or nation" (13).[2] In this chapter, I explore ways in which examples of Native writing "deals with the world" as a nonreductive means of negotiation and exchange, asserting its values and beliefs, rather than accepting those imposed by colonizing powers and traditions.

128

Recalling Spivak's negative colonial worlding discussed in the introduction, what I suggest here, following Jodi Byrd's interpretation of LeAnne Howe's work, is the potential to "imagine worlds with *relational spirals* and a center that does not so much hold as stretches, links, and ties everything within to worlds that look in all directions" (2011, 20; emphasis added). Vine Deloria (Standing Rock Sioux), echoing the philosophical ideas of Édouard Glissant employed throughout this book, describes such relationality as "everything in the natural world has relationships with every other thing and the total set of relationships make up the world as we experience it" (1999, 34). More recently, Tommy Orange (Cheyenne/Arapaho), discussed later in this chapter, wrote, "Everything here is formed in relation to every other living and non-living thing from the earth. All our relations" (2018b, 11).

What matters, according to Adam Arola (KBIC Ojibwe), is not humans acting alone, but rather "the web of relations in which it participates in a particular place at a particular time" (2011, 559). Using the example of a bird, Arola explains that one can know the "personality" of that bird only through the part it plays in a structure larger than the body of the bird itself. This would mean knowing and understanding the whole "world" in which the bird participates (eating, breeding, nesting, and so forth), the world that sustains it and that it in turn reciprocally sustains.

THREADS THAT CONNECT THE WORLD

Robin Wall Kimmerer explores just such a "web of relations" in *Braiding Sweetgrass*, written from the dual perspective of a scientist and enrolled member of the Citizen Potawatomi Nation. She offers "a braid of stories meant to heal our relationship to the world…woven from three strands: indigenous ways of knowing, scientific knowledge, and the story of an Anishinabekwe scientist trying to bring them together in service to what matters most" (2013, x). Worlding for her is an "intertwining" of "old stories and new ones," working together to create different and better relations toward a particular "worldview" (x, 163) to put alongside others determined by science and the academy. In 2020 her book suddenly appeared on the *New York Times* best-seller list and has since sold more than five hundred thousand copies worldwide.[3]

For Kimmerer, Native creation stories, like that of Sky Woman, are stories of arrival, "immigrant" stories connected with all arrivals to America "since 1492" (8). What differs, however, is their relationships to the land, with colonialists viewing it as "property, real estate, capital, or natural resources" in contrast to "[Native] kinship with the world" as a "gift in motion," a continuing process, and not a static outcome (17, 31). The science taught at university felt "reductionist, mechanistic, and strictly objective" when the questions she wanted to ask of the world are very different, open, reciprocal, and expansive: "Who are you?" and "What can you tell us?" (42). *Braiding Sweetgrass* functions not only as natural history but also as an intense ceremony reacquainting readers with a living world in which "matter and spirit are both given voice" (346). Her sense of the world runs counter to the established rational views of the scientific community, being defined instead through "an architecture of relationships, of connections…the shimmering threads that hold it all together," the "threads that connect the world, to join instead of divide" (46; 42). She writes, "When I stare too long at the world with science eyes, I see an afterimage of traditional [Native] knowledge," and so, it is vital that "we see the world more fully when we use both" (46). As Arola explains, this relational thought extends to a broader sense of Native community, since "an individual cannot be said to exist without the 'people'…understood as *the whole web of existence* in which any singular being inheres" (2011, 560; emphasis added).

Kimmerer's shared and interlinked understanding of the world echoes Häkan's "mentors" in *In the Distance* whose two traditions filter into his life (see chapter 2). In Native terms, Paula Gunn Allen (Laguna Pueblo) expresses this as a "sacred hoop" to "embody, articulate, and share reality, to bring the isolated, private self into harmony and balance with this reality," and, consequently, understand the world as "a circular, dynamic universe in which all things are related and are of one family…[forming] a sense of relatedness to (instead of isolation from) what exists" (1992, 55, 60). Kimmerer terms it a "dance of cross-pollination that can produce a new species of knowledge, a new way of being in the world" (2013, 47), like a powerful hybrid form of what Donna Haraway calls "situated worlding…neither traditional nor modern" (2016, 91). In Arola's words, "We learn from our brothers and sisters, the more ancient animals, and only thereby acquire knowledge of how to interact with others in the world. The knowledge gained in this way is always knowledge of a particular place with particular relations of particular particulars" (2007, 5).

The strong indigenous base of Kimmerer's worlding shares much with Haraway's drawing upon Native knowledge because "decolonial indigenous peoples and projects are central to…stories of alliance" (2016, 71). Haraway's "science art worldings" combine various knowledges "like knots of diverse intra-active relatings in dynamic complex systems," resembling the wondrous woven threads of a Navajo rug (60). We become, as a result of such visions and memories "at stake in each other" (97), entangled and knotted together as humans and nonhumans in place, in the world as *the whole web of existence*. However, as this book explores, existence is undermined by reductionism, recklessness, and greed, or what Kimmerer calls the "contemporary Windigo-mind" (2013, 374–75), combated by the "need to unearth the old stories that live in a place and begin to create new ones, for we are storymakers, not just storytellers. All stories are connected, new ones woven from the threads of the old" (341).

For LeAnne Howe, "Native people are certainly the ghost writers for the event and story of America" (1999, 123), functioning as an intimate shadow within American culture, often overlooked, but uncannily present. Gerald Vizenor (Anishanaabe) writes, "Shadows of heard stories are the paramount verities of a tribal presence…active and intransitive… remembered as survivance" (1994, 56, 58). As Howe's *Savage Conversations* shows later, the (Native) ghostwriters of America are its shadows, ever linked and related, bound together as memories and traces, prompts and visions, to "counter the dominance of histories and the dickered testimonies of representations" (63) and project a powerful, active future.

GRAFTING ECHOES INTO HARMONY

Kimmerer's demand for a world seen through "a lens of stories" (2013, 346) is a challenge taken up by LeAnne Howe, whose interest in story making and storytelling is both multiple and complex, interdisciplinary and, inherently, worlding.[4] As she has written, "Native stories have always been enormous in scope and in the telling of all creation, [although] in a little over a century our stories have been pressed into the minuscule size of a grain of sand. A stereotype in feathers. So I hope to (re)complicate matters with international stories" (37). Her writing opens up Native experience, history, and stories to the world, underlining the fraught and complex relations that constitute what Vizenor calls "active presence" (1998, 15). If, as Byrd asserts, Natives have become "past tense presences," a "paradigmatic Indianness to facilitate…imperial desires" (2011, xx, xxi), then in writers like Kimmerer and Howe, something contrary and awkward emerges as a counterposition of presence.[5] Their transgeneric writing aims "to make visible what imperialism and its resultant settler colonialisms and diasporas have sought to obscure," and, therefore, "to activate indigeneity as a condition of possibility" and then "deploy" it as a force against the colonizer's production of Indianness-as-otherness (xxx, xxxix). Echoing Glissant once again, Byrd writes that "the Indian is a ghost in the system, an *errant* or virus that disrupts the virtual flows by stopping them, redirecting them, or revealing them to be what they are and will have been all along: colonialist" (19; emphasis added).

In Howe's and Kimmerer's work, "science is not more capable than or superior to native thinking, but is rather cousin, brother and sister, daughter and son to Indigenous knowledge" (Meland 2014, 31). Referring to scientist Lynn Margulis, Howe argues her concept "symbiogenesis" reflects Choctaw beliefs and practices, stressing "continual cooperation, strong interaction, and mutual dependence among life forms…co-opting others, not just by killing them" (20).[6] For Howe, this is a Choctawan "way of looking at the world" and critical to an understanding of "tribalography," with one foot in traditional stories and the other in science, shifting us away from colonialist thinking toward what she calls "an ethical Native literary praxis" (2008, 338). Thus, tribalography is a worlding process, "a looking back along the world lines of the past and seeing worlds other than the one trumpeted by a triumphal American exceptionalism and the Native victimage it imagines" (Meland 2014, 37). When Jill Doerfler explained her use of tribalography as a methodology, she expressed it as a poem about weaving a sweetgrass basket. Like Kimmerer, the weaving metaphor allowed her "to create a single piece using multiple distinct elements" in a collaborative, dynamic production of material, not as a simple unity, but rather as a productive tension stressing "the diversity, complexity, and adaptability" of Native identities (2014, 72). Following Howe, Doerfler summed up this approach as interdisciplinary, telling "stories that include all…elements and also work in collaboration with the past, present, and future," teaching and showing "us our place within our families, communities, nations, and the world" (2013, 229). Central to this approach are reciprocity and responsibility moving from the past into the present and future, understanding connections across time and space, in what Doerfler calls "the spaces between reality and rumors of memory" (2009, 295).

Howe's "The Story of America" explains tribalography as the means to "pull all the elements together…meaning the people, the land, multiple characters and all their manifestations and revelations, and connect these in past, present, and future milieu. (Past, present, and future milieu means a world that includes non-Indians)" (2013, 31). The task of the Native author, therefore, is "to make connections across difference through an imaginative act…that acknowledges the effects of colonialism on both the colonizers and colonized," but to do so in such a way that stories alleviate the past pain by invoking "cross-cultural and cross-national alliances" (Romero 2014, 22, 23). As Byrd points out, although tribalography is associated within Chickasaw and Choctaw "structures of relationality and governance," it "*looks out toward* a region, a hemisphere, to a world" (2014, 56; emphasis added), as an active process of worlding defined by Wilson earlier as "openings of time and consciousness to other values and multiple modes of being, projection, and survival" (2018, 8). This explains Howe's desire "to (re)complicate matters with international stories" (2013, 37), forming a "worlded criticism [that] seeks new and emergent connections to and articulations with region, place, area, and trans-species forms" (Wilson 2018, 8).

Like Kimmerer's view of "a new way of being in the world," Howe's tribalography emphasizes alliances and collaboration, "bringing things together…making consensus…symbiotically connecting one thing to another" as if into "an expanding global covenant" (2013, 31, 36).[7] In this way, Native stories "know the world as a neighbourhood" (Kimmerer 2013, 56), being both local and global, retaining and sustaining tribal histories, ceremonies, and humor, while also reaching outward and making connections with what Howe calls "other realities." Tribalography asks, "What story do we want to tell? What work do we want that story to do? What kind of future does the story construct?" (Doerfler 2014, 67).

Working across genres, Howe and Kimmerer find common ground, "integrating oral traditions, histories, and experiences into narratives and *expanding* our identities," so that "tribalography is a story that links Indians and non-Indians" (Howe 2013, 36; emphasis added). Reviewing Howe's *Evidence of Red*, Craig S. Womack (Creek-Cherokee) commented, "The significance of Howe's imaginative act is an insistence that Indians have something to say about the world beyond Indian country, that Native studies is not inherently parochial, that tribally specific approaches have global implications" (2005, 158).

In exploring this "world beyond Indian country," Howe's writing is often surreally chaotic, shifting between spatial and temporal frames, one identity to another, nation to nation, consciousness to unconsciousness. As she has written, chaos is that which "occurs when Indians and non-Indians bang their heads together in search of cross-cultural understanding. The sound is often a dull thud, and the lesson leaves us all with a bad headache" (2013, 41). She disrupts the flow of empire through *huksuba*, a chaotic, disruptive perspective that Howe favors, for challenging one-dimensional constructions of fact and fiction (such as the dominant narrative of Indian disappearance and US Manifest Destiny), through the utilization of intricate and diverse Native experiences or the multidimensional ways Native Americans often construct their stories. As Howe argues, "All histories are stories that are written down. The story you get depends on the point of view of the writer. At some point histories are contextualized as fact, a theoretically loaded word. Facts change, but stories continually bring us into being" (31). Thus, the layered experience of Howe's work (like Kimmerer's) enables the questioning of norms through colliding realities, teasing us to see the world and its many relations differently. History, for example, is not static or fixed within tribalography, but "a collaboration with the past and present and future" (Howe 2008, 333), reconsidered and revised through the telling and creating of new, resonant stories, as, for example, in Howe's "Choctalking on Other Realities," discussed later. Such a mix of styles, or *huksuba*, aims, according to Kimberley Blaeser, to "incite the reader to an imaginative reevaluation of both the accounts and processes of history" (quoted in Doerfler 2014, 72).

Chaos, as seen in the work of Glissant, for example, is uneasily marked by "the immeasurable intermixing of cultures," the "unimaginable turbulence of Relation," and erratic deterministic systems (Glissant 1997, 138). It is frictional and complex, as in *huksuba*, which Byrd calls "a generative, creative force as well as a potentially destructive one," from which emerges an indigenous critical theory "that emphasizes interconnectedness and grievability embodied within and among relational kinships created by histories of oppressions" (2011, xxvii, xxviii). As we have seen, Howe's goal is to "activate indigeneity" and then "deploy it" against these multiple oppressions, but without sacrificing "indigenous worlds and futures" in the process. Here, I am drawing together these oppressed "relational kinships," in Byrd's words, to "imagine cacophonously" (xxxix) a landscape of worldings that refuses to impose any single authoritative worldview. What these writers argue through their versions of activated indigenous knowledge is that we are all related and that we are our relations. Howe comments that "the past is ever present whether it's through the ceremonies, ghosts, land, because the land is past tense and present tense all at the same time...a wonderful space in physics that is all things at once, past, present, and future....I can't imagine a worldview without it" (Krivokapić 2019, 529).

For Howe, tribalography's traditions of alliance, collaboration, and diplomacy provide an antidote to recent political tendencies of US and other governments, "helpful in getting our country past the nightmare of binaries that the Bush administration has created," while witnessing "the rise of fundamentalism, homophobia," and other forms of separatism in Indian country (Squint 2010, 216, 224). Although Howe recognizes the importance of tribal sovereignty, it cannot be at the cost of inwardness and turning away from the world, since, as we have seen throughout this book, the dangers of reductionist thinking, or simple binary divisions, are fundamentally unproductive.[8]

OTHER REALITIES, OTHER WORLDS

In *Choctalking on Other Realities* (2013), Howe's tribalography deliberately crosses between geographies, identities, and beliefs, spinning strange travel stories that are both humorous and jarring. Its form and content are provocative and unsettling, fluctuating from essay to memoir through weird fiction, ancient storytelling to film scripts, in kaleidoscopic fragments. In "How I Lost Ten Pounds," the narrative stops and restarts with the words "But, I digress" (72), and it is the digressive that makes these pieces tribalographic and worlding. Susan Stewart argues that narrative digression "stands in tension with narrative closure. It is narrative closure opened from the inside out" and so, "instead of offering the reader transcendence, the digression blocks the reader's view, toying with the hierarchy of narrative events" (1993, 30). Howe's digressive, transgeneric playfulness discourages "transcendence" with its connotations of superiority by plunging her readers into the creative destructive "chaos," or *huksuba*, where worlds collide and interact: Indian and non-Indian; Upper, Lower, and Between Worlds (2013, 41); the United States and other nations. As with narrative digression, the effect is nonreductive, expansive, and errant, serving to "multiply worldings that occur *all at the same time*," as Byrd puts it (2011, 66).

Throughout *Choctalking* Howe's transnational contacts "multiply worldings," breaking away from the closed, colonial discourse of the marginalized, invisible, or erased Indian. Howe encounters the world beyond the United States, as American, Native, and woman, to "learn more about my ancestors and myself in order to create" and "inform ourselves and the non-Indian world about who we are" (2013, 3). Accordingly, she continues, "My characters are doing some of the same things that Choctaws have done in the past. They link the stories they've heard about their ancestors with the stories they are living." In turn, this *alliance* of narratives "breathes meaning into their world (as well as breathing life onto the pages of written stories)" (Womack and Justice 2008, 331).

Crucially, Howe refuses the invisibility of Indians, insisting that "America is a tribal creation story" (2013, 13) in which indigenous knowledge helped immigrants survive in the New World, advising which crops to grow and uniting diverse peoples into a coherent political structure. She insists the tribal story, often dismissed as primitive or fantastical, is "one of America's authors" and "brings forth knowledge and inspires us to make the eventful leap that one thing leads to another" (30, 18). Despite the efforts over time of physical and cultural removal, Native Americans persist as "authors" (or "ghostwriters") of the nation with their histories and presence central, not marginal, to America's meaning in the world. Like Margulis's symbiogenesis, Natives are entangled and related, rather than separated by lines of division, prejudice, history, race, and gender, with Howe paralleling the "Choctowan way of looking at the world" with the new science "of continual cooperation, strong interaction, and mutual dependence among life forms" (20–21). However, written history, as discussed earlier, remains dominant through repetition and unquestioned acceptance, shaping "nation-state stories" (Howe 2008, 332), while other voices are squeezed out, forgotten, or erased. This is why tribalography matters, reminding, prompting, surprising, connecting, and countering such dominant patterns by employing erratic or errant stories "to affectively and intuitively read through and beyond the colonial rumors that have been layered onto Indigenous lands…to confront, challenge, and reconfigure the stories colonizers like to tell about themselves and their place in the world" (Byrd 2014, 62). Tribalography consistently unsettles this *assumed* place and *assumed* world.

To demonstrate this, Howe discusses Irvin Morris and Susan Power as tribalographers, showing how their Native stories "transcend [their] own memories, but include those of relatives and tribal community," connecting to "the shiny and glittering world," providing a "multi-generational story" that "unfolds" as the "reader is taken backwards in time" and into the future (2013, 34–35). These intense acts of collaboration reveal "other realities," asserting, "We were there. Always there. Still here" (35). These elements emerge in the story "Choctalking on Other Realities," beginning in Jerusalem, the epicenter of conflict, ethnic division, and "the wars of heaven," where Howe is visiting as an "academic tourist," encountering Palestinian protesters whose aim is "to change the status quo" (2013, 79,

80). The scene immediately slides through time and space, taking Howe back into her past, as a child running from another authoritarian injustice, bullied by a white classmate in Bethany, Oklahoma. "I am still running" (81), she writes, drawing us into the continuum of the story's overlapping worlds where diverse people run from and confront different oppressions. The setting draws parallels too between the sovereignty-seeking struggles of Native Americans in the 1970s and of the Intifada of 1992 Jerusalem.

In the 1970s, the "story she really wanted to tell" (81) is in the transit zone of an airport, where people, nations, and beliefs cross over and intersect; a "non-place" or "out-of-place" in Marc Augé's formulation, "like palimpsests on which the scrambled game of identity and relations is ceaselessly rewritten" (1995, 79). In tribalography's ideal space, "a whole mass of relations" are mediated, "with the self and with others" (94), through Howe's cast of intersecting female characters: a German Catholic, an African American, a Russian Jew, and herself, an Oklahoman Choctaw. In varied ways, they have all experienced historic oppressions and racism, Nazism, slavery, anti-Semitism, and US colonialism, yet they still live in a new age of imperial wars and violence marked by the presence of "one hundred Vietnam draftees" arriving at the airport on their way to war. As Howe points out, "It's not news… that the Vietnam War is being fought disproportionately by the poor… red and yellow, black, and poor white boys" who pass through on their way to the front line (82). She wants to tell them to run, as she once had from her childhood bully, but does not. In the "urgency of the present moment," this nonplace is where such identities are reassessed and undone, as if within "immense parentheses" removed from the secure notion of place as a "closed world… whose stability is supposed to be assured" (104, 111, 44). At this moment she recalls the words of the teacher when she was hiding from her childhood bully, "*No one gets hurt if they do what they're told*" (Howe 2013, 82; italics in original), and suddenly the fragments relate, as if talking to each other across time, with the personal and the political coalescing. Bullying, coercion, and violence knot together, and even the multicultural cast fight and argue over old wounds. Howe, the waitress and union steward, is caught between them trying to "intercede" (83), but everywhere in 1970 seems chaotic, with "Vietnam on television nightly," while Indians occupy Alcatraz, "fed up with colonialism," longing to "change the status quo," echoing the earlier scene of the protesting Palestinian women. Howe is not the hero of her own narrative, however, for she feels "powerless to change anything," simply parroting a version of the earlier line, "No one will get hurt if they do what we're supposed to do"

(84). This refrain of compliance and docility becomes the story's reverberating core, reinforcing the very status quo it hopes to change.

In Jerusalem Howe meets a woman who claims some Indian ancestry and with whom she feels "remarkably alike" (86), both in the way they look and in their histories of migration and violence. In a key moment in the story, their worlds interfuse, "bringing things together" (31), as tribalography always does: "To place her in our past, to put myself in her beginning, and intertwine our threads of history—for we are nothing without our relationships. That's Choctaw" (86). This "intertwined" process is akin to a *decolonial* worlding through which oppressed communities find common ground and shared concerns to set against the apparently dominant world. As Howe puts it, "We're on the side of societies that have reduced us to grief" (88), yet it can be a revelatory grief, a sense of commonality that, in Judith Butler's words, "delineates the ties we have to others, that shows us that these ties constitute what we are" (2004, 22). Howe's story, with its scenes of conflict, strife, and misunderstanding acted out across time and space, returns to these relational ties through which "my fate is not originally or finally separable from yours," since "the 'we' is traversed by a relationality that we cannot easily argue against" (22–23). Yet the battle, as her story suggests, is with the "overwhelming" power of colonial imposition and control, like the song she was taught in kindergarten whose lyrics she ironically mishears as *"Red and yellow, black and white, we are separate in his sight, Jesus loves the little children of the world"* (Howe 2013, 90; italics in original). "Separate" replaces "precious" in her rendition, underlining how communities remain divided in her experience, denying the relational ties she understands as critical to tribalography as active worlding.

As the story closes, Howe wants to see how, even in Jerusalem, there might be some "relationship" across communities of Jews and Palestinians, imagining she sees Nina, the survivor of Babi Yar from the airport kitchen, protesting with the Palestinian women. As an Arab minister arrives, "with his palms facing toward the Sun" (92–93), in a gesture linked throughout with prayer, worship, and peaceable understanding across cultures, she hopes his prayer is one of hope and reconciliation, bringing together all the fragmented identities of her story, Jewish, Palestinian, Vietnamese, Mayan, and Black women suffering at the hands of oppressive regimes. Through difference and across time, Howe's worlding tribalography connects rather than divides, relates, and heals in the face of the other: "She is The People, our grandmothers, our mothers, our sisters, our ancestors, ourselves" (93). For Howe, tribalography was always about "integrating oral traditions, histories, and experiences into narratives and expanding our identity" so that what is created is "a story that links Indians and non-Indians in an expanding global covenant chain" (2013, 36). By invoking the latter concept, she draws on the tradition of alliances and agreements in early Indian-Anglo relations, forming what Bruce Morito calls a "culturally hybrid institution" forging "an ethic of mutual respect" (2012, 13). Tribalography, you will recall, is similarly "an ethical Native literary praxis," *expanding* Indian identity into other worlds and other realities through connection, mutuality, and alliance. As in Glissant's work, the idea of "expanse" is a critical opposition to what he calls "filiation," or the transfer of power through imposed lines of inheritance (as in patriarchal families) (see 1997, 57–58). Tribalography too seeks *expansion*, an "inexhaustible tangle" like that of a complicated, extended family, "circular and meshed," standing against "reductive transparency," favoring what Glissant calls "opacity" (58–59). For Howe, as in Glissant, there is the possibility to "link the stories they've heard about their ancestors with the stories they are living" (2008, 331) and so be "considerate of all the threatened and delicious things joining one another (without conjoining, that is, without merging) in the expanse of the Relation" (Glissant 1997, 62).

Ultimately, as Romero correctly states of Howe, "Her concept of 'tribalography' urges a fuller representation of the past, one that recognizes and honors not only historic grief but also stories of collective resistance. Tribalography advocates that individuals and tribes expand their identities and political practices, adopting early tribal traditions of diplomacy and inclusiveness more actively to resist intergenerational trauma" (2014, 24).

THE WORLD AS IT TRULY IS

If, as discussed earlier, "the Indian is a ghost in the system, an errant or virus that disrupts" and "Native people are…the ghost writers for the… story of America" (1999, 123), then Howe's *Savage Conversations* actualizes a powerful disturbance. In it Mary Todd Lincoln, wife of President Abraham Lincoln, is locked in an asylum where she "conjures" (or not) a ghostly "Savage Indian" who torments her nightly (2019, 94).[9] As Howe says, Mary is "very much the Donald Trump of her day," a person representing the system of capitalism and governance, yet filled with troubled memories, self-doubt, and delusions, while deflecting weaknesses onto others (in this case embodied in the Savage Indian). As one reviewer put it, the experience of the text is of "a striking hybrid, a play in verse never meant to be staged, a novel that resists prose structure, a series of scenes that encompass the unseen" (Lapointe 2019). Like so much of Howe's published work, it is perplexing and unsettling, with parallels to ceremonial mounds built "by layering different kinds of soils one upon the other… represent[ing]…the stories we layer," connecting worlds above and below, before and after (Howe 2013, 178). As such, it reframes personal and public history, highlighting its erased elements and blank spaces (like the missing images within the text itself, suggesting an incomplete document). Such is the book's effect as it layers the "soils" of history, myth, prejudice, guilt, and violent redemption into an *unfinished*, haunting tribalography, mixing past, present, and future in a complex *danse macabre*.

Her Savage Indian is a brutal reminder of Lincoln's little-documented racial violence ordering the hanging of thirty-eight Dakota Indians on December 26, 1862, in Mankato, Minnesota.[10] Mary, haunted by this past and institutionalized by her son, began to speak of visions that threatened to unravel Lincoln's, and by implication America's, mythic narrative. In Howe's generic mixture of Beckett-like absurdist drama and poetic fragments, Mary's hallucinations of the Indian cutting bones from her face and sewing open her eyes becomes almost ceremonial, an ecstatic ritual of "assent," a spiritual cleansing or penitence, like some sublime and terrifying act of an Old Testament God. It is as if Mary yearns to free herself from the *personal* guilt and pain she feels for her own troubled marriage, dead children, and loss of status, but also the *political* guilt attached to her husband as the esteemed father of the modern nation, its American saint.

Howe finds something revelatory in Mary's visions, inviting readers to revisit a history that condemned the first lady's madness and ignored her husband's anti-Indian policies, while also revisiting the silenced memory of Native American dispossession. Mary's "old wounds" reveal a past of self-harm, laudanum addiction, and possible filicide, "When I felt nothing, / I used a kitchen knife" (2019, 41), she says. Savage Indian becomes part of her own pained being, cutting through the shame she feels for the life she has lived as a beneficiary of sustained colonial attitudes and structures. Although a simplified stereotype, Savage Indian is nonetheless the product of Mary's imagination, steeped in the history she learned as a girl growing up "western" (born in Kentucky), reinforced through colonial discourse, and the politics of war and genocide practiced by her esteemed husband. As a result, Savage Indian is savage only in Mary's conception of him, "the savage counter to the promises of liberal democracy" (Byrd 2011, xxxvii). Unnamed, he functions within the psychodrama, as Mary's "shadow" that "climbed out of the abyss" (Howe

2019, 82). As discussed earlier, it is as if the Savage Indian is "not bound by the measures of time and space," becoming rather the "unsaid presence in names, the memories in silence, and the imagination of tribal experiences" (Vizenor 1994, 78, 73). Throughout the book, his "shadow" falls over Mary, opening up and confronting the past as he flays her flesh, opening her eyes to erased histories. As Vizenor writes, "Shadows tease and loosen" dominant narratives, disrupting the "ruins of representation" written into conquerors' archives and policed by the lies of the powerful, like Lincoln himself. As Bergland explains, "Europeans take possession of Native American lands, to be sure, but at the same time, Native Americans take supernatural possession of their dispossessors" (2000, 3). Savage Indian exists to remind Mary and contemporary readers that erasure leaves traces for which we all bear responsibility.

His ironic "possession" of Mary is enacted through entangled and surreal acts of exchange (or "expansion"), which underline their curious relational bond. They spar "like amateur boxers," "twirl around the room to a waltz," while he "places her wedding ring on his little finger," grooms the nits from her hair, and even wears her clothes (Howe 2019, 10, 54, 14, 13, 66). Through their hallucinatory "marriage," with its touching intimacy, sexual frisson, and sadomasochistic torments, Mary "swallows" (14) all the Indian offers up, as though she is undergoing a revelatory communion through the return of the repressed Indian *into* her consciousness. In a classic reversal of what Bergland has called "the national uncanny" (2000), the always "absent or dead" Indians of American nationalist discourse return in *Savage Conversations*, talking back to political power. So rather than "sustain" the acceptable *world* of American nationalism, as Bergland has it, Savage Indian's *otherworldliness* serves as "constant reminders of the fragility of national identity" and "call it into question" (4–5). In Howe's gothic psychodrama, the spectral Indian "cannot be buried or evaded, and the spectre of their forced disappearance haunts the American nation and the American imagination" (5). Nightly, the ghostly Indian shackles Mary, or "Gar Woman," as he calls her, to a chair and tortures her: "*Oh!* At last," she cries. "I can see the world as it truly is" (17).[11] *Through* her Indian fantasy of ritual violence—"they prick my skin, slash my will" (19)—Mary's sense of the world is gradually unsettled and undone.

In the Indian's longest speech in "Savage Indian Laments," he emerges from behind the veil of simulation and cultural assumptions to express a more complex identity. "I know isolation. / Silence," he says, as if to signal his identification with Mary, but, as Vizenor explains, "the shadows of tribal memories are the active silence, trace, *différance* in the literature of survivance" (1994, 71). From these "shadows" come entangled lessons for the distraught and broken Mary: "I have crippling doubts," he says, "but I surrender nothing, not even in death" (Howe 2019, 28). In such moments of intimate empathy, their exchange is both touching and profound, like a coming together of worlds: "When I look at your world, I weep / Because in the end, even your life is a captivity account. / Maybe we are all captives of one sort or the other" (29). "We are a pair, you and I, / Relics to be studied," Mary proclaims (101), a "pair" entangled in history, a "we" languishing "in a room filled with betrayal," as if relating her own situation (betrayed by her son) to that of the Indian (betrayed by Lincoln and the US government).

Despite Mary's social grandeur, wealth, and power, she is a captive too of her gnawing guilt and terrible sense of loss. Yet she and by implication America "can never cover the past," since within both person *and* nation there exist dark secrets and repressed memories. "Gar Woman," the Indian says, "you are not who you claim to be," for she has, according to this ghostly voice, killed her own children, as brutally as Lincoln and his armies had killed his kin—"everything you touch leaves a bruise" (30). She is culpable and responsible, complicit in the "scriptures of manifest manners," as Vizenor terms the discourse of colonialism (1994, 5), but it takes the slow possession of the Savage Indian to open her world to such recognitions.

As Mary "assents" to her eyes being opened by the torments "she craves" (Howe 2019, 20), Howe's drama works across time, past, present, and future, as her writing inevitably does, reminding contemporary readers of the ongoing violence, racism, and injustice within the United States that have deep roots in the trauma of the past. As Howe told an interviewer, "I write about issues and events that have taken place in the past but resonate with the present" (Macklin 2017). Indeed, "In the future" is oft repeated throughout *Savage Conversations*, marking Mary's visions as prophetic, predicting the endless chain of violence committed in America's name, like "a reflection of national conscience" (Montgomery 2019). Ironically, her "husband's spirit," the great emancipator of slaves, predicts future racial violence, where "metropolitan police of the district / Will shoot black men / And black children on / The streets of Washington like moving targets" (Howe 2019, 56). In Mary's prophetic words, "Our world indeed is a bitter gasp" (63).

Mary also dwells on the date of her release from the asylum, September

11, 1875, commenting, "I vouchsafe September 11 to the nation that / My husband saved, / Died for. For centuries to come, let freedom ring" (82). Continued racial violence, oppression, foreign wars, terrorism, and social division all question freedoms guaranteed by Lincoln, and, ironically, she "condemned the nation on September 11" (83). As the Rope, a symbol of capital punishment and of brutal repression, "searches for his legacy" and place within American history, he describes himself with an appalling, everyday innocence: "I float in the wind like a flag on holidays. / I inspire national pride" (47).

The force of remembrance comes through the Savage Indian whose "words vibrate from the past to / Future constellations," as he lies beside Lincoln's "catafalque" like a bizarre alter ego, proclaiming the worlding weight of Howe's resonant and prophetic drama. Charting attempts to destroy the Native presence in the Americas from 1492, Savage Indian concludes that tribal life remains "undaunted" because, as he cries out, "We live / We live" (48).

Mary, however, tells him in a moment of bitter anger that he "can never escape the past" and will forever remain unfree "in this land" (72). However, such sentiments are not exclusive to 1875; once more there are parallels with contemporary US politics, still troubled by a cultural psychosis, permitting those in power to construct partial narratives such as Trump's defense of racial violence in Charlottesville in 2017, Kenosha and Portland in 2020, and the insurrection at the Capitol in Washington, DC, in 2021. Howe's haunting narrative refocuses on a national inheritance that is contradictory and even criminal, where presidential power is abused, marginalized bodies destroyed, and shameful stories erased in favor of the glorification of a man and a narrow vision of nationhood. As Montgomery writes, "Historical relics and monuments and walls, sanity and control—these are still what haunt us." "The world will little note, nor long remember what we say here," Lincoln assured America in his Gettysburg Address, "but it can never forget what they did here." As Montgomery explains, "But forgetting, Howe insists, is precisely what the country has done. History has focused on the myth instead of the terror that remains for marginalized bodies" (2019).

HISTORIES WRITTEN WRONG

Toward the end, Mary, now freed from the asylum, claims ambiguously, "Yesterday my shadow climbed out of the abyss" (Howe 2019, 82), indicating "a new beginning" apart from her tormentor. As we soon discover, he is still present in her sister's home in Springfield, Illinois, saving Mary from suicide: "He cuts her down and holds her in his arms like a lover" (85). Together in the abyss, they fulfill Glissant's words on the nature of suffering as "the best element of exchange" (8). Out of the painful "matrix abyss" (203) Mary wrestles with the past, present, and future, her sorrow, guilt, and rage for herself and for her country. As Glissant states, such a "projection" moves us from "exception" to "Relation," because "peoples who have been to the abyss do not brag of being chosen…do not believe they are giving birth to any modern force." Instead, as their "memory intensifies" through the abyssal journey, they come toward "Relation," to "shared knowledge…the best element of exchange" (8). As Drabinski explains, "The fecundity of the pain of history and memory…underscores the chaotic swirl of relationality across time and geography…but it is *also* world-making" (2019, 163).

Through their ambiguous intimacy of relation, Mary and Savage Indian are indeed world-making, or perhaps sketching out a tentative, fragile, and different sense of the world born from suffering their mutual abyss. Their relation and exchange, dialogue and action—their "savage conversations"—create a rhythmical *to and fro*, slowly revealing their irresolvable entanglement. Savage Indian exposes Mary's racism, Confederate sympathies, and anti-Indian feelings because he knows the letters she has written that will, in time, be burned, "purifying your image for history's sake" (Howe 2019, 96). She sides with General John Pope, who led the army in the Dakota war and wrote of exercising "punishment beyond human power to inflict" and that Indians should be "treated as maniacs or wild beasts."[12] The Indian desires Mary's confession—"The truth, say it" (97)—and to see the hanged Dakota bodies above her head as grievable, which, according to Byrd, "calls people to acknowledge, to see, and to grapple with lived lives and the commensurable suffering" (2011, 38). Following Judith Butler, what Howe dramatizes through Mary's captivity and torment is how those "framed as being already lost or forfeited" (like Native Americans or Chinese, or Irish) become acknowledged as "grievable" and, therefore, as worthy of life (2010, 31).

Without doubt, Savage Indian *calls* Mary to *acknowledge* her past and requires her to *see*. After all, he sews her eyes open every night, demanding that when she says, "Grief became my friend, my work" (Howe 2019, 100), she might actually learn to extend this "work" beyond her own life, to the lives of others, like the hanged Dakotas and all those killed by her husband's army. "Hear me now, woman, now and forever," Savage Indian demands, reminding us that these 1875 troubles resonate across time up to and beyond the present. As Orange writes in *There There*, "Stray bullets and consequences are landing on our unsuspecting bodies even now" (2018b, 10). Native and non-Native are bound up tensely in the larger narrative of the United States, just as Mary and the Indian are, ultimately "a pair. / Abused. Abuser" (Howe 2019, 102). Howe's "dialogic imagination," as she calls it in *Evidence of Red*, "re-pairs" a sense of the world in which sharing, connection, and relation become the watchwords of the future, born out of the calamity and pain of the past.[13] "Everywhere you are, I am" (95), he says.

Returning to Butler's new ethics, *Savage Conversations* activates loss on both sides, appealing to the possibility of a "tenuous 'we,'" "for all of us have some notion of what it is to have lost somebody" (2006, 20). A world "re-paired" in this manner holds out the possibility of what Glissant calls "Relation" and, for Butler, "the ties we have to others…ties [that] constitute what we are, ties or bonds that compose us." Mary and the Savage Indian are *tied* in a similar way, "differentiated and related," "traversed by a relationality" (22) that has bound them in the past through the figure of Abraham Lincoln and now by "a room filled with betrayal" (Howe 2019, 59). Mary is possessed in order to be dispossessed, since through spectral torment her "unknowingness" is exposed and she is "undone" (Butler 2006, 28, 23) by the rememory he provokes in her. Finally, she acknowledges, indeed *studies* the hanged men" above her head, referring to herself as "a woebegone," willing to "embrace all my bad deeds" and conceding "the truth" (Howe 2019, 97, 99; emphasis added). Mary has progressed from "the narcissistic preoccupation of melancholia" toward "a consideration of the vulnerability of others" (Butler 2006, 30) and to a conception of the world based less on self and more on its multiple relations to others: "I cannot muster the 'we' except by finding the way in which I am tied to 'you.'…You are what I gain through this disorientation and loss. This is how the human comes into being, again and again, as that which we have yet to know" (49). In *Savage Conversations*' surreal and macabre dance when Mary admits "we are a pair. / Abused. Abuser," she recognizes the ambiguity of the two words side by side, indicating the possibility of "shared precariousness" and what Butler calls "the interdependency of persons" (2010, 28, 19).

This odd "pairing" is a reminder of the broader implications of tribalography's attention to mutuality, connection, and the ways "one thing leads to another" (Kirwan 2016, 269). Gaps and silences, erasures and "the nothingness of histories written wrong" (Orange 2018b, 10), have to be confronted, since, as Byrd argues, "elisions and refusals challenge us *to remember otherwise and against* the repetitive memes that obscure the continued persistence of Indigenous presences within the realms of the sensible, the political, and the digital" (2014, 61). *Savage Conversations* ends with the word "Yes" (spoken by the executioner's Rope), suggesting the possibility inherent in tribalography "to confront, challenge, and reconfigure the stories colonizers like to tell about themselves and their place in the world" (62) and, as a consequence, to perhaps world differently and better. After all, as Howe asserts, "A story is active and a story changes the world" (Macklin 2017).

STORIES THE WORLD IS RICHER FOR

Orange's *There There* draws together, like Howe's writing, past, present, and future but for a younger urban audience, a Facebook generation, producing what has been termed "digital tribalography" (Ross and Sexton 2020). Orange's prologue too bends genres, establishing a tragic tone through a contextualizing frame foreshadowing violence, from the TV test pattern's "Indian head…surrounded by circles that looked like sights through riflescopes" (2018b, 3) to King Philip's War, or the Pequot massacre with Indian heads on spikes, in jars, or kicked down the street "like soccer balls." Such acts testify to settler-colonial dispossession of Native peoples, "like flags to be flown, to be seen, cast broadly" into the world as symbols of authority, conquest, and control (5). Today, on "the screens of the New World" (6), media representations continue "a different kind of violence" (Gates 2018), defining Native life as a well-rehearsed set of stereotypes and tropes: "The copy of a copy of the image of an Indian in a textbook" (Orange 2018b, 7). Consequently, Orange's tribalography works against "the historical monolithic Native American that everyone thinks of, and that…the only real way to be a real Native American is to be historical or have a headdress or look this one way. It's deeply damaging to a people to not have a dynamic range of ways to be that are still acceptable as Native" (Orange in Hughey 2019).

As discussed earlier, Howe points out that such monolithic images extend to sports mascots and logos, even once to heads on coins, which "like the truth of what happened in history all over the world are…now out of circulation" (Orange 2018b, 7). Orange, like Howe, wants to put different and better images into "circulation" via dynamic and diverse stories, creating a version of tribalography for the Internet age. In refusing reductionist images of Indian life, Orange continues the battle against "assimilation, absorption, erasure" (8), taking the fictional fight into the cities, where in the twenty-first century most Indians live. For example, Opal Viola Victoria Bear Shield explains her mother's "hypercritical" approach as preparing "them for a world made for Native people not to live but to die in, shrink, disappear" (165). The Native world has been "shrunk" through the violence of colonialism, controlled and reduced by others' interpretations and history, curtailed onto reservations, and excluded from mainstream culture except as mascots and logos. The very title of the novel reinforces this central notion, since "for Native people in this country, all over the Americas, it's been developed over, buried ancestral land, glass and concrete and wire and steel, unreturnable covered memory. There is no there there" (39). Hence, "Indianness" becomes a static entity, a monolith, as Orange refers to it, and so easier to manipulate, define, and control. The novel counters this with stories, as all tribalography does, because, as Howe wrote, "Native stories are power. They create people. They author tribes" (2013, 13), or as Ross and Sexton explained, "Native stories help all of us remember who we were, recognize who we are, and imagine who we will become" (2020, 583).

As *There There* acknowledges, "We are the memories we don't remember, which live in us, which we feel, which make us sing and dance and pray the way we do," played out negatively *and* positively, in contemporary Oakland lives (Orange 2018b, 10). The counterargument to reductionist thinking is evident in Dene Oxendene's film project and exemplified by his dying uncle Lucas, who "looked off, out the living room window, across the street, or farther, off to where the sun had set, or past that, back at his life maybe, and then he got this look in his eyes…something that looked like remembering and dreading at once" (32–33). In this moment, Orange's revamped tribalography spreads out *expansively* from the local, "off…off" out into the world and *simultaneously* inside individual and collective memory, across the flow of time "to where the sun set" in the West, and then spiraling back. In this intense geography, Orange expresses the novel's capacity for worlding in which indigeneity is varied, complex, and *expansive*, established "as a fact of the present, with a real future" (Ross and Sexton 2020, 584).

Dene explains his film project as "inherited" from Lucas, like a digital archiving of stories otherwise lost, gathering up "every kind of story" people wanted to tell, "with no direction or manipulation or agenda" (Orange 2018b, 40). However, it goes further too, since "Dene indigenizes new technology, expanding what counts as tribal elements and asserting an evolving sense of being Indigenous" (Ross and Sexton 2020, 586). This archive functions as a bulwark against the hegemonic narrative of disappearance so prominent in history textbooks, Hollywood cinema, and popular culture, and, as Dene puts it, it's "just what our community needs considering how long it's been ignored, has remained invisible" (Orange 2018b, 40).

In the interlude, where the same third-person narrator of the prologue addresses the reader, we are told, "We've been fighting for decades to be recognized as a present tense people, modern, relevant, alive," yet, in a phrase that foreshadows the novel's ending, we "die in the grass wearing feathers" (141). The prologue alerted readers to the impossibility of escaping historic colonial violence and trauma through its imagery of bullets as "premonitions, ghosts from dreams of a hard, fast future." As in Howe's work, these symbolize the ghostly traces of violent settler-colonialism scarring present-tense Indian lives, tethering, as tribalography always does, the past to the present and future. Predicting the cataclysmic violence at the Oakland powwow, the prologue states, "They took everything and ground it down to dust as fine as gunpowder, they fired their guns into the air in victory and the strays flew out into the nothingness of histories written wrong and meant to be forgotten. Stray bullets and consequences are landing on our unsuspecting bodies even now" (10).

Bullets from the past are still in flight in the present violence and oppression of the twenty-first century, from the Standing Rock Sioux Dakota Access Pipeline protests to the American Indian Movement flags in Minneapolis after the death of George Floyd or on the streets of Portland, Oregon.[14] As Orange wrote, "Violence is crucially related to both what is happening in America now, and what happened in its bloody and brutal history," revealing "this country's underhanded, undermining underbelly of an unconscious" in its treatment of nonwhite citizens. "Black Americans and other Americans of color," he continued, "are already carrying the weight of cruel, unreckoned-with histories on their shoulders; so to live amid unmitigated, too often racially motivated violence with little or no accountability on the horizon feels a lot like abandonment" (2018a).

It is against this background that Orange, writing in the age of Donald Trump, sought to challenge these "unreckoned-with histories" and the "underhanded, undermining underbelly of an unconscious" with contrary stories of other and different worlds.[15] In *There There*, during the occupation of Alcatraz, Opal recalls a laminated card with an image of "sad-Indian-on-a-horse-silhouette" on one side and on the other a quotation from *Crazy Horse's Prophecy*: "'Upon suffering beyond suffering; the Red Nation shall rise again and it shall be a blessing for a sick world. A world filled with broken promises, selfishness and separations. A world longing for light again'" (Orange 2018b, 48). Not locked in the past, the "sick world," as Orange demonstrates, nonetheless persists in the everyday lives of Native communities today. As Opal says, recalling her mother's words, "We should never not tell our stories" (57), from wherever they come, for they reach back as well as forward, mapping worlds others would silence, diminish, or erase. As Dene says of his film-archive project, they will be "all put together, all our stories," to counterbalance "reservation stories, and shitty versions from outdated history textbooks…to start telling this other story" (149). For Orange, this is an urban story that nonetheless retrieves the past, linking with earlier generations, for as Ross and Sexton point out, "In *There There* digital technologies enable tribalographies of the immediate present and imminent future, shot through with recent and long pasts both tribal and settler-colonial" (2020, 587).

Consequently, *There There* is a polyphonic and multigenerational assemblage of "independent and unmerged voices and consciousnesses…*each with its own world*" (Bakhtin 1997, 6; emphasis added), working together to construct a complex identity for indigenous peoples to interrupt the static, hegemonic images that see Native culture as monolithic and monologic.[16] Bakhtin's "interaction and interanimation of languages" describe a process akin to tribalography, "like mirrors that face each other, each reflecting in its own way a piece, a tiny corner of the world," which "force us to guess at and grasp for a world behind their mutually reflecting aspects that is broader, more multi-leveled, containing more and varied horizons than would be available to a single language or a single mirror" (414–15). In their indigenous versions of worlding, Howe and Orange refute the "single language" that too often shrinks the Native world, opting instead for something "broader, more multi-leveled," like *There There*'s "living mix of varied and opposing voices…developing and renewing itself" (49). Thus, Orange's characters use the Internet, social media, modern dance, and hip-hop, along with traditional powwow music and dancing, in a dialogic, polyphonic, hybrid form of storytelling and story making that deliberately refutes reductionist stereotypes of "New Age" spirit and romantic healing associated with Native culture. Not tied to their historic pasts, or even to their parents, Orange's complex and ambiguous characters move forward, working life out as they go, rarely finding all the answers.

Such polyphony is alive in Edwin Black's discussion of the music of a Tribe Called Red, revealing a hybrid mix of past and present Native and non-Native sources, while raising questions about identity and community: "the most modern, or more postmodern, form of Indigenous music I've heard that's both traditional and new-sounding. The problem with Indigenous art in general is that it's stuck in the past. The catch, or the double bind, about the whole thing is this: If it isn't pulling from tradition, how is it Indigenous? And if it's stuck in the past, how can it be relevant to other Indigenous people living now, how can it be modern?" (Orange 2018b, 77). *There There* walks this line, gathering up stories, forming layers, and spiraling from and around the Indian Center (a real community site *and* a symbolic one), mixing historical violence and removal with the painful realities of addiction, domestic violence, and family division, but always alongside hopeful stories of survival, reunion, and sacrifice.

Orange has said that his "view of life is that it's tragic" because "Native history has been tragic," and so he "wanted to represent [that]" in his work, yet, despite this, "I have hope, too. I think both things can exist. And I wanted both things to come across in the novel" (Goldstein 2019). Thus, alongside the novel's violent conclusion at the Oakland powwow, there are tentative moments of hope: Tony Loneman's refusal to carry out the robbery, turning on his own gang; Opal's rescue of Orvil; and Blue's discovery of her mother and father amid the chaos. In one of the final moments of the novel, Tony recalls his love of Transformers as if referring to the strength, resistance, and survival of communities that, with all their human flaws, the novel portrays: "We're metal, made hard, able to take it. We were made to transform" (Orange 2018b, 289–90). As Terese Marie Mailhot (Seabird Island Band) has written, tragedy cannot be avoided when writing about Native people in the Americas, but it does not have to fix identity "in grief," since "the word is pregnant with meaning," reminding us that in "a tragic life…there is a magnitude to my character, my loss, and it is all toward some end—a denouement." Above all, as a tragic character with magnitude and purpose, one is enabled "to see the human in the work," she writes, yet, she continues, "I am not a hopeless illustration, something for non-Natives to witness. *This world is larger for us in it*, because we saw things the white settlers didn't—we had maps and taxonomy, an interior knowledge of the Earth that our colonizers wilfully tried to erase and negate…stories the world is richer for" (2018; emphasis added).

As with Kimmerer, Howe, and Orange, what Mailhot reminds us of is the *expansive* nature of Native writing and how, through its dialogic relations, it connects endlessly with worlds. It is never a comfortable or secure process, as Mailhot testifies, but it is vital and generative: "I don't know what to do with my definition of tragedy in the face of theirs. But I think the answer is always story. The duplicities in our identities as indigenous people are key" (2018).

In 1999 Gerald Vizenor spoke of his "interest" in encouraging "serious literary artists who create new myths and stories about natives in diverse situations, and who do not solely rest on *indian* simulations or romantic revisions of traditions to move a character" (Vizenor and Lee 1999, 155). Although from different generations, Kimmerer, Howe, and Orange fulfill Vizenor's hope, becoming "diverse storiers," not marginal or romantic, but always at "the start of any national or continental history… with other natives and diverse cultures" and, as Mailhot suggests, with the whole world (178–79). Their writings, in whatever genre, are tribalographic because, in Vizenor's terms, they are "transmotional," potentially *transformative*, through humor, memories, "survivance over dominance," and the sheer diversity of stories they conjure (1998, 184).[17] Transmotion is sovereignty beyond mere territory, rights beyond land, for it is an "active presence," "tacit and visionary," "personal, totemic, and reciprocal," always moving against what Vizenor calls the "*indian*" or the static simulation of "aesthetic victimry" (15, 190, 16, 21). As I have shown throughout this chapter, tribalography is always moving and making worlds.

"The Story and the Archive of the Story"

Valeria Luiselli's *Lost Children Archive*

> The archive is never closed. It opens out of the future.
> —Jacques Derrida, *Archive Fever: A Freudian Impression*

AN ERRANT ARCHIVE

In *Tell Me How It Ends* (2017), the nonfiction basis for her novel *Lost Children Archive* (2019), Valeria Luiselli describes how the Border Patrol pulled over her family on a road trip from New York to the southwest borderlands. On presenting their documents and telling the officer they were writers, rather than reveal the real nature of their interests in the refugee crisis, they lied, "We are writing a Western, sir," to which he replied, "So you come all the way down here for *the inspiration*."[1] In what follows, Luiselli corrects this assumption to herself: "No, we do not find inspiration here, but we find a country that is as beautiful as it is broken," and she feels "broken with it…ashamed, confused, and sometimes hopeless" (24). Luiselli's combination of feelings reflects upon the original lie about a western while offering a vital clue to the important work undertaken in her writing, in particular her first novel in English, *Lost Children Archive*. The novel is a worldly reworking of the presumed "inspiration" of the western and its place in US cultural history, becoming a layered and complex countertext to the ideologies and mythologies of the frontier, Manifest Destiny, and internal colonialism that remain alive and active in US political culture today (see the introduction). In an essay for the *New Yorker* (2019b), Luiselli visited Tombstone's OK Corral "Wild West re-enactment" show, exploring the persistence of these myths in the lives of contemporary Americans. What she found was "a loop of embodied repetitions" enacted in "a space where the past had been replaced by a peculiar, repetitive, and selective representation of the past" that conveniently overlooked "historical accuracy in the broader sense," such as the "genocidal campaigns against Native Americans" taking place around the same time as events of the OK Corral.

These myths, as the country the family travels through in *Tell Me How It Ends* and *Lost Children Archive*, are both beautiful and broken, chock-full of long-held and powerfully evocative stories, which nonetheless gloss over a whole *other undocumented* history that actually constitutes the US West. At Tombstone, for example, she reflects on the "heroes" archived in the town like Wyatt Earp and Doc Holliday alongside those treated differently, asking "why some people get to have a name in history while others remain a generic category, why some identities are mapped into history and others are mapped out." In the reenactments witnessed at the OK Corral, these "mapping-outs" are very evident, with women made invisible and "non-whites…completely erased from the popular narratives." For Luiselli, the performance clearly has a contemporary political resonance, tracing "a connection between these places which glorify and commodify a violent frontier past and the violence that is so frequently directed toward undocumented immigrants in the area." Unsurprisingly, prominently displayed in the bookstore at the OK Corral is a large "poster of Donald Trump dressed as a cowboy, with a gun under his belt, and the slogan 'Keeping America Safe Again'" (2019b).

As Luiselli explains, there is a "foundation myth in the US, the understanding of the expansion of the West in terms of east to west…a country being invented, conquered…an East-West narrative," yet there exists simultaneously another "silenced foundation myth" of "Hispanic presence" and the "displacement of the Native-American population" that cannot remain hidden (Luiselli 2018). As we have tracked throughout this book, the denial of such hidden histories alongside the endless repetition of frontier myths of the "gunfighter nation" fuel Luiselli's politics and practice. Like a terrible return of the repressed, she has commented upon the "rather cyclical nature of history but not in an abstract, philosophical way. Not in a Hegelian, dialectical way either. But more what happens when a country or countries don't really take the time to think about reparations, to come to terms with the political violence of their past, to try to heal those wounds. What happens I think when you ignore violence that way, is that it just comes up again and again and again. When you don't address historical trauma properly, it always returns" (Floyd 2019).[2] Her comments echo my discussions in previous chapters because Luiselli understands the crisis on the US-Mexico border not as an isolated incident, but rather part of this "cyclical nature of history." Trauma is an endless repetition of historical violence, from conquest, slavery, Indian removal, border wars, the insidious actions of successive US administrations over Central America and Mexico, right up to the current migration crisis and Trumpland's politics of suspicion (see Luiselli 2019a, 133).[3]

Critically, Luiselli's "western" is *worldly* because it understands this border crisis as not only a national problem, but also something "deeply embedded in our shared hemispheric history…a transnational problem that includes the Unites States…as an active historical participant in the circumstances that generated that problem" (Luiselli 2017, 85).[4] Whether it is the drug trade, arms sales, or political interference, the United States is directly involved in the "roots and reach" of the crisis as it forms a "complex global network whose size and real reach we can't even imagine" (86). To absolve this responsibility for what Judith Butler calls "global obligations" (2020, 44), retreating from global networks behind a physical wall and engaging in ideological posturing are to ignore the consequences and interrelationships of such historical actions. So how do you open up this closed mind to tell instead a *worlding* story when history, politics, and the media so closely control its formative narratives? Having initially expressed the story via nonfiction in *Tell Me How It Ends*, Luiselli felt its formal "limitations" because "you can only ever document immediate presence," and, therefore, "it's hard to go beyond the urgency of that" (Washington 2019). In a similar vein, in *Lost Children Archive*, the mother is perturbed by how her daughter's school teaches her to write stories using a simple grid system of four boxes: "'Character,' 'Problem,' 'Setting,' 'Solution'" (Luiselli 2019a, 61).[5] Thus, to "go beyond…immediate presence" is the challenge of Luiselli's fiction, permitting the imagination to draw upon different narrators, narrative threads, symbols, temporalities, and histories, to create something closer to what the father calls an "inventory of echoes" in which "everything will remain unnarrated, a collage of environments and voices telling the story on their own, instead of a single voice forcing it all together into a clean narrative sequence" (97). The overall affective charge of *Lost Children Archive* is, therefore, an accumulative process, *a collage of environments and voices* working on the reader to fashion a reverberating echo-world.[6]

From the beginning, the first narrator (the unnamed "mother") decides to comprehend the world going on around her, if only for her children: "We'll need to tell them a beginning, a middle, and an end. We'll need to give them an answer, tell them a proper story" (5). In complex times, however, what is a "proper" story? As the novel unfolds, it seems less and less a "proper" story with a beginning, a middle, and an end and more an "improper" one, akin to what we earlier defined as errant: "a kind of thinking that is never closed, thinking that prefers indecision and *errance*—wandering, errantry—to definition, which delimits and immobilizes" (Rosemberg 2016, 3). Through such errant thinking, the novel explores methods of worlding, achieved in part by Luiselli's generic playfulness as she adopts and distorts American genres like the road novel and the western. Through this process she reengages the reader with the wider "transnational problem" of political responsibility and "global obligations" while simultaneously disrupting what Pheng Cheah calls "the crisis of narrating the nation" (2016, 213). As Luiselli has said, "You can think of playing with genres that are typical of a literary tradition and subverting them through a foreignization of the genre itself. This is a road trip that then brings a foreignization to the genre or the sub-genre of road trips. It subverts it through a foreign gaze. It is a partly foreign family" (Floyd 2019).[7] Seeing the world differently, *foreignly* as she terms it and as we discussed in chapter 2, opens up the idea of American myth-history to other worlds with alternative perspectives and variant histories and thereby interrupts the nation's well-rehearsed story about itself. This notion of the "foreign" derives from Luiselli's work as a translator and her interest in translation as a process. Walter Benjamin famously commented on the "mode" of translation as a type of dialogic process by which one language was "powerfully affected by the foreign tongue" in such a manner that a translator "must expand and deepen his language by means of the foreign language" (1992, 81). Paul de Man, in turn, wrote, "We think we are at ease in our own language, we feel a coziness, a familiarity, a shelter in the language we call our own, in which we think that we are not alienated" (2002, 84).[8] In *Lost Children Archive*, genres, traditions, and histories are "affected by the foreign tongue," breaking out of this "shelter," to afford different points of view as a practice of worlding.

As Luiselli's novel moves westward, this assumed "language" of certainty and "coziness" is undone and "disarticulated," as we "are made aware of certain disjunctions, certain disruptions, certain accommodations, certain weaknesses, certain cheatings, certain conventions, certain characteristics which don't correspond to the claim of the original, so that the original loses its sacred character" (de Man 2002, 97), revealing a different America below the promise of its surface. In the novel, the family becomes increasingly "alienated," as if "in movement, they're displacing themselves through America, and therefore, somehow, also displacing America, looking at it out of context" (Floyd 2019). To strengthen this point, Homi Bhabha develops Benjamin's metaphor of original unity "like a fruit and its skin" by adding that through the power of translation there is an absolute displacement, like the "splitting of skin and fruit through the *agency* of foreignness" (1994, 76, 228).

Worlding the Western argues that central to the United States' "original" story, its "fruit and skin," is the idea of the West as a beacon of foundational politics—Manifest Destiny, progress, and individual achievement constructing a closed horizon through an indomitable archive. As Jacques Derrida put it in *Archive Fever*, the concept of an archive seems to always "presuppose a closed heritage and the guarantee sealed, in some sense, by that heritage."[9] The *closed* and *sealed* archive refers to the past, to "consigned memory," and exists "to recall faithfulness to tradition" (1998, 33).[10] Derrida claims the archive "commands" because "there is no political power without control of the archive, if not of memory" (4n1). As discussed in earlier chapters, the world cannot simply be the version approved and archived by those who hold power and, therefore, influence the media and write its histories, and for Luiselli the role of the writer is, above all, to intervene and "displace" those sustaining narrative conventions that carry such canonical authority. As she put it in *Sidewalks*, "A writer starts from the fissures and the holes" (2013, 78), in an interruptive process close to Jean-Luc Nancy's notion of "unworking" (discussed in chapter 1).

Indeed, one reviewer called *Lost Children Archive* an "upside-down Western" (Haas 2019) precisely because of its attention to interruption, reversal, and the countering of such well-established narratives.[11] Thus, the "lost children" of the novel's title refer to those who cross the border looking for a new life in the West, like the narrator's friend Manuela's daughters, as well as those who disappear trying, "lost" in the deserts or the labyrinthine US detention system. As Luiselli has it, however, "They weren't looking for the American Dream, *as the narrative usually goes. The children were merely looking for a way out of their daily nightmare*" (2019a, 19; emphasis added). The novel's structure and purpose as "upside-down Western" are, above all, to challenge our underlying assumptions ("as the narrative usually goes") and unwork the various "worldviews" it presumes, and by so doing "bringing into existence an entire layer of the world previously ignored" (124, 99). Ultimately, it is a *worlding* western of "*avowed* interdependency" (Butler 2020, 45).

TELLING A PROPER STORY

In *Tell Me How It Ends*, Luiselli comments on the difficulty translating and articulating experiences of child refugees on the border in any conventional linear manner, referring directly to the first page of *Lost Children Archive* discussed above: "The problem with trying to tell their story is that it has no beginning, no middle, and no end" (Luiselli 2017, 7). This raises the book's central concern, which Luiselli terms "the politics of documenting" (Oliva 2019). How, therefore, to tell this story without being "mentally colonized by Western-Saxon-white categories" (Luiselli 2019, 79)? In contrast with her efforts to *translate* migrant experiences for the official record of the courts as "written words, succinct sentences, and barren terms," the children's stories she hears are structured by "hesitance… distrust, [and]…fear…always shuffled, stuttered, always shattered beyond the repair of a narrative order" (Luiselli 2017, 7). Carried forward into Luiselli's novel, this conveys the struggle of the narrator to create a sound archive of the migration crisis capable of testifying to the children's journeys, and beyond that, to the author's own attempts to create an appropriate narrative structure. At the same time, her husband is working on a soundscape of Apacheria, creating "an inventory of echoes…about the 'ghosts' of Geronimo, Cochise, and the other Apaches…to capture their past presence in the world, and making it audible despite their current absence" (Luiselli 2019a, 140–41).

Eventually, in the many layers and echoes of the novel's form and content, what emerges is far from an orderly archive of sounds and stories, but instead something nearer to a "shuffled, stuttered, always shattered" form, mirroring that of the migrant children's testimonies. In the mother's mind, the migrants and Apaches become intertwined, since "the more I listen to the stories he tells about the country's past, the more it seems like he's talking about the present" (133). Throughout *Worlding the Western* the entangled and imbricated past and present swirl around with histories and myths retold and reworked in contemporary life and politics. Luiselli's novel, with its multivalent qualities, translates these echoes of past, present, and future into a complex shape that *worlds* the western in provocative and extraordinary ways: "There are things that can only be understood retrospectively, when many years have passed and the story has ended. In the meantime, while the story continues, the only thing to do is tell it over and over again as it develops, bifurcates, knots around itself. And it must be told, because before anything can be understood, it has to be narrated many times, in many different words and from many different angles, by many different minds" (Luiselli 2017, 96–97). To express this in another way draws on the analogy of maps that Luiselli uses in her book *Sidewalks*, referring to mapping as "a fixed superimposition on a world in perpetual motion" (2013, 26).[12] Equally, the mother-narrator of *Lost Children Archive* is forever looking at maps and plotting routes, as if narrativizing the landscape into a controllable order and shape. Her son even refers to their lives before their road trip as if the family "all lived inside the same map" (2019a, 193). The reality, however, is of a more errant world in perpetual motion where, to echo Benjamin, the "flesh of the fruit has, in fact, overflowed far beyond its skin," and, therefore, its representation always exceeds any attempt at its accurate, ordered mapping (Luiselli 2013, 27).

From *Tell Me How It Ends* to *Lost Children Archive*, Luiselli layers "overflowing" multiple stories of migration, loss, violence, and survival into a cumulative, alternative "archive" of US history, "as it develops, bifurcates, knots around itself," allowing all its "different angles" to emerge as an "inventory of echoes," or what I referred to earlier as an "echo-world." Hence, it not only becomes the mother-narrator's struggle for a documentary form, but also records a family narrative of a disintegrating marriage ("an echo of the political crisis" [Luiselli in Owens 2019]), the parents' shifting relationships with their children, and, alongside these intimate personal stories, broader interrelated ones about Indian removal, western migration, the history and myth of the West, and the current migration crisis on the border. Worlding interlinks these echoes in a "poetics of relation" in which personal and public histories become inseparably intertwined and materially real, so that, for example, the lost children of government migration policies resonate with the very lives of two children lost in the desert Southwest.

Mistrusting a single narrative, Luiselli's novel enacts a story "narrated many times," shifting from the adult view of the parents to that of their children, supplementing both with a series of digressions and asides (its echo-world), reflecting upon and critiquing the nature of storytelling itself. As she has said, "I guess everything is an echo of another thing. It's not necessarily clear who emits the original sound. It's like an echoing where the original source is lost. I like the kind of fiction that is often self-conscious about its artifice.… I'm talking about a kind of fiction that is *porous*, that documents, but also observes itself" (Rollenhagen 2019; emphasis added). Recognizing the novel's worldliness, she argues, "The question that beats in the center of the novel is about storytelling, about how to tell the story of 'now,' whatever that story is, and make sense, through that narrative, of the world—a very confusing and painful world" (Floyd 2019).

The mother's narrative is likewise dominated by deliberations over form and technique and how best to capture the complex nature of American history in the twenty-first century when "the present has become too overwhelming, so the future has become unimaginable." Stories capable of expressing such "a very confusing and painful world" seem frustratingly limited so that "our ways of documenting the world have fallen short. Perhaps if we found a new way to document, we might begin to understand this new way we experience space and time." She goes on to list all the disciplines, from journalism and movies to molecular biology and quantum physics, that fail to "capture…how space and time exist now," stressing once again the need to find a new way to document "this strange, beautiful, dark country" (Luiselli 2019a, 103). This new way returns to the idea of "porous" fiction, with its echoes of Walter Benjamin's notion of porosity as a type of "interpenetration" and "stretching of frontiers" where "the stamp of the definitive is avoided…[and] no figure asserts its 'thus and not otherwise'" (1997, 175, 169–70).[13] Crucially, porosity "involves the discovery of what lies concealed" when clear boundaries disappear, merge, or become disrupted (Gilloch 1997, 28). Luiselli's fiction is porous too, permeated by multiple forms, from photography, book lists, and streams of consciousness to critical analysis, history, and storytelling, as well as temporal and spatial shifts, between past and present, East and West, far away and nearby. The *interpenetration* of these differences creates a complex meshwork or labyrinth of fragmented stories resembling Benjamin's *Arcades Project*, whose alternative perspective reveals "what lies concealed." As with all labyrinths, however, there is also the possibility of becoming lost. Just as the characters in the novel become literally and metaphorically lost, with a marriage breaking up, children running away, and migrants stranded in the desert, detained, or deported, the reader too undergoes a disorienting experience *within* the reading of the text, looking for hints, clues, and routes forward in the referential archive boxes that structure the novel ("like an appendix of us" [Luiselli 2019a, 24]). As Gilloch reminds us, however, "Porosity as ambivalence, as hesitation, as paradox" (1997, 36), is how such disorientation works and why, in the case of Luiselli's novel, as in the *Arcades Project*, the reader is constantly disconcerted. As she puts it in *Sidewalks*, as if preparing us for these readerly challenges, "Walter Benjamin: a one-way street walked down *against the flow*" (Luiselli 2013, 77; emphasis added). As with the task of reading Benjamin, so too in Luiselli, since the challenge is piecing together fragments, insights, and juxtapositions across time and space, defying the assumed mythic delusion of progress and history, to uncover an altogether different echo-world.

ARCHIVE FEVER

In *Orientalism* Edward Said explains how documentary control can work to shape worldviews: "Orientalism was a library *or archive* of information commonly and, in some of its aspects, unanimously held. What bound the archive together was a family of ideas and a unifying set of values proven in various ways to be effective…allow[ing] Europeans to deal with and even to see Orientals as a phenomenon possessing regular characteristics" (1991, 41–42; emphasis added). Similarly, the American West has been *archived* with particular stories selected and emphasized for inclusion, while others are omitted or erased, and as a result, "a mentality, a genealogy, an atmosphere" has emerged that, as I argue throughout this book, has helped define the United States. Under this process, certain memories are maintained and endorsed, while others, such as Native Americans, African Americans, immigrants, and women, for example, are buried or erased in the archive's "family of ideas and…unifying set of values." Thus, the "violence of the archive," as Derrida calls this process of erasure, helps to perpetuate colonial and nation-building projects like those in the West (1998, 7).

Setting off on a road trip into the West, the mother-narrator and her husband aim to create a different archive, yet, despite their best intentions, they too are engaged in mechanisms of control through what they tell their children: "I'm not sure which parts of our story we might each choose to pluck and edit out for them, and which ones we'll shuffle around and insert back in to produce a final version (Luiselli 2019a, 5). Their own "archive" is constructed by many voices or representations from elsewhere (writers, photographers, maps, images, notes, and more), creating a discourse defining and ordering a world with "a certain narrative distance" (24). Like Benjamin's gathering-up process in the *Arcades Project*, this archive presents a different critical perspective on the "future ruins of later capitalism" (102) that they travel through, drawing on an intellectual landscape produced by others' images and values, books read and referenced throughout the journey, from Susan Sontag and Walt Whitman to Robert Frank and Ezra Pound.

However, as the mother-narrator's journey unfolds, she realizes that "what I see is not quite what I see. What I see is what others have already documented" (102). To discover *another* archive, her "mind twists and spirals down into the thought of children lost" (140), encountering a range of stories from elsewhere (her friend Manuela's children, the detained and deported migrants, her own lost children, and the book she reads, *Elegies for Lost Children*) that together construct a different, less "distanced" worldview. *Elegies*, for example, describes a traumatic journey of children along "a single straight line moving up across the barrenlands…a thin crack, a long fissure slicing the wide continent in two" (143). Although not specified as in the Americas, their mythic quest northward on a train (like La Bestia), "up against the iron wall" (315), resonates with the current migrant trail with its "long series of uncertainties" and a "history soaked in blood" described by Óscar Martínez in *The Beast* (2013, 50, 53).

As Marco Pustianaz argues, "An archive is defined by its own partiality, which stands for everything else that has been lost," since whatever is in the archive box is merely a part of the whole. We presume an archive stands against loss, against all the fear of forgetting the past, yet, in truth, it is "born out" of loss (Palladini and Pustianaz 2017, 15). In relation to Luiselli's novel, loss is everywhere, and the archive ultimately formed by the novel itself is a complex response to this process of loss. Luiselli's "porous" fiction refuses to impose a single vision on its subject matter, drawing together diverse archives to create an alternative one questioning what Said called the "unanimously held…family of ideas and…unifying set of values" framing western American history and contemporary US politics.

The novel is part of a wider dialogue, constantly engaging in conversations with its time, other literature, and general political discourse, and, as a result, expanding the "closed box" archive that the narrator carries with her. She asks, "What does it mean to document something, an object, our lives, a story?" only to conclude that however one records the world, whether by "camera, on paper or with a sound recording," is "really only a way of contributing one more layer, something like soot, to all the things already sedimented in a collective understanding of the world" (Luiselli 2019a, 55).

The mother-narrator realizes the problem of "pragmatic storytelling" or conventional documentary work when dealing with the "chaos of history repeated…[its] debris, dust, erasure," knowing such moments require new stories for "those whose voices can no longer be heard." To achieve this, she needs "to start looking somewhere else" (146), toward what I call here an "affective archive," borrowing from Palladini and Pustianaz, to suggest the novel's movement away from both the traditional archive of mythic western history and the intellectually structured archive of the husband and wife. Instead, what emerges is a fuller, more inclusive, and complex version containing both "archives" and more: "a horizon, a limit, a possibility always ready to be enacted and released."[14] Such an affective archive "wavers between materiality and immateriality, between conservation and transformation," acknowledging "the impulse that both creates and mobilizes the archive as an endless process" (Palladini and Pustianaz 2017, 12). Luiselli's intervention is to construct a novel becoming this "somewhere else," a site of multiply inflected overlapping "ghosts and echoes" (2019a, 146) through which the reader travels, assembling and "translating" across its various "languages" (texts, images, intertexts, asides, paratexts).

Luiselli's affective archive (her "porous" archive-novel) draws in voices from outside the couple's boxes, self-consciously challenging us as readers with its unconventional structure, fragmented sections, and, above all, extensive range of unusual materials. As she explained, "So having different bits and pieces of things in the novel—not just straightforward text but an image, the pictures at the end, the things in the archival boxes throughout the book, and particularly the migrant mortality reports—forces us as readers, I think, to not only stand differently, but to stop and wonder, 'How do I read this?'" In keeping with many of the novels discussed in this book, Luiselli sees such textual variations as "interruptions," enabling "a more active form of reading…intentionally pulling you in, forcing you to stop and interrogate the work. Because if this was just a straightforward four-hundred-page family saga, it would be a different experience of reading. You would let it sweep over you" (Leblanc 2019). Thus, the novel becomes an alternative archive, gathering, ordering, sifting, reproducing, and saving material, while simultaneously commenting on the process of archiving more generally, since, as Luiselli clarifies, "The novel is both the story and the archive of the story" (Floyd 2019). This dialogical structure allows her to raise questions for the active reader about the processes of history, as witness, as official record, and as storytelling. As we read the novel, with all its "interruptions," textual asides, and intertextualities, a layered archive emerges, which, as Derrida pointed out, by its very nature would be "more troubled and more troubling" because it functions "always at the unstable limits between public and private, between the family, the society, and the State" (1998, 90). The consequences, as Arlette Farge suggested, of such a radical archive is that they "bring forward details that disabuse, derail, and straightforwardly break any hope of linearity or positivism. This eruption of words and actions shatters established models, broadens the norm, displaces conventional wisdom once and for all, and often adds a certain confusion to things that had been previously considered simple" (2013, 42). The novel shares much with the mythic tropes of US western expansion: the journey west away from New York by a type of pioneer family unit, "Ma," "Pa," and two children in a wagon (here, a Volvo station wagon), in the cautious but hopeful search for a new home; the presence of Native Americans; the desert landscapes of the Southwest and borderlands; and encounters with law and order. However, it is, ultimately, a centrifugal text, spinning outward from its apparently "American" base to more worldly (or foreignized) perspectives. Unlike traditional westering stories, this journey is "driving toward a future we most probably won't share" (Luiselli 2019a, 121) and, therefore, not to the ideal of familial settlement. As Luiselli has said, echoing Diaz earlier: "The way that I think of this book, it's very much written as a typical American road novel, but it's also a reverse or an upside-down road novel that plays against the foundational myth of the U.S. being invented in this expansion toward the West. It does so by crossing another narrative, which is the movement upward from the south, whose presence is often ignored, but is not really ignorable. The road trip, which is kind of a horizontal story, is intersected by this vertical narrative that moves upwards" (Owens 2019).[15] Through the novel's "verticality," it resists the straight tracks and assumptions of American myth-history, circling around, "knotting," and delving down in order to, as Luiselli says, "make sense, through that narrative, of the world—a very confusing and painful world" (Floyd 2019). To bring these two points together, Luiselli's self-conscious interest in the archive and archiving is a means of, as Susan Stanford Friedman puts it, "defamiliarizing the familiar archive [of the US West] by looking anew through a different lens" (2018, 76).

Consequently, "The question of the archive is not, we repeat, a question of the past," since it is always about the future, "the question of a response, of a promise and of a responsibility to tomorrow" (Derrida 1998, 36). Noticeably, in the novel, the parents keep two empty boxes in the car "for the children's future archive" (Luiselli 2019a, 42), as if predicting the importance to an affective archive from the child's point of view. That which the conventional archive excludes is "spontaneous, alive and internal experience," coming in part from the various children (real and imagined) within the novel for whom "the archive is never closed," since "it opens out of the future" (Derrida 1998, ii, 68).

What Luiselli's novel reflects upon, repeatedly, "as it develops, bifurcates, knots around itself," is the problem of such a synchrony or unity in the "gathering together" of US western history as a sealed archive. What *troubles* this effort of the archive to gather, order, shelter, and "command" most, according to Derrida, are "secrets and heterogeneity," or all that exists "under" the system, biography, autobiography, and theory (4–5). Once admitted, "the limits, the borders, and the distinctions" are "shaken by an earthquake from which no classificational concept and no implementation of the archive can be sheltered" (5). Luiselli's "earthquake," discussed at length in the novel, derives from Greek "En, theos, seismos" ("in, god, earthquake"), suggesting the word "enthusiasm" as a "kind of inner earthquake produced by allowing oneself to be possessed by something larger and more powerful, like a god or goddess" (2019a, 173). What the novel demonstrates is how "something larger and more powerful" erupts, like an earthquake, into her characters' world, into their supposedly ordered "archive" (symbolized by the regulated and numbered boxes packed into their car) and into the assumed progression of western history. The reality of the migrant crisis and familial disruption shakes the foundations and order of their family, their worldviews, and the very "limits, the borders, and the distinctions" that frame their "own fragile structures" (160).[16] "It is a book," Luiselli has commented, "about documenting and representing—worrying about how documenting our world can affect our relationship to it. It mediates the relationship to the world. When you take a picture or record something…then you're not only doing that, you're also intervening in your experience of it" (Floyd 2019). Beyond the materiality of the boxes in the back of the Volvo, beyond the efforts of the wife and husband to narrativize the journey west, and beyond the wider myth generated by the history and landscape itself, another "relationship to the world" is made possible, a *world* emerging not from established views but through the hidden archive of children.

THE UNINTERPRETED WORLD

With this in mind, the novel shifts its narrator midway through, moving from the mother to the son, the adult to the ten-year-old child, in keeping with the novel's intention to jar its readers and unsettle any single perspective or voice. As Luiselli commented, "It's a novel about the intergenerational mechanisms of storytelling and how a view of the world is articulated and passed on to the next generation. But then also how that generation re-articulates it and also sort of hands it back. It's a kind of circular process of conversation—in this case, a circular process of a story-making" (Breen 2019).

Her sense of how the "world is articulated and passed on" from parents to children parallels with the ways by which cultural stories are transmitted or *translated* across generations and, as a result, myths formed. Central to this exemplary novel and to others considered in this book is how history favors some groups and marginalizes others, archives some documents, while ignoring others. As the boy recollects his father telling him, "Some people get proper graves, because most lives don't matter. Most lives get erased, lost in the whirlpool of trash we call history" (Luiselli 2019a, 215).[17] That which eludes history and its official archives ("the whirlpool of trash") is the lived experience of events and of loss that, in the novel, derives from the child narrator and the intertext of *Elegies for Lost Children* spanning both halves.[18] Rather like the rag-picker in Benjamin's writings rifling through history's ruin, these voices redeem those elements lost "from the oblivion of forgetting, with collection and recollection" (Gilloch 1997, 166). This circular narrative process rejects the authority of the archive posited in the first half of the novel, allowing in lived experience and marginal voices (the "lost" of the novel's title) or what is "hidden or destroyed, forbidden, misappropriated, 'repressed'" in official archives (Derrida quoted in Steedman 2002, 8).

Thus, the boy's role is to "rearticulate" or "reenact" his parents' "pragmatic storytelling," juxtaposing it with all the numerous stories he overhears, invents, reads, and experiences, and then "hands…back" throughout the second half of the novel that he is recording for his younger sister (Luiselli 2019a, 81, 99). One way to think of this second narration is as a *translation* of the first, relaying and replaying the mother-father story in a different, accented light. As discussed earlier, Luiselli, as a translator herself, has embraced the process of translation, discussing it within the novel via references in the archive boxes to Walter Benjamin and Lawrence Venuti, placing it at the center of an earlier novel, *Faces in the Crowd* (2012), and exploring it as an actual job in *Tell Me How It Ends*. Translation for Luiselli is a "mode," as Benjamin termed it in "The Task of the Translator," a way of creating from the "original" an "afterlife"—a "transformation and a renewal of something living" (1992, 71, 72, 73). As Paul de Man wrote in his commentary on Benjamin's essay, translation has a series of precise functions: "To put the original in motion, to de-canonize the original, giving it a movement which is a movement of disintegration, of fragmentation. This movement of the original is a wandering, an errance, a kind of permanent exile if you wish, but it is not really an exile, for there is no homeland, nothing from which one has been exiled" (2002, 92).

In another example of errance or errantry explored in this book, echoing Glissant's assertion that it "emerges from the destructuring of compact national identities" while "taking up the problems of the Other" and questioning the world summarized as "one presupposed sense and one destiny" (Glissant 1997, 18, 20), the boy's "translation" creates a type of echo-world that replays and "reenacts" the "sounds" he has received and processed during his parents' journey (his errantry) across the West. As the mother comments, the children "combine the stories, confuse them. They come up with possible endings and counterfactual histories" (Luiselli 2019a, 75). With parallels to Howe and Orange in the previous chapter, the children are closer to the position of the reader who must wrestle with the multiplicity of narrative voices, textual interruptions, and fragmented structure, trying to uncover some satisfactory meaning. In *Tell Me How It Ends*, Luiselli comments, "I find myself not knowing where translation ends and interpretation starts" (2017, 62), as if, as Benjamin writes, translation always moves "beyond transmittal of subject matter" becoming "the echo of the original" (1992, 76–77). Like Luiselli's constant use of echoes and reverberations in the novel (in its structure, section titles, the husband's project, and even the name of the finale's canyon), Benjamin uses similar images in his essay, explaining that translation is "the echo…the reverberation of the work in the alien one" (77). Of course, the child's point of view muddles, troubles, *reverberates*, and "supplements" (79) the stories overheard, blurring their boundaries across time and space, and in so doing questioning them as discrete episodes, seeing instead patterns, relations, and repetitions that the "adult" view seems to exclude in its rush to document, order, and narrate. The parental stories are, therefore, in de Man's words, *decanonized* in their retelling and, therefore, made *alien*. As the boy explains to his sister about his relentless questioning, he "kept insisting, asking more and more, until I think I got them both a bit annoyed" (Luiselli 2019a, 232). Luiselli relates this to the wider function of children in the novel: "Maybe [the children's] confusion—they confuse stories of American soldiers in the Indian Wars with Border Patrol agents—is a fertile one, because it's a way in which history can be understood as a larger, more multilayered, and complex arc, how the present can be understood not only in its exceptional urgency, but also through what came before it" (Washington 2019).[19] Within the novel itself, the mother ponders different literary sources in books that deal with "adultless children" like *Lord of the Flies* (a constant reference point in the novel) or *Huckleberry Finn*, yet she recognizes nonetheless that "they are in fact stories about an adult's world when there are children in it, about the way children's imaginations destabilize our adult sense of reality and force us to question the very grounds of that reality" (Luiselli 2019a, 160). As the boy and girl interject their views, questions, "backseat games and reenactments" into the fabric of the novel, "their imaginations leak through the cracks of our own fragile structures," presenting new and different pictures of the world that "tell the story of the lost children" (180, 160, 180). Indeed, as the boy renarrates the novel's later sections, he takes on the characteristics of the "pre-habitual gaze of the child" that "problematize[s] the habitual, forgetful vision of the adult," in Benjamin's writings, providing "the lost perspective," dereifying the world through a more "incisive, yet 'mistaken knowledge'" (Gilloch 1997, 65, 83, 65). Children do not "know" the adult world in a formal sense, like the children in the novel, who are often confused and muddled, yet, as in Benjamin's analysis, precisely because of this they offer something askew and, therefore, refreshing "which disconcerts the stable, distant adult gaze" (62), upsetting what Luiselli calls "the scaffolding to his world" (Luiselli 2019, 161). Gilloch refers to the "error-filled knowledge of the child" that for Benjamin can "reveal hidden facets…and may unmask the false appearance of things, the mythic facades that hold the adult observer enthralled" (1997, 63).[20] The mother responds to her children's reenactments and games, feeling that everything they do "charges our world…with a weird electricity" (81). Unlike the adults' efforts to order and control, like the father whose archive is described as "an all-male compendium of 'going a journey,' conquering and colonizing," with its inherent "instrumentalism" (Luiselli 2019, 43, 79),[21] children enjoy a privileged proximity to landscape and things, fully immersed in the surrounding world.[22] Susan Buck-Morss explains that for Benjamin, children's consciousness was too often "badgered out of existence by bourgeois education," whereas his work sought to "redeem…in a new form" the "unsevered connection between perception and action" through "an active form of mimesis." As we have seen, such mimesis takes the form of reenactment in the novel, or what Buck-Morss calls "spontaneous fantasy" (1993, 263) as the children errantly "echo" their parents' archives, stories, and conversations into games and challenges.

Luiselli dramatizes this alternative perspective in different ways, for example, when the boy places his Polaroid pictures inside the pages of *Elegies for Lost Children*, the book his mother reads. It is as if he mixes the reality of the present (the photographs—"another species of archive" [Derrida 1998, 70]) with the fictionalized account of children journeying from a timeless South retold in the book. This shares much with Luiselli's concept of the "intralinear" references punctuating the novel, functioning as "markers that point to the many voices in the conversation that the book sustains with the past" (Luiselli 2019a, 381). Between the structured lines of the book the boy holds in his hands exist the Polaroids with their ghostly representations of the present intersecting and commenting upon the words on the page, and in that moment of juxtaposition and "conversation," the world seems opened up to creative and different interpretations and possibilities. Such an uncanny juxtaposition of worlds recalls Derrida's point that "the structure of the archive is *spectral*" because it always refers to and activates the presence of the absent dead, like "a trace always referring to another" (1998, 84).

A second example of how the boy's perspective functions in the novel is through the contrast of the documents his mother and father make and the scary "worldsounds" (Luiselli 2019a, 265) the children notice all around them in the desert. Once the boy decides to take his sister in search of the lost children and leave their parents behind, they step outside of a controlled environment (the car, the motel rooms, the diners, their stories, the parents' crumbling marriage), and, as a result, in Benjamin's words, they "must wake up from the world of [their]…parents" (quoted in Buck-Morss 1993, 112). The order of the parents' archive of boxed and contained notes, books, and tapes, set within the parameters of their own journey along well-mapped roads, is in stark contrast to the "desert worldsounds" (Luiselli 2019a, 323) impinging on the lost children: "birds crying, rocks shifting, footsteps trudging, people imploring, voices begging for water before fading into silence with a final whimper, then darker sounds, like cadavers diminishing into skeletons, skeletons snapping into bones, bones eroding and disappearing into the sand." These are the *undocumented*, raw, unprocessed sounds, like those of the migrants whose footsteps the two children follow, "the sound of all the dead in the desert, all the bones there" (324). Reminiscent of the "other living" in *Inland*, or the ghostly Savage Indian in Howe's work, it forms an *other* archive beyond that imposed by their parents, beyond the frame of political gestures, and beyond the established narratives of history and myth.

This is, ultimately, an "uninterpreted world where everything is unnamed for them" (328), a potent world of experience and tactility, where thirst, heat, and hunger structure their journey as it brings them ever closer to the affective world of Manuela's lost children and to the fictional children of the *Elegies*: "We walked into the unreal desert, like the lost children's desert, and under their blazing sun, you and me, over the tracks, and into the heart of light, like the lost children, walking alone together" (293). Here, as real and unreal worlds converge, it is as if they enter what Óscar Martínez calls "the cemetery of the nameless" (2013a, 62). Without adults, the children exist within an "ancient domain of sensuous correspondences" (Gilloch 1997, 86) where finally, in the remaining eighteen pages of the novel, punctuation disappears in a stream of consciousnesses, languages, and feelings. As Luiselli has commented about this section, "It's a march in the desert. There's no interruption. People don't get a break from that. Time…is this ongoing, brutal, unbroken paragraph" (Floyd 2019).

A third function of the boy's narration is to mediate the different perspectives of his parents (the documentarian and documentarist), identifying, for example, intersectional issues of racism drawn from the "sensuous correspondences" of their journey. For example, as he watches the plane full of deported migrant children take off from the airfield in New Mexico, his mind connects (or "corresponds") their plight with "the Apache cemetery" they had visited, and the poor black neighborhood they had driven through in Memphis (Luiselli 2019a, 194). Rather than follow the directions laid down by his parents' individual and closed obsessions, the children's "mapping" of experience engages in transformative, creative play, redirecting and connecting their worlds differently. For instance, listening to his father's history of Apaches, the boy is "drawing a map of his history with my finger on the back of the driver's seat, a map mostly full of arrows, arrows *pointing everywhere*… half arrows *disappearing like ghosts*" (205; emphasis added). Such "imagined maps," finger-maps, as he calls them, produced "beautiful routes" he might "refollow, or kind of" (205), and, above all, they refuse to conform to established lines or authorized commands, instead *pointing everywhere* and *disappearing like ghosts*. Of course, one of the routes the children follow is that embodied by the "little red book," *Elegies for Lost Children*, with which their own journey gradually merges as they too cross the "unreal desert" and "into the heart of the light…under the same sun." The novel's ghostly layers pull together the groups of children into a frenzied climax, "trapped in a circle, and all circles are endless" (319). Here, the novel's repetitive structures remind us of a bigger picture, the endless cycles of oppressive, violent histories of conquest, slavery, and migration discussed earlier that remain the under-archive of US history, like a "secret account," "burned" "on the other edge of repression," because, as Derrida puts it, "the secret is the very ash of the archive" (1998, 101, 100).

As the boy and girl move across the burning desert toward Echo Canyon, their journey converges with that of the fictional lost and migrant children, staring as they all do at the eagles in the black, stormy sky, while their narrative space becomes simultaneous and shared.[23] From this moment, points of view become fluid, shifting between children, as the everyday horrors are amplified by the banality of bureaucracy: from the Border Patrol finding the bodies in the desert with retrieved items "in transparent plastic bags" (Luiselli 2019a, 322) to the "methodical old lady" inputting deaths into a computer to mark "red death spots over everything…hundreds of red dots," while listening to an audiobook by Lynne Cheney, wife of Dick Cheney, who with George W. Bush helped militarize the border (323). Removed and remote from the terrible scenes of heat and exhaustion outside, it is the "desert worldsounds," discussed above, that the children hear that exist for the bureaucrats only as "unregistered, unheard, and finally lost" (324). The bureaucratic "archive" of Border Patrol reports and computer files is in stark contrast to the affective archive of the lost children teeming with "strange sounds," "all our feelings and bodies changing like the wind," and "heat always getting heavier" (325). All are now "descending…sinking into an airless heat" of an abandoned village and the "deeper echoes of the things that were once there and were no longer…the uninterrupted murmur of other children who had died there before them" (325, 326). In this hellish convergence, "they walk among the echoes of other children, past and future," drawing the reader toward a terrible recognition of the cycles of history as suffering and loss, where childhood is no longer a time of playfulness, but rather "a world completely foreign," a world of violence, exploitation, and brutality (328).

CONCLUSION—IT IS FICTION BUT ALSO IT IS NOT

The unnamed family at the heart of the novel echoes western settlers journeying across the landscape to establish roots, desiring some pattern to anchor their lives and achieve order and security binding them together for the future. As Luiselli writes, "New families, like young nations after violent wars of independence or social revolutions, perhaps need to anchor their beginnings in a symbolic moment and nail that instant in time." In such moments, "chaos became a cosmos" (2019a, 12). For the United States, that moment, its creation story, had been the opening up and settlement of the West that Luiselli's novel, as we have seen, interrogates and unsettles in so many ways. Like the pink cowboy hat the boy carries out of the fictional world of the *Elegies* at the end of the novel, the tropes of the western are both referenced and subverted throughout *Lost Children Archive*, *translating* them into an imperfect affective future archive. Perhaps ultimately, as the narrator tells the border guard in the novel, it has been a type of "spaghetti western" (130), "gesturing toward wider communities" to "construct a collective worldview" that refutes the terrible legacies of Manifest Destiny (Oliva 2019).

The self-conscious search for an appropriate form for such a "western" is front and center of *Lost Children Archive* because, as Luiselli put it in *Tell Me How It Ends*, "it has to be narrated many times, in many different words and from many different angles, by many different minds" (2017, 96–97). Activating these multiple layers of narrative, Luiselli requires her readers to become *translators*, taking the various threads, perspectives, and "languages" performed in the novel as a whole and trying "to read the world as part of a narrative plot" (101). However, there is no single plot to the world, no history that represents every twist and turn, as the mother suggests, herself echoing Walter Benjamin, defining the ideal form for her project as a complex relationship between the archive (the past and the known) and the future: "I suppose an archive gives you a kind of valley in which your thoughts can bounce back to you, transformed. You whisper intuitions and thoughts into the emptiness, hoping to hear something back. And sometimes, just sometimes, an echo does indeed return, a real reverberation of something, bouncing back with clarity" (Luiselli 2019a, 43). By the end of the novel, as I have shown, the echo and reverberation come back "transformed" through the lost children, both her own and those real and unreal desert wanderers.

Rescued from their ordeal in the desert, unlike the migrant children, the boy and the girl finally present their own archive boxes VI and VII. Filling the once-empty box VI are the fragments and echoes of the girl's ("Memphis") impressions, her onomatopoeic memories gathered here as an active, performative remembrance of "all the different paths" (Floyd 2019) of their journey: play, word games, and associated sounds. In box VII come the Polaroids the boy ("Swift Feather") has taken throughout the journey, each a ghostly echo whose bleached-out light suggests the novel's sense of loss and disappearance, which along with his tape recording of events form his own archive. He spells out its purpose for his sister's future: "You could get at least two versions of everything and know things in different ways, which is always better than just one way" (Luiselli 2019a, 349). Earlier, the mother, realizing her son's capacity for understanding, comments, "It's his version of the story that will outlive us…be passed down.…He'd understood everything much better than I had.…He'd listened to things, looked at them—really looked, focused, and pondered—and little by little, his mind had arranged all the chaos around us into a world" (185). As Ben Anderson and Paul Harrison explain, such worlds "are not formed in the mind before they are lived in, rather we come to know and enact a world from inhabiting it, from becoming attuned to its differences, positions and juxtapositions" (2010, 9). The boy's *making of a world* refuses the limiting archives of his parents and of official history, understanding that through the "pulse…gaze…[and] rhythm" of his affective archive, he intuitively knows that "stories don't fix anything or save anyone but maybe make the world both more complex and more tolerable. And sometimes, just sometimes, more beautiful" (Luiselli 2019a, 186). The resultant archive, the "Lost Children Archive" of the novel's title, has, as Derrida suggested, little to do with the past, because like all archives, "they are there to launch a future. In the archive, we never encounter the past but only what remains of it, after the fire" (Pustianaz in Palladini and Pustianaz 2017, 19).

Ultimately, this is also the reader's vital position in the novel, for having undergone the various layers of the archive, from its "ashes" or "remainders" you make a world, and having finally arrived, you acknowledge, perhaps with some hope, "There will be no rest in this archive, now that you have come" (Palladini and Pustianaz 2017, 10).

‹ 8 ›

Exit West

Conclusions Perhaps

The age is off its hinges.
—Jacques Derrida, *Specters of Marx*

What is certain is that we can no longer tell ourselves the same old stories.
—Bruno Latour, *Facing Gaia*

Only when we have travelled to each other's "worlds"
are we fully subjects to each other.
—Maria Lugones quoted in Gloria Anzaldúa, *Interviews / Entrevistas*

A WORLD FULL OF DOORS

In Mohsin Hamid's *Exit West* (2017), there is a deliberately ambivalent relationship to the idea of "West," taking us back to a point made in the introduction about the "West and the Rest." On the one hand, Hamid refers to the broad global geographic division between the "West" as a center of global colonial powers in Europe and North America and the "Rest" of the world from which migrants "exit" their homelands in search of a better and safer life. On the other hand, he alludes specifically to the mythic lure of the United States as an Edenic "West," identified in the novel as California (San Diego, San Francisco, and "Marin"). This blurring of Wests is of interest to this project, for it underlines the cultural associations and assumptions that tie these spaces together in people's minds. Hamid has spoken of how in his fiction the various meanings of West can be both interrogated and deployed:

The idea of "go west young man and young woman" is very much a part of this. The pull so many millions and billions of people feel to go to Europe and North America, to head west as it were—that's very much in this novel. *But is there a west?* I really think about that term. When somebody from the east lives in London, is London a

173

western city any more? *When lots of people from the east live in London, what is west?* I think part of what's happening now is that this notion of the west is becoming more difficult to sustain. *It's becoming less coherent. That's not a bad thing.* (2018b; emphasis added)

In *Exit West*, these questions arise as apparently stable geographies and demographics become "less coherent" through migrations that unsettle preconceived categories, just as the novel's speculative realist style undoes the reader's sense of unwavering reality. In the novel, people move freely through magical black doors that shift them in and out of nation-states. As Esra Coker Korpez puts it, "Hamid challenges the reader to envision a world where everyone, irrespective of class, color, or religion, internalizes something of the quality of being a foreigner, an immigrant, a refugee" (2020, 165). The novel raises crucial questions through the eyes of the other: What is West? asks Hamid echoing the confused boy at the end of Diaz's *In the Distance* who asks, "What West?" (2017c, 335) or Ba in Zhang's *How Much of These Hills Is Gold*, querying, "West of where? It was just our land, and we were just people" (2020b, 162; see chapters 2 and 3). Through what we earlier called "foreignizing," and subsequently developed as worlding, the novels in this book explore the uprooting of generally accepted terms and their associated ideological weight, specifically and most weighty of all the notion of the West as a fixed and stable point in the history of the United States and in the world as a whole. As Hamid suggests, fiction might undo what historians tell us: "Geography is destiny" (2017, 9).

As we have seen throughout *Worlding the Western*, migration and motion have an intense positive and negative transformative quality, from the multiple migrations of Obreht's *Inland* and Barry's *Days Without End*, to the south–north flows in Luiselli's *Lost Children Archive*. Hamid summed it up as "both like dying and like being born" (98). In a similar vein, Glissant's concept of errantry, employed throughout this book, indicates "a wandering that guides us" (2020c, 9), opening up the idea of migration and movement as a vital philosophical concept. As Hamid explains:

> I think that if we can recognize the universality of the migration experience and the universality of the refugee experience—that those of us who have never moved are also migrants and refugees— then the space for empathy opens up.…And that means we can

recognize the refugee not as some strange other person who's had a weird experience of crossing the Mediterranean on a boat, or crawling under barbed wire to Texas, but instead we see somebody who's had an experience that emotionally reminds us of our own experience. (Chandler 2017)

Here, Hamid places geographies under pressure, with nations questioned and regions rethought, because "it seemed that as everyone was coming together everyone was also moving apart. Without borders nations appeared to be becoming somewhat illusory, and people were questioning what role they had to play" (2017, 155). In these unstable moments, the "space for empathy" might just emerge.

Krista Comer explains, "'The West' or 'the Western World' is posited against some presumed non-West, a world of Others" (2007), and *Exit West* explores the possibilities of communities within which the so-called Others are migratory bodies reshaping and challenging those previously defined spaces. As a result, norms slide away, for in Hamid's "exited" West, slowly emptying itself of its assumptions, the notion of progress, for example, as ever associated with "westernization" and western power, is often interrogated or undone. Ironically, it is as if Hamid recalls Frederick Jackson Turner, quoted in the introduction, defining the West as offering "an exit into a free life and greater well-being...into the midst of resources that demanded manly exertion, and that gave in return the chance for indefinite ascent in the scale of social advance" (1961, 91). Hamid's "exit West" recontextualizes these assumptions of "indefinite ascent" through the problematic experience of transformative migration, shifting his characters Saeed and Nadia away from their night-school classes on "corporate identity and product branding" (2017, 1) toward a new "space for empathy" and alternative ways of being.[1]

Therefore, toward the end of their migratory journey, they arrive in Marin, a new city emerging on the California coast overlooking the Golden Gate Bridge and close to, but very different from, the wealthy high-tech neighbor, San Francisco. Here the hills are "overwhelmingly poor" (192) and composed of stratified shantytowns with makeshift and simple amenities.[2] Hamid has discussed how his intention was to challenge the established "essence" of the West in the novel: "The west as a geographic direction will always be with us, but the west as something fundamental, with a different essence, has always been a kind of myth. There have always been easterners in the west, and southerners in the north. The fact that this notion is itself being challenged is central to the book." Inherited from Turner and subsequent iterations, this "myth" for Hamid is a form of paralysis that creates a "false permanence" about the region and nation and, consequently "leads us to nostalgic politics and nostalgic psychological dysfunction," preventing the imagination of a "desirable future" (2018b).[3] As we have seen throughout *Worlding the Western*, myth, as Glissant puts it succinctly, forms "the hub of…collective existence" through stories that emphasize "filiation and legitimacy" as the "pillars…of divine Right of property" (2020c, 21). For this reason, as I argue in chapter 1, the interruption of myth is crucial.

Similarly, "the category 'westerners,'" as Comer reminds us, "conceives a unity of peoples who share residential origins, racial heritage, and civilization" (2007), yet in Hamid's reimagined "exited" West, this essentialist category is under pressure too, eroded and transformed by migration, with community defined by "the mix of its people" with "almost no natives" (Hamid 2017, 193, 195). Here, Hamid's choice of the term "natives" reminds us of its ambiguous meanings, with "nativeness being a relative matter," depending on the claimers of origin or settlement. In his futuristic novel, there are "layers" (196) of nativism, of "tribes" with claims to their respective place in the world, whose stories, recalling LeAnne Howe's description of tribalography, will "render all our collective experience into a meaningful form," in order "to make a united nation by combining people from various tribes" (2013, 3, 14). In *Exit West*, natives include those who have "died out or been exterminated long ago" or who barely survive in "impromptu trading posts" (Hamid 2017, 195), but nonetheless live on as in Orange or Howe. As Orange puts it, "We've been moving for a long time, but the land moves with you like memory.…Being Indian has never been about returning to the land. The land is everywhere and nowhere" (2018b, 11). Thus, native stories have a magical resonance in this new age of migration and dispossession: "Tales were told at these places that people from all over now gathered to hear, for the tales of these natives felt appropriate to this time of migration, and gave listeners much-needed sustenance" (Hamid 2017, 196). Such stories are *appropriate* to the possibility of worlding sketched out by Hamid and tracked throughout this book, since, as Orange explains, "the more you don't know, the more innocent you can stay" (2018b, 139). However, recalling Carys Davies's discussion of Trump's "indigenous natives" in the introduction, Hamid goes on to say that "nativists" also exist in the US West, rejecting such combinations and holding on to their "innocence," claiming their rights as "native to this country," by which they mean "their existence here did not owe anything to a physical migration that had occurred in their lifetimes" and most often were "those with light skin who looked most like the natives of Britain" (2017, 196).

Hamid's third layer of nativeness relates to those descended "from the human beings brought from Africa to this continent centuries ago as slaves," who "had vast importance, for society had been shaped in reaction to it" through acts of "unspeakable violence," yet this layer, once more echoing Glissant, "endured, fertile, a stratum of soil that perhaps made possible all future transplanted soils" (197). Through this archaeology of "nativeness," Hamid sketches a contemporary version of what Glissant calls the "poetics of Relation," as a complex, uneasy bringing together of peoples, cultures, languages, and traditions, often specifically due to colonization and migration. As we have seen elsewhere in this book, Glissant's arguments enable a rethinking of assumptions and norms through a vision of a "creolized" world where diverse groups interact in unpredictable ways. Critically, "Creolization is not a fusion, it requires each component to persist, even while it is already changing. Integration is a centralist and autocratic dream.... A country that creolizes is not a country that becomes uniform" (Glissant 2020c, 130).[4] This "elusive worldness," as Glissant calls it, is the "possibility of the imagination" to relate our place or what, with echoes of Jean-Luc Nancy, he terms our "common place" (those shared spaces) with the wider world (12).

Within Hamid's *exited* West, with its various layers of nativeness, emerges a sense of *worlding*: unruly, troubled, and countermythic, while retaining, through these commingled natives, some prospect of survival, endurance, and what Bruno Latour termed "a system of engendering," by which what matters are "transmission, inheritance, or revival, and thus, of transformation" (2017, 87–88). Hamid's protagonists, Nadia and Saeed, are multiple migrants reflecting on their own losses of people and place and finding within their displacement a universal or *worldly* humanity that transcends division, hate, and envy *engendering* forces of hope and possibility. We are told that Saeed

> prayed fundamentally as a gesture of love for what had gone and would go and could be loved in no other way. When he prayed he touched his parents, who could not otherwise be touched, and he touched a feeling that we are all children who lose our parents, all of us, every man and woman and boy and girl, and we too will all

be lost by those who come after us and love us, and this loss unites humanity, unites every human being, the temporary nature of our being-ness, and our shared sorrow, the heartache we each carry and yet too often refuse to acknowledge in one another, and out of this Saeed felt it might be possible, in the face of death, to believe in humanity's potential for building a better world, so he prayed as a lament, as a consolation, and as a hope. (Hamid 2017, 201–2)

What he finds through love and prayer is connection to other lives in "lament...consolation, and as hope" (202), to the "shared" lives of others who are lost in death yet persist as timely reminders of the "temporary nature of our being-ness." As Nancy put it, "Community is revealed in the death of others; hence it is always revealed to others. Community is what takes place always through others and for others. It is not the space of the *egos*—subjects and substances that are at bottom immortal—but of the *I's*, who are always *others* (or else are nothing)."[5] This is what Saeed feels through his prayers: a new, fluid "community" based not upon "ego," but "always through others and for others" (1991, 15). In Naomi Klein's words, Saeed senses an alternative community not "based on endless taking— from the earth and from one another—[but rather] a culture based on caretaking, the principle that when we take, we also take care and give back" (2017, 241).

Saeed's acknowledgment of precarity or "temporariness" sharpens his desire for a "better world," reminding him of the entangled "value of things" distilled in the aura of Marin, "the new settlement," whose hybrid or "creolized" and therefore unpredictable sounds fill the air "like a festival, music and voices and a motorcycle and the wind" (204, 205). In this new space, there is a strange echo of the Oakland powwow in *There There* that Orange describes as "a place to be together....The messy, dangling strands of our lives...pulled into a braid...coming for years, generations, lifetimes, layered in prayer...braided, blessed, and cursed" (2018b, 135). In Hamid's West, the myth has been interrupted, or "exited," and California reimagined, not as the culmination of the American dream of success, wealth, and endless summer, associated with Hollywood movies and lifestyle magazines, but as a space born of the "ecology of fear" (M. Davis 1998), of racial and class divides, yet, nonetheless, out of this painful birth come "intermittent optimism" and "coexistence" (Hamid 2017, 192, 164) or even what Klein calls "an economy built on love" (2017, 241).

Earlier in the novel, Saeed takes some magic mushrooms and expresses something of this changed perspective: "for we are so fragile, and so beautiful, and surely conflicts could be healed if others had experiences like this, and then he regarded Nadia and saw that she was regarding him and her eyes were like worlds" (Hamid 2017, 44). As Glissant states, thinking about the seeming impossibility of life after the abysmal horror of slavery, "it became something shared and made us," because "peoples do not live on exception….This experience of the abyss can now be said to be the best element of exchange." Coming out of the abyss, Hamid likewise gestures not to "exception," as the Great Western Myth always had, but toward Glissant's "game of the world," "gambl[ing] on the unknown" with "exchange," "shared knowledge," and "Relation" embodied now in the ramshackle shanties of Marin, California (1997, 8).

Once more, recalling Glissant's creolization, Hamid has said, "The essence of nature is hybridity: different things coming together and mixing, and out of that something new coming into existence. That's why so much of procreation involves two parents" (2018b). But rather like Nancy's refusal to settle for an idea of community as fixed or "completed," Hamid presents Marin as "singular beings…constituted by sharing,…distributed and placed, or rather spaced, by the sharing that makes them others" and to understand this place as an "incessant incompletion" of worlding (Nancy 1991, 25). Looking down over the settlement, it is for Nadia and Saeed, as if "everything in the world" (Hamid 2017, 206) is spread out there in a form of *errant* community engaging in "destructuring…compact national identities" and simultaneously "taking up the problems of the Other" (Glissant 2019, 18).

Through his magical realist dispersal of people and place, Hamid enables us to look differently at issues that polarize communities, finding there something emergent, fresh, and hopeful. In discussing this in an interview, Hamid helpfully reflects on many of the concerns of *Worlding the Western*:

> Part of the great political crisis we face in the world today is a failure to imagine plausible desirable futures. We are surrounded…[by] violently nostalgic visions. *Fiction can imagine differently.* Wrenching climate change will happen. Mass migration will happen, on a vast scale. But maybe our children and grandchildren can still inhabit a world where they have a chance at hope and optimism. Fiction can explore this possibility, it can make us feel something other than the sense of either doom or denial that is so prevalent in our nonfiction discourse. It can make human beings less unmoored by the endless nature of change. (Leyshon 2016; emphasis added)

As we have seen, Glissant calls this "the thinking of wandering" or errantry that "releases the imagination, [and] projects us far from the imprisoning cave in which we were huddled" (2020c, 39). Rejecting "nostalgic visions" in favor of shaping a "desirable future" in Marin, Saeed and Nadia discover a "great creative flowering…especially in music," like a "new jazz age" gathering people in different and innovative ways, echoing Glissant's "creolization" of Orange's powwow, with "all kinds of ensembles, humans with humans, humans with electronics, dark skin with light skin with gleaming metal with matt plastic…tribes that had not existed before" (Hamid 2017, 216). Glissant too expresses his "diffracted poetics" of creolization in musical terms, referring to "harmony" and "disharmonies," "echoes" that "mix into the mechanical, humdrum little tunes of our progress and our driftings" so as "to change the sound of the world" (2020c, 8). In a similar vision of worldliness, Nadia, as she becomes sexually involved with a woman chef "who reminded her a bit of a cowboy," experiences "all sorts of old cuisines" and, at the same time, is introduced "to new cuisines that were being born, for many of the world's foods were coming together and being re-formed in Marin" (Hamid 2017, 217).

Hamid's fiction, with its magical realist twists and charged juxtapositions, performs this sense of "possibility" in a similar manner to many of the novels discussed in this book: "We talk about being 'moved' by a book: that word means having a strong emotional reaction, but also, literally, being shifted. I think novels shift people in very interesting ways" (Seaman 2017). As readers too, we "migrate" through language "which diffracts the unity of the meaning," shifting our perspectives and views, creating what Glissant calls "a different kind of vertigo" or "a writing that dances" (2020c, 124, 122). At one point in the novel, Saeed shows Nadia the photographs of French artist Thierry Cohen's series *Villes éteintes* (*Darkened Cities*, 2010–) on his phone (he is not named in the novel). Cohen says of his photographs: "By combining two realities, I am making a third that you cannot see…but it exists!…I am not showing you post-apocalyptic cities…merely bringing back the silence" (quoted in Brook 2014).[6] In the photographs, the city in daytime and a night sky shot elsewhere combine to form an uncanny image of beauty and unease. Nadia interprets them as "achingly beautiful, these ghostly cities," showing "the same sky, but a different time," and "whether they looked like the past, or the present, or the future, she couldn't decide" (Hamid 2017, 54–55). Like Glissant's "vertigo," Hamid's novel echoes Cohen's images, combining competing realities, blurring time and space, cognizant of the past while able to imagine a possible future both ghostly and beautiful. Corresponding to Cohen's images, Hamid asks his readers to see metaphorically *both* the earth and the sky, day and night, the city and the wilderness as somehow always interrelated, coexisting as his migrants might in the newly configured worlds they emerge into within the novel.

With this in mind, *Exit West* engenders a new ethics of "collaborative survival" (Tsing 2015, 4) based upon being "at stake with each other" and with the world (Haraway 2016, 97), born out of loss and mourning, as Saeed realizes above, because "loss unites humanity, unites every human being." Echoing back to earlier discussions of Barry and Zhang, Donna Haraway too understands through the writing of Thom van Dooren that "genuine mourning should open us into an awareness of our dependence on and relationships with those countless others being driven over the edge of extinction." What Saeed understands, in Haraway's words, is that "grief is a path to understanding entangled shared living and dying; human beings must grieve with, because we are in and of this fabric of undoing. Without sustained remembrance, we cannot learn to live with ghosts and so cannot think" (39). As many novels in *Worlding the Western* have shown, learning to live with the ghosts of hidden histories, undocumented lives, and the secrets of the "other living" is critical to fully appreciating "collective life or an individual life—as a series of worldings that have laid down tracks of reaction, etched habits…of composition onto identities, desires, objects, scenes and ways of living" (K. Stewart 2013, 32).

Thus, Hamid's novel counters the Trumpian fear of migration as "apocalypse," an alien contagion engulfing America's long-cherished values and beliefs—though "the apocalypse appeared to have arrived and yet it was not apocalyptic" (2017, 215). Although the world was shaken by migration and its many consequences, "they were not the end, and life went on, and people found things to do and ways to be and people to be with, and plausible desirable futures began to emerge" (215–16). Like Nadia, Saeed moves on to a new relationship with a part African American, part Indian "preacher's daughter," who senses in him the embodiment of a "plausible desirable future," captured in "the expansiveness of his gaze upon the universe, the way he spoke of the stars and of the people of the world" (218–19). But at the same time, she "prompted him to want to listen and speak" and to be politically engaged in new forms of governance and justice that gave a voice to all of the community, "unlike those other entities for which some humans were not human enough to exercise suffrage" (219). In this "entangled shared living" where perspectives

shift from intimate exchanges to universal expansion, Hamid imagines
a community no longer rooted in the past, or in the overworked patterns of life laid down by tradition, institutions, and nations, but proposes something different and more worldly, akin to Kathleen Stewart's
"dense and textured worldings" that function as "both a promissory note
and an imperative that demands a response" (2013, 32).[7] It is ultimately,
as the novel outlines, a world where "everyone migrates, even if we stay
in the same houses our whole lives.…We are all migrants through time"
(Hamid 2017, 209). Our "migrations" are *individual* within the "time" of
our own lives, from child to adult, from experience to experience, life to
death, but also vitally in our *relations with others* through time, negotiating, exchanging, and "being-with" in the unending creation of new forms
of shared community.

NEW TRIBALISM

We are deserts, but populated by tribes, flora and fauna.
—Gilles Deleuze in Deleuze and Claire Parnet, *Dialogues II*

What *Worlding the Western* has shown, in the words of Gilles Deleuze, is
the political value of imaginative fiction, "not…of addressing a people,
which is presupposed already there, but of contributing to the invention
of a people."[8] In the past, "the master, or the colonizer, proclaims 'There
have never been people here,'" and so legitimate communities or peoples
go "missing," excluded or erased by the dominant, majoritarian language.
The novels discussed here give voice to the missing through what Deleuze
called "minor literature," "hidden by the mechanisms of power and the
systems of majority" (1989, 217). Evident in these new epic, errant tales
from below is a landscape less of "tyrannical unity" and more of "several
peoples, an infinity of peoples" coexisting like a "plurality of intertwined
lines" or worlds (220). Critically, what emerges in this process of what
I have called errantry or alternative mappings is, as Deleuze explains,
"Not the myth of a past people," with their established mythic narratives of individualism and progress, but "the story-telling of the people to
come," operating "like a foreign language in a dominant language" (223).
From the echo-world of these disparate voices, the American West tells
worldly "stories for a time yet to come," as Robin Wall Kimmerer puts it
(2013, 207).

Stories, like those in Hamid's speculative Marin, a shantytown community of communities or a "people to come," are born from the intersecting

lines of *deterritorialized* globalization. Such "minor" writing places majoritarian language and myth "in a state of continuous variation," which is, according to Deleuze and Guattari, "the opposite of regionalism" with its tendency to be inward-looking and closed, and instead, opens it up to missing and forgotten elements "different from that of the constant." Such a movement against the constant, major, and dominant power is an "outsystem" that "deviates from the [unanimist] model" (1996, 105) and critically instigates a process of "continuous variation" that resists political sedimentation or domination in favor of "the becoming-minoritarian of everybody, as opposed to the majoritarian Fact of Nobody." To overcome the authoritarian "Fact of Nobody" is to recognize it as "constant and homogeneous" operating by "regionalizing or ghettoizing," whereas "becoming-minoritarian" stresses "connecting…conjugating" and so "invents a specific, unforeseen, autonomous becoming" (106). Glissant was endlessly stimulated by Deleuze and Guattari's radical ideas, returning often to the rhizome as opposed to the root identity, and seeing within it a notion of identity and community defined by the vital concept of "a root reaching out to other roots." In this, he felt "the *difficult* constitution of a *relational* identity…an opening up to the other, without risk of dilution" (2020b, 11).

Returning these relational concepts to the American West, Chicana writer Gloria Anzaldúa understood the need for "becoming-minoritarian," finding in her writings "continuous variation" that enabled a "language to speak about new situations, the new realities" rather than simply recycle the major language "based on the old concepts." She explains, "I use the word nos/otras to illustrate how we're in each other's worlds, how we're each affected by the other, and how we're all dependent on the other" (2000, 215).[9] Thus, through challenging dominant language, we move beyond the designated world (the Fact of Nobody) toward an autonomy through relations with others and a deep appreciation of their worlds. Appropriately, given my earlier discussion of LeAnne Howe's work on "tribalography," Anzaldúa calls this being in each other's worlds "New Tribalism," functioning by "propagating other worldviews…redefining what it means to be una mexicana de este lado, an American in the U.S., a citizen of the world" (2015, 141).[10] This echoes back to Barry's motley "tribe" at Grab Corners in *Days Without End* or Hamid's new settlement of Marin in which "tribes that had not existed before" came together (2017, 216) to form new democratic assemblies, which "might at first have only a moral authority, but that authority could be substantial, for unlike those other entities for which some humans were not human enough to exercise suffrage, this new assembly would speak from the will of all the people, and in the face of that will, it was hoped, greater justice might be less easily denied" (219).

As Josephine Carter argues, "These creative and political forms of assembly are borne of an ethical impetus to meet, share, discuss and actively strive to connect with strangers. They demonstrate a form of community that emerges through being prepared to risk the uncertainty of relating to others, rather than defending against vulnerability." What these "new tribes" demonstrate is "a form of community whose togetherness is based neither on an appeal to sameness nor on the impulse to defend against a precarity that has been misplaced onto already vulnerable bodies" (2020, 636). Hamid's Marin community is uninterested in people's inherited native status bolstered by defensive walls and exclusionary practices and refuses to see borders as closed doors. Fundamentally, "New Tribalism" is for Anzaldúa and Hamid "about relatedness—to self, others, world," crossing the slash between *nos* and *otras*, or, as ever, crossing "the bridge—the best mutuality we can hope for" (Anzaldúa 2015, 151). As noted in the introduction, with powerful contemporary political resonance, Anzaldúa explains, "To bridge means loosening our borders, not closing off to others. Bridging is the work of opening the gate to the stranger, within and without....To bridge is to attempt community" (Anzaldúa and Keating 2002, 3).

What she proposes shares Naomi Klein's political vision at the end of *No Is Not Enough* in which a community made of "connections, not competition" (2017, 238), emerges, learned in part from the experience of the Standing Rock Reservation protest against the Dakota Access Pipeline. Here a new tribalism, akin to Marin in *Exit West*, forms as "a network of camps" comes together "to figure out what connects the crises facing us, and try to chart a holistic vision for the future," despite the "diversity...of tough exchanges" (239, 232, 233).[11]

Through such communities, we might "finally decide to make space to dream together...imagining the world we want" (233–34). Being open in this manner demands an "interconnectivity, a mode of connecting similar to hypertexts' multiple links" that draws people across and beyond lines of race, gender, and class into relations where in the past there were none (Anzaldúa 2015, 151). Recognizing we are all vulnerable makes us more responsible for the well-being of others, who, we understand, are vulnerable too. To build up defenses against this vulnerability "at the expense of every other human consideration is to eradicate one of the most important resources from which we must take our bearings and find our way" (Butler 2004, 30). Ultimately, though risky, it is a bridge toward "a larger vision, a less defended identity": a worlding (Anzaldúa 2015, 152).

THE ELSEWHERE IN THE HERE AND VICE VERSA

Poetry reminds us there are worlds everywhere.
—Billy-Ray Belcourt, *This Wound Is a World*

A world is always as many worlds as it takes to make a world.
—Jean-Luc Nancy, *Being Singular Plural*

Although this book has employed the framework of the Trump era as a device for grouping together certain western novels published during and in response to that time, it is important to recognize, as David Shields has said, "If we're to understand Trump, we need to understand ourselves, American culture, and human nature. Trump is symptom, not cause" (Alter 2018). As Klein argues:

> Trump is not a rupture at all, but rather the culmination—the logical end point—of a great many dangerous stories our culture has been telling for a very long time. That greed is good. That the market rules. That money is what matters in life. That white men are better than the rest. That the natural world is there for us to pillage. That the vulnerable deserve their fate and the one percent deserve their golden towers. That anything public or commonly held is sinister and not worth protection. That we are surrounded by danger and should only look after our own. That there is no alternative to any of this. (2017, 257)

Indeed, as this book has argued from the beginning, these "many dangerous stories" are often rooted in frontier mythologies, the drive westward, and its subsequent history. It is a history that reaches back to what Patricia Nelson Limerick famously called "the legacy of conquest" (1987), and, as we have seen, much of the rhetoric, ideology, and policy of the Trumpian moment stems from a perpetuation and distortion of what Frederick Jackson Turner summarized as "intellectual traits of profound importance." As he explained in typical lyrical style, "Since the days when the fleet of Columbus sailed into the waters of the New World, America has been another name for opportunity, and the people have taken their tone from the incessant expansion" (1961, 61). Under these frontier conditions, "The self-made man was the Western man's ideal…the kind of man that all men might become" and accordingly, "the frontiersman's dream was prophetic" (69, 70). Turner's democratic frontier vision, discussed in the introduction, became rapidly tainted by sustained destruction undertaken in the name of opportunity and destiny in the West, with its deep consequences on people and place. The "prophetic" element of the frontier myth, as Richard Slotkin put it, was "*exclusionist* in its premises, *idealizing* the White male adventurer as the hero of national history," celebrating inevitable progress, while promoting it as a source of "regeneration of personal fortunes and/or of patriotic vigor and virtue" (1993, 655, 12; emphasis added).

As a consequence of this exclusionism and exceptionalism, as Edward Said famously noted, there is a paradox at work in the United States, which as an "immigrant society composed of many cultures" maintained nonetheless an image of itself "free from taint…[and] unified around one iron-clad major narrative of innocent triumph." The result of this has been that the United States "disaffiliates the country from its relationship with other societies and peoples, thereby, reinforcing its remoteness and insularity" (1994, 381).

The novels considered in this book, while circling around the specific and local histories of the American West, counter this "one iron-clad major narrative" through "a poetics of Relation" with historical, imaginative, and epic reach, striding nations, languages, ethnicities, and cultures telling challenging new stories. However, as the epigraph to this section says, "Poetry reminds us there are worlds everywhere," and ultimately, this has been a book about worlds, about the worlding of what might seem local and regional—the American West—when in truth it is shot through with innumerable interrelated and entangled worldings. These novels express worldings as *interruptions* of western myth, reclaiming and re-presenting its components through different, often silenced voices, or new and diverse forms. As I describe them throughout, they are productively *errant*, opening up hidden worlds and counterarchives in a manner best described by Jean-Luc Nancy as "something else": "When a voice, or music, is suddenly *interrupted*, one hears just at that instant something else, a mixture of various silences and noises that had been *covered over by the sound*, but in this something else one hears again the voice or the music that has become in a way the voice or the music of its own interruption: *a kind of echo, but one that does not repeat that of which it is the reverberation*" (1991, 62; emphasis added). To borrow a phrase from

Luiselli, what *Worlding the Western* composes is "an inventory of echoes" that does not repeat that of which it is a reverberation, since the created sound returns changed in subtle and unpredictable ways. Holding on to Nancy's musical metaphor, one might argue that this "kind of echo" reverberating through these novels of the West, resembles what Said once called "an atonal ensemble" (1994, 386).[12] Unsurprisingly, Said, making an impassioned plea for "contrapuntal" thinking, or what he termed "worldliness," chose the image of the echo in the closing lines of *Culture and Imperialism*. He calls for "the connection between things" rather than division and essentialism, for "in Eliot's phrase," as he writes, "reality cannot be deprived of the 'other echoes [that] inhabit the garden'" (408).

As I have argued elsewhere, despite its mythical call to unity, the West has always been a rhizomatic garden of echoes with entangled roots, from multiple sources, intertwined yet always, as Glissant reminds us, reaching out to other roots. As he wrote, a rhizome is an "enmeshed root system" that "maintains…the idea of rootedness but challenges that of a totalitarian root." As we have seen throughout this book, rhizomatic thought is intimately connected to Glissant's model of errantry, and "the Poetics of Relation, in which each and every identity is extended through a relationship with the Other." Worlding is central to this "poetics" because it activates, explores, and interrogates relationships with the Other, questioning those who would turn away from the world in favor of the "intolerant root" (1997, 11), defending identity and nation against what it perceives as a threat.

As Robert Macfarlane wrote, history "no longer feels figurable as a forwards-flighting arrow or a self-intersecting spiral," for we have come to see it differently, as "a network branching and conjoining in many directions" (2019, 103). Likewise, nature is better understood, as Kimmerer testifies, "in fungal terms: not as a single gleaming snow-peak or tumbling river in which we might find redemption, nor as a diorama that we deplore or adore from a distance—but rather as an assemblage of entanglements of which we are messily part" (Macfarlane 2019, 103). The novels discussed here testify to this "messiness" when history and the world it makes are viewed in what Nancy calls an "unworked" manner, stripping away mythic narratives with their focus upon individual triumphs, destiny, and a consequently fixed definition of the "people" and the "nation." To see around these categories, to "unwork" them, is to uncover and deploy an alternative and messier sense of community—rather like what Nancy later called a "mêlée." He defines "the place of a *mêlée*" as "a crossing and a stop, a knot and an exchange, a gathering, a disjunction, a circulation, a radiating" (2000, 148), a dynamic movement of sharing rather than a collection of already constituted subjects with a common substance.[13]

The migrant errant futures sketched out across these chapters from Diaz to Hamid, from Obreht to Luiselli, from Barry to Howe develop recurrent concerns and patterns about how we might rethink and renew our sense of the world. As Devisch puts it, "We share the sense in which we exist, but we do not own it" (2000, 247), since in order to live with others we must recognize deep and abiding kinships beyond the self, beyond the imperial "I." To deny this vital interdependence, this sharing with others, is to exist as a type of egotistical, tyrannical self "who preserves itself and only those who belong already to the regime of itself." As Judith Butler argues, with clear reference to the Trump era, "Such a self belongs only to itself or to those who augment its sense of itself, and so stands worldless, threatening this world" (2020, 149). To "stand worldless" or unworlded, as Nancy put it, is also to deny not only one's communal obligations, but also one's global obligations, viewing the world as an arena for exercising individual power over those lives deemed "unlike me," unworthy, or "ungrievable" (Butler 2020, 11).

In the complex, errant journeys of *Worlding the Western*, disregarded lives are seen to matter, to be worthy of grief, mourning, and care, like the deracinated body of Lurie at the end of *Inland*, the fragmented corpse of Ba in *How Much of These Hills Is Gold*, the queer bodies of McNulty and Cole in *Days Without End*, or the ghostly Savage Indian in *Savage Conversations*. They all suggest a "politics of equality" in which all lives, of whatever race, sexuality, gender, or class, might count in the stories of the American West, in the United States, and, consequently, the Whole-World's future. Butler's words at the end of *The Force of Nonviolence* speak to the concerns of these writings that demand, in different ways and through diverse stories, that every life be grievable and that, as a result, "all lives ought to be able to persist in their living without being subject to violence, systemic abandonment, or military obliteration" (2002, 202).

As Butler explains, this struggle against "worldlessness," with its "lethal phantasmagoria," stands for the constant creation of a "sustaining world" (203, 200) and as such, according to Rebecca Solnit, "is always, first and last, storytelling work, or what some of my friends call 'the battle of the story.' Building, remembering, retelling, celebrating our own stories is part of our work" (2017b). If, as I have suggested, following Naomi Klein,

Trumpism was "not a break with…[the United States'] underlying stories, but their fulfilment…a dystopian fiction come to life," then these new stories must counteract and interrupt "the stories that ineluctably produced him" (2017, 258). In order to achieve this, as the novels in *Worlding the Western* attest, there must be a struggle to create "a new imaginary… an egalitarian imaginary that apprehends the interdependency of lives," perhaps even *utopian* fictions.[14] However "unrealistic and useless" such fictions might appear within this global "battle," their function is always "a way of bringing another reality into being that does not rely on instrumental logics and the racial phantasmagoria that reproduces state violence" (Butler 2020, 203).[15]

As I have shown, these writings produce errant worldings whose often surreal expansiveness challenges the contained and framed unanimity of mythic America.[16] They conjure what Iain Chambers calls "the aesthetics (and ethics) of disturbance that reveals a gap, an interval in the world, that signals a limit and establishes a transit, a passage elsewhere" (2018, 52). In this "interval" within the assumed order of *the* world, other worlds open up, often refusing "to make sense or speak in a prescribed way" (53). Chambers employs terms I have used throughout this book to describe the process of worlding, writing of the "art of the interruption" whose "diverse worlds" create "the promise of interrupting such an order, of punctuating the homogeneous, historical time of 'progress,'" enabling us to recognize the limits of "our prescribed state," while also "revisiting, reciting (in the sense of reworking) and re-siting (in the sense of transporting)," shifting toward some "elsewhere," perhaps toward Butler's "new imaginary" (52–53).

What Butler calls the "unrealism" of this imaginary is best illustrated through the interruptions of art, with its infinite capacity for "ongoing, worldly interrogations" (54). As the works discussed here demonstrate, despite the lure of "the presumed sovereignty of individual identity… striving to harness and homogenise the world" (54, 56–57), there exists the possibility for a tentative *interdependence* in which "'each' is, from the start, given over to another, social, dependent," and at the same time able to "live with the living, mindful of the dead" (Butler 2020, 203).[17]

THE "OTHER IMPULSES OF LOVE"

With this in mind, I wish to return to the work of Édouard Glissant, whose writing has been a theoretical echo chamber throughout this book, offering new poetic approaches to my developing sense of worlding. He calls this Whole-World, explained as "our universe as it changes and lives on through its exchanges and, at the same time, the 'vision' we have of it," meaning that we are always involved or entangled in those changes imaginatively and productively, as "physical diversity" and "in the representations that it inspires in us."[18] Glissant was, however, always a writer of place, a writer of Martinique. For this reason, above all, he is helpful in comprehending my use of the American West in this project. As I wrote in the introduction, my use of the West is not to reinforce its sense of exceptionalism, or what Glissant terms "the exclusivity of place," because such a "sole norm…prefigured or accompanied…Conquest." As he explained, "We are no longer able to sing, speak or work based on our place alone, without plunging into the imagination of this totality" (the Whole-World). Indeed, this pendular movement between place and world offered for him a "new way of writing," a "Worldness" (2020c, 108), which is not negative globalization, but rather about relational diversity and respect for the other. What matters is "place in Relation, opening up its subject matter, questioning its limit, destabilizing its limits" (112). In the process, Glissant asserts, "you rise to that knowledge" because "everyone is embarking, at every moment, on a Treatise on the Whole-World" (109). Through his powerful, poetic vision, each "treatise" is constituted by relations in which "human cultures exchange while living on, change without losing themselves" so that "at the same time" one might be, crucially, of one's place *and* of the world (110).[19]

In this regard, each chapter in this book is a form of "treatise" of entangled relations, exploring history, community, and nation, *rising to the knowledge* of place (or regionality) with all its diversity engaging with the world. Recalling Latour's words from earlier, place becomes an "agitated history in which we are participants among others" (2018, 42), a *regionality-as-worlding*, defined by Glissant as "a poetics of sharing in the Whole-World" (2020b, 94). He termed this interlinked thought "archipelagic," like islands separate yet connected, as in the Caribbean, "a thought of trembling, of non-presumption, but also of openness and sharing," in a manner strangely appropriate to a postwestern poetics that understands tribal lands, states, cities, neighborhoods, and individual geographies within new frames of reference. In Glissant's words, "The regions of the world become islands, isthmuses, peninsulas, advances, lands of mixing and passage, yet which still remain" (143, 111).[20]

Celia Britton argues that such a vision is indeed a "new form of political action in the globalized world," combining "local action with global consciousness of Relation—summed up most recently in the slogan 'Act in your locality, think with the world'" (2009, 9). Once more, these words echo Latour's vital Terrestrial "balancing act" between the politics of the local and the global, the earth and the world (2018, 93). A failure to see the value of such political action and of a shared responsibility for the other is spelled out in western terms in *The Line Becomes a River*, Francisco Cantú's contemporary account of the US-Mexico border: "This reality is quite often a reality of fear, a reality that makes us—individually and as a society—crazy, isolated, filled with distrust for our fellow human beings, the people who share our neighbourhoods, our cities, our country, our borders, our intractably and intimately interwoven global community— the people with whom we share our very lives" (2018, 158). What is at risk because of this debilitating fear is this book's central concern, *regionality- as-worlding* or Latour's Terrestrial. What Cantú calls an "intractably and intimately interwoven global community" comes close to a shorthand for the complex web of shared relations that the novels examined refer to and imagine. Within these fictions, the West becomes a site not for exceptionalist nation building or narrow-minded racial, gendered, or ecological thinking, but for multiple stories like threads of something better, "down to earth," and perhaps more hopeful. This is best summed up by Mikhail Bakhtin's thoughts on the radical potential of the novel form itself: "It is entangled, shot through with shared thoughts, points of view, alien value judgments and accents…[that] weave in and out of complex interrelationships, merges with some, recoils from others, inter- sects with yet a third group" (1990, 276). As a view both of fiction's poten- tial and, more significantly, as a vision of worlded community, Bakhtin's words resonate with theoretical ideas employed throughout this book, from Glissant and Nancy, to Said, Latour, Butler, and Wilson. In Amitav Ghosh's words, "The body of the nation can no longer be conceived of as consisting only of a territorialized human population: its very sinews are now revealed to be intertwined with forces that cannot be confined by boundaries" (2016, 144).

In the final paragraph of Ghosh's *The Great Derangement*, discussed briefly in the introduction, there is nonetheless a clear, if qualified, hope for change and for a future vision of the world, echoing Cantú's and Bakhtin's words: "I would like to believe that out of this struggle will be born a generation that will be able to transcend the isolation in which humanity was entrapped in the time of derangement; that they will redis- cover their kinship with other beings, and that this vision, at once new and ancient, will find expression in a transformed and renewed art and literature" (2016, 162). Despite the violent histories discussed throughout *Worlding the Western*, there is a similar hope to be found in the potential of worlding, since, as Solnit explains, "hope is a belief that what we do might matter, an understanding that the future is not yet written. . . . Hope looks forward, but it draws its energies from the past, from knowing histories, including our victories, and their complexities and imperfections" (2017b). Through Deleuze's "people to come," Ghosh's "kinship with other beings," and Solnit's forward-looking hope, there emerges a resource for the future, between families, communities, individuals, within nature and across time. The idea of a "society based on endless taking and depletion to one based on caretaking and renewal" with "relationships . . . grounded in those same principles of reciprocity and care . . . are our most valuable resource of all" (Klein 2017, 247). In Zhang's *How Much of These Hills Is Gold*, for example, this surfaces as Lucy's "feeling a sorrow kin to love," in which her relation to the West is deeply intertwined with the hills she travels through: "A part of her is buried there, a part of her lost in them, a part of her found and born in them." However, while others claim the land as territory, for conquest and gold, "there is being claimed by it. The quiet way. A kind of gift in never knowing how much of these hills might be gold." In this unknowable and unpredictable relation with the world, "like and unlike an echo" (2020b, 245), lies something "kin to love," an irreducible and opaque force, as Glissant might have it, not a "grasping" like "hands that grab their surroundings and bring them back to themselves . . . [in a] gesture of enclosure if not appropriation." In Glissant's terms, this is "the gesture of giving-on-and-with" that both exposes us and simultaneously opens us to the Whole-World (1997, 192). "In this," he wrote, "we are inventing different forms of networks, another relationship to the Other. And perhaps other impulses of love?" (2020a, 25).

Clearly, this is not romantic love, not a fusion of opposites, or a joining of separate identities into some mystical union, for it is closer to Jean-Luc Nancy's discussion of "shattered love."[21] In Nancy's work, love is a reminder of the multitudinous or "shattered" possibility of identities, exposing and exceeding the self, so that "in love with" (echoing Glissant's "the gesture of giving-on-and-with") suggests an acknowledgment and sharing of one's finitude with the other, whom one comes to recognize in love as also finite. Thus, love "shatters" self and other, and in this mutual gesture of opening up or vulnerability, relation forms.[22] Love undermines the tendency of thinking to totalize, categorize, and hierarchize and instead relishes touching and caressing as gestures that initiate contact and relation (as in Glissant), but resist possession and domination.[23] As always in Nancy's philosophy, however, he is illuminating the possibility of community as a similarly shared coexistence of "being-with": "That which exists, whatever this might be, coexists because it exists. The co-implication of existing…is the sharing of the world. A world is not something external to existence; it is not an extrinsic addition to other existences; the world is the coexistence that puts these existences together" (2000, 29).[24] Hence, love is an opening of the already fragmented self and an obligation to the equally shattered other—"Love's uncertain light shows being not as a brute totality, but exposes it as singular and plural, completely incomplete" (Abbott 2011, 160).[25] As McNulty puts it in *Days Without End*, "I guess love laughs at history a little" (Barry 2016a, 77).

With these multifaceted ideas on love, sharing, and community in mind, I want to return finally to Solnit's political vision, written before the Trump administration yet, with its powerful call for new communal values, a prescient rallying cry to the world. Her words reflect Baldwin's description of love as "a state of being," "the tough and universal sense of quest and daring and growth" (Baldwin 1981, 82): "I call it public love, in contrast to the private loves of family, romance and home life. The public loves encompass the love of place, of civil society, of meaningful work and a role in making the world, of hope about the future, of a sense of possibility. They involve a larger sense of home that includes the neighbors, the village, or city, or region, the culture and community, or even humanity" (Solnit 2014). With this "public love" in mind, recall Saeed's meditation on love and loss in *Exit West* with his sense that "loss unites humanity, unites every human being" in "the temporary nature of our being-ness, and our shared sorrow, the heartache we each carry and yet too often refuse to acknowledge in one another." Echoing Solnit, Nancy, Butler, and Glissant, therefore, it might be possible, in the face of love and death, vulnerability and loss, to believe nonetheless in "humanity's potential for building a better world" (Hamid 2017, 201–2). As the resilient fictions of *Worlding the Western* have shown, this might be a Whole-World in which many incomplete worlds coexist, even more engaging and hopeful for their portrayals of diversity, unpredictability, possibility, and love.

> For me everything still remains to come and to be understood.
> —Jacques Derrida, *The Work of Mourning*

Notes

Introduction

1. Maguire's call found answers in works published since 2002. See the works cited for works by Paul Giles; MaryEllen Higgins, Rita Keresztesi, and Dayna Oscherwitz; Marek Paryż and John R. Leo; Susan Kollin; Krista Comer; Lee Broughton; Stephen Tatum; Stephen Teo; and Christopher Conway, as well as my own works.

2. The upsurge in interest in the West demonstrates a growing disruptive relationship with earlier conventions, in films like *Slow West* (John MacLean, 2015), *Hell or High Water* (David McKenzie, 2016), *Wind River* (Taylor Sheridan, 2017), *Lean on Pete* (Andrew Haigh, 2017), *The Rider* (Chloé Zhao, 2017), *News of the World* (Paul Greengrass 2020), and *The Harder They Fall* (Jeymes Samuel 2021). Alongside novels discussed here, see Carys Davies's *West* (2018), Marlon James's *A Brief History of Seven Killings* (2014), or a crop of Australian works such as the futurist *The Rover* (David Michod, 2014), the colonial outback film *Sweet Country* (Warwick Thornton, 2017), the Aboriginal "westerns" *Mystery Road* and *Goldstone* (Ivan Sen, 2013, 2016), or Paul Howarth's outback epic *Only Killers and Thieves* (2018). See my essays on Marlon James and Carys Davies in the references.

3. Chapter 1 discusses worlding in more detail.

4. The term "melee" comes from Jean-Luc Nancy: "On the other hand, it is not 'one': in a *mêlée* there are meetings and encounters; there are those who come together and those who spread out, those who come into contact and those who enter into contracts, those who concentrate and those who disseminate, those who identify and those who modify—just like the two sexes in each one of us" (2000, 151).

5. I am using only novels written in English.

6. Minoritarian relates to "becoming" and "continuous variation" as opposed to the fixity of the majority, the aspirational, radical "becoming-minoritarian of everybody," rather than the "Fact of Nobody" associated with the majority (Deleuze and Guattari 1996, 106). See the conclusion for more on this.

7. Glissant wrote, "The wretched other side of worldness is what is called globalization…the rush to the bottom, standardization, the imposition of multinational corporations…circles whose circumference is everywhere and whose center is nowhere" (quoted in Mignolo 2000, 40).

8. Robert Wright in *Wired* summed this up with one line, "back in the good old days, we didn't take orders from foreigners" (2019).

9. See how Latour's remarks overlap with those discussed in chapter 1 from Jean-Luc Nancy with regard to "sharing" and "being-in-common."

10. In a 1958 episode of the western TV series *Trackdown*, the late actor Lawrence Dobkin plays a con man named Walter Trump, who enters a dusty town in Texas to scare the locals into believing that the world will end in a rain of cosmic fire

unless they let him build a giant wall to protect them. "I am the only one. Trust me," says Trump. "I can build a wall around your homes that nothing will penetrate" (Nguyen 2017).

11. Ironically, "Project Alamo" was a database of voter information created for Trump's 2016 presidential campaign and an associated fund-raising and political advertising operation on social media platforms. *Vanity Fair* reported in 2019 that Trump aides referred to the wall as "the president's personal Alamo" (Sherman 2019).

12. See Berenson 2016. On western themes, see also Viala-Gaudefroy 2018a.

13. Victor Hanson wrote in a similar vein: "The real moral question is not whether the gunslinger Trump could or should become civilized (again, defined in our context as becoming normalized as 'presidential') but whether he could be of service at the opportune time and right place for his country, crude as he is. After all, despite their decency, in extremis did the frontier farmers have a solution without Shane, or the Mexican peasants a realistic alternative to the Magnificent Seven, or the town elders a viable plan without Will Kane?" (2018). In a 2018 article on fashion shifts in the age of Trump, he was described as "something of a go-it-alone cowboy in politics, he has lassoed the land of America and is dragging it like a hog-tied Holstein to slaughter—or, as he thinks, to the metaphorical grasslands of not the early frontier days but the just-as-vanished era of factory jobs and middle-class plenty" (Young 2018). Also Gershom Gorenberg: "Donald Trump, a city boy, born rich, has managed to cast himself as a self-made, rugged individual, a man with no regard for convention and no need for government to do anything but to get out of his way. This is the American myth expressed in its purest form in the classic Western from an age before irony—especially the films in which evil forces threaten an isolated town, the sheriff is useless and the townspeople recruit an outlaw in his place. The old gunslinger will know when to pistol-whip a baddie, when to kick below the belt" (2016). In the days after Trump's defeat to Joe Biden, *Guardian* journalist Nesrine Malik summarized his appeal in similarly Wild West terms, like a Man with No Name: "Into that stagnant bog, Trump came to stir the muck. His incoherence was seen as a kind of unpractised honesty; his ignorance as a mark of accessibility; his vileness as a sign of his fighting spirit. He wasn't nice, but he was going to shake things up" (2020).

14. Speaking at the United Nations in 2019, Trump said, "The true good of a nation can only be pursued by those who love it: by citizens who are rooted in its history, who are nourished by its culture, committed to its values, attached to its people, and who know that its future is theirs to build or theirs to lose. Patriots see a nation and its destiny in ways no one else can."

15. In stressing these characteristics, I draw parallels to many of the authors in this book who are "tribalographers," telling communal stories lost in Trump's America. They function as reminders of the "other realities" that constitute the nation, whether Native, Irish, gay, Chinese, women, Mexican, Muslim, or Syrian Arabs.

Chapter 1. On Worlding

1. As Rob Wilson explains, unworlding or deworlding "suggests enduring impacts of empire, colonialism, and turbo-capitalism upon other life-worlds and

ways of being (as Ghosh portrays through the transoceanic India in *The Great Derangement*)" (2018, 10).

2. As Eric Prieto reminds us, Glissant's struggle is against exceptionalism too: "Glissant's emphasis on Relation…has been built on the premise that we must recognize the specificity of every community while also putting an end to all forms of exceptionalism" (2010, 114).

3. Errantry is later discussed at length.

4. Nancy's work, like much of postwar French philosophy, is a response to totalitarianism and Nazi Germany. So his thoughts on myth, community, and the world reflect back upon the dangers of extreme nationalism, reductionist thinking, and the construction of unicity. "Fascism was the grotesque or abject resurgence of an obsession with communion; it crystallized the motif of its supposed loss and the nostalgia for its images of fusion" (1991, 17).

5. Phalanstery is a group of people living together in a community and holding property in common.

6. In Nancy "singularity" has a very precise meaning: "Therefore, it is, at one and the same time, infra-/intraindividual and transindividual, and always the two together. The individual is an intersection of singularities" (2000, 85).

7. "Sharing is always incomplete, or it is beyond completion and incompletion. For a complete sharing implies the disappearance of what is shared" (Nancy 1991, 35).

8. See Judith Butler's (2004) ideas on the politics of relationality and others discussed elsewhere.

9. Iain Chambers argues that it is only through "the oblique gaze and the excessive and errant language of poetics" that we are able to harness a new way of thinking (2018, 69).

10. See Pratt 1995. As Drabinski explains, "Rhizomes live from many roots. Mangrove thinking, thinking at the shoreline—the Caribbean inflection and creolisation of Deleuzian thought" (2019, 163).

11. "Wherever founding myths appear, in what I am calling atavistic cultures, the notion of identity grows up around the axis of filiation and legitimacy, which gives no room to the Other as a participant" (Glissant 2002, 289).

12. See, for example, Stegner 2003.

13. "The same is true of the Epic, which singles out a community in relation to the Other, and senses Being only as in-itself, because it never conceives of it as relation" (Glissant 1997, 50).

14. Some might, however, term these "epics" as "speculative realism" or "peripheral realism." The term "peripheral realism" derives from Sharae Deckard's essay on Roberto Bolaño's *2666* (2012). There is no space to discuss *2666* in this book, but the novel is a further example of the new epic (sometimes called "monumental") novel. It is, of course, a novel interested in the western.

15. In discussing Glissant's work, Drabinski asks, "What is this world" he conjures through Relation? The answer stands as a remarkable insight into the ways Glissant's work might also illuminate the American West as a powerful *regional-to-worlding* space: "The movement toward it [the world] is what I call the geography of reason, the location of thinking in a particular place that intersects the folds of time

(specific historical experiences and their attendant memories) with the rich implications of spatiality (landscape, climate, sites of memory, ruins, living languages, expressive life, but also the nation and aspirations for a liberated state)" (2019, 165).

16. Note the parallels to Diaz and Hamid here with the use of "horizon" and "exit."

17. Nancy's "sense" has a very particular usage: "So, what does 'sense' mean? Sense means 'relationship.' A sense does not 'exist' as a thing. A glass of water does not make sense. A person, by itself, does not make sense. What makes sense? Sense is made (we use the verb 'to make'). In French we say 'une chose fait sens.' The sense is something that someone makes, it is a dynamic, it is a relationship to something or someone else. As Bataille says, there is no 'sense' only for 'one' person. Even if we think of the 'one' and 'unique' God, he does not make sense and he has not sense" (2015).

18. Resonance here is closely related to my discussion of echoes in Luiselli in chapter 7.

19. See my *Affective Critical Regionality* (2016) on this.

20. As Nancy writes, "The world springs forth everywhere and in each instant, simultaneously" (2000, 83).

21. I discuss Spivak's "vulgar" sense of worlding in the introduction. See also Cheah 2016, 8.

22. The idea of the "journey" is in itself interrupted in the Trump-era fictions I discuss, since the linear, goal-oriented notion of the epic voyage associated with classical literature is questioned and retraced in *In the Distance*, *Exit West*, and *Inland*, all of which propose "vertical," circular, or unfinished travels as a mark of their narratives.

23. For Mignolo, for example, this involves "delinking" from those taken-for-granted ways of thinking associated with coloniality in order to assert that "thinking-otherwise is possible (and necessary) and that the best solutions are not necessarily found in the actual order of things under neo-liberal globalization" (2005, 117).

Chapter 2. "What West?"

1. Macfarlane does not mention Glissant in his work, but they are both fascinated by webs, networks, and the rhizomatic, as opposed to rooted relations of the natural and human worlds. Macfarlane, for example, writes of the "mycorrhizal network" among trees and the isotope's "unexpected intricacies of interrelations" (2019, 90). Macfarlane discusses "trace fossils within us" (79), and Glissant writes of the significance of "trace thought" that "sings its relativity" and is "opposed to systematic thought" (2020c, 9, 50, 9). The sense of "Relation" is everywhere alive in both writers.

2. See the final chapter on Mohsin Hamid's *Exit West* for more on this sense of migration.

3. Latour comments that "people everywhere call for returning to the land of old! But the land of old is in no way the Earth of ecologists and activists. It is the old utopian site of the nation state and ethnic communities—in Poland, Hungary, France, Italy, as well as in the England of Brexit or the Trumpian US" (Latour et al. 2018, 2–3).

4. "Local-minus" is Latour's term for a localism "that promises tradition, protection, identity, and certainty within national or ethnic borders" (2018, 30). It has much in common with Trumpism.

5. In Glissant's work, according to Eric Prieto, "The goal…is to reconcile the local and the global, to gain this totalizing perspective but without losing track of the particulars" (2010, 116).

6. In science studies and the work of Donna Haraway, "worlding" refers to the cooperative and conflictual ways of "world-making" in which different species, technologies, and forms of knowledge interact. According to Bruno Latour: "We would have to be able to introduce an opposition, not between nature and culture this time (since the incessant vibrations between the two are what drives us crazy), but between Nature/Culture on the one side and, on the other, a term that would include each one of them in a particular case. I propose to use the term world, or 'worlding,' for this more open concept, defining it…as that which opens to the multiplicity of existents, on the one hand, and to the multiplicity of ways they have of existing, on the other" (2017, 35).

7. In his "Book Notes" essay on music, Diaz remarks that like Brian Eno reworking three-hundred-year-old music, "building something new on a tradition by manipulating its legacy is a crucial part of *In the Distance*" (2017a).

8. The idea of the epic is discussed at length in chapter 1. Glissant argues that although epics were put to work as national narratives, in truth they were more complex, because, as he puts it in *Poetics of Relation*, like *In the Distance*, "These are books of errantry, going beyond the pursuits and triumphs of rootedness required by the evolution of history" (1997, 16).

9. Latour refers to "the arrow of time" as a component of modernity's sense of progress, and so "to debate…to hesitate, negotiate, take one's time, was to doubt the arrow of time, to be old-fashioned" (2018, 88).

10. In Glissant's work, invading nomadism links to rooted identity and the consequent belief in uniqueness (or exceptionalism) that generated colonization and the desire to spread that superiority throughout the world. He also links together "the absolute of ancient filiation and conquering linearity, the project of knowledge and arrowlike nomadism, each used the other in its growth" (1997, 56).

11. Glissant's attention to difference, "Relation," and "opacity" are all aimed against what he calls "reductive transparency" and "uniformity" (1997, 55, 191), that is, a sense of the world as understandable, knowable, and, therefore, "graspable" (191). He says, "Displace all reduction" (190). Similarly, Latour argues that to be Terrestrial is to be "learning to be dependent. No reduction. No harmony" (2018, 87).

12. Lorimer is based on John Muir and Ralph Waldo Emerson.

13. There is no space to discuss here the parallels to Jean-Luc Nancy's *Being Singular Plural* (2000), but they are picked up in later chapters.

14. This resembles Glissant's notion of *donner-avec*, which is usually translated as "gives-on-and-with," suggesting both generosity and "looking out toward" (see Wing in Glissant 1997, 212). See the conclusion.

15. John Drabinski explains that "Glissant deploys *tout-monde* in his late works as simultaneously about the world as a whole (totality) and concerned with sustaining what can never be total (irreducible fragmentation, the archipelago as a figure of thinking)" (2019, 168). Like many of Glissant's concepts, it is an open system, radical and different. "The writer and the artist invite us to it" (quoted in Drabinski 2019, 168).

16. Glissant uses the idea of the "graft" to express his sense of "Relation": "Onto the imagination of single-root identity, let us graft this imagination of rhizome-identity" (2020c, 11).

17. Glissant's term "creolization" is not a simple fusion or mix of cultures, as it is sometimes used, but is well described by Birgit Mara Kaiser: "Due to centuries of (again most often forced) displacements, violence and migration in the backwash of colonialisms, and intensified entanglements across the globe in the past decades, he sees our contemporary time as marked by a 'massive and diffracted confluence of cultures,' analogous to what occurred in the historically specific context of the Caribbean" (2014, 279).

18. There are clear historical echoes of the Mountain Meadows Massacre, a series of attacks on the Baker-Fancher emigrant wagon train, at Mountain Meadows in Utah. The attacks began on September 7, 1857, and culminated on September 11, 1857.

19. In a further interruption of western traits, there are hints of a homosocial relationship in the novel, whereby Asa "would lie by his side," and when Hawk asks why he had run away with him, Asa replies, "Because of you.... Because I saw you and knew" (Diaz 2017c, 238, 244).

20. As Drabinski explains, "Glissant borrows from Deleuze and Guattari and creolises their work first through critical engagement with Caribbean experience, memory, and landscape and then, in the late work, through an extension of that experience to a sense of a global and globalising future" (2019, 168). What Glissant understands is that the rhizome has many roots (not just a single root) and so moves and entangles in multiple unpredictable ways. It is his bulwark against single-rooted, essentialist, universalist, nationalist, and colonialist thinking. Errant thought is relational and rhizomatic.

21. Echo-world is a concept in Glissant's work (see 1997, 93–94). See chapter 7 for more on this.

22. Glissant adds, "History with a big H is really the daughter of the Founding Myth and on the path that leads to history myth will be accompanied, then hidden, and finally replaced by myths" (2002, 289).

23. See Rash 2017.

24. Diaz has commented on his own playlist that accompanied the writing of the novel: "If there is an emphasis on American composers, from Charles Ives to James Murphy, it is for the obvious reason that I was trying to inhabit and feel an American space. Most of these pieces have to do with openness, repetition, and variation, which are crucial elements in my book. Some of this music was more influential than any of the books I read during the writing process." Specifically commenting on Feldman, "His music can be so slow that it renders movement imperceptible—we don't hear the harmony changing or the patterns transforming. Suddenly, we just notice a change of state. We have been displaced. This does *not* mean 'now we are here; then we are there' (that, in fact, would be the very definition of development). It means, rather, 'now we are here; now we are here'—different nows, with no then in between. I tried to convey this kind of temporal disorientation in my prose" (2017a).

Chapter 3. "What World We Making?"

1. As in Diaz's *In the Distance* (discussed in chapter 2), this shifting of geographical norms in the western is crucial to the subversion of the genre and the deliberate questioning of its underpinning ideologies.

2. Barry's son Toby was the inspiration for the story, having come out as gay at the age of sixteen. Barry commented that "the nature of his love between him and his boyfriend" was profound, "something to be revered, emulated, cherished, something we can learn from" (Gross 2017). Barry also wrote an open letter to the readers of the *Irish Times* on May 12, 2015, in support of same-sex marriage. He based his support for marriage equality on personal reasons, defining himself as "the more than proud father of one shining person who happens to be a member of the LGBT community," as well as referring to "all the hatred, violence, suspicion, patronisation, ignorance, murder, maiming, hunting, intimidation, terrorising, shaming, diminishment, discrimination, destruction, and yes, intolerance, visited upon a section of humanity for God knows how many hundreds of years, if not millennia" (Moss 2017).

3. Susan Lee Johnson (2000) uses the idea of a "shadow story" to express the complex social world of the gold camps that included "cross-gender" confusions and homosociality of various forms (see 339).

4. There is a possible reference in her name to Pauline Hopkins's novel *Winona: A Tale of Negro Life in the South and Southwest* (1902–3), which also deals with issues of identity, mixed race, gender, and community in America.

5. "Queer" is a word much used in the novel, referring both to the sexuality of its two central characters and, more widely, to the ways America and the West are unsettled and questioned throughout—queered, in this sense. For example, early on McNulty tells of coming across an abandoned piano in the desert, commenting, "It was a might queer thing to see a black piano in the half-true desert" (Barry 2016a, 15–16). Or later, "There's no soldier don't have a queer little spot in his wretched heart for his enemy" (95).

6. See the conclusion for a more detailed philosophical discussion of love, drawing on the work of Jean-Luc Nancy in particular, where his notion of "shattered love" shares something of this idea of dispossession.

7. Kimberlé Crenshaw's work on intersectionality examines how "inter-secting patterns of racism and sexism" must be understood in order to highlight "the need to account for multiple grounds of identity when considering how the social world is constructed" (1991, 1243, 1245).

8. There is an interesting relationship between Barry's sense of kinship in the novel and Donna Haraway's *Staying with the Trouble*. She writes of the urgent need "to make kin in lines of inventive connection as a practice of learning to live and die well with each other in a thick present" (2016, 1).

9. In Lakota *wíŋkte* is the contraction of an older Lakota word *winyanktehca*, meaning "wants to be like a woman," suggesting male-bodied people who adopt the clothing, work, and mannerisms that tribal culture usually considers feminine. In contemporary Lakota culture, the term is more commonly associated with simply being gay. While historical accounts of their roles vary, many see the *winkte* as full members of the community and not marginalized at all. Other accounts hold the

winkte as sacred, occupying a liminal, third gender role in the culture, often fulfilling ceremonial roles that cannot be filled by either men or women.

10. See Flaherty 2015.

11. In *A Thousand Moons*, the sequel to *Days Without End*, Winona comments on her mother's sense of time as "a hoop or a circle, not a long string," and "if you walked far enough…you could find the people still living who had lived in the long ago" (Barry 2020, 31).

12. Barry commented to Gross, "I had just thought recently if you wanted a reality TV star for a president, why didn't you choose RuPaul? I think she would have been a much better choice, but let's leave that there" (Gross 2017).

Chapter 4. "The World in All Its Workings"

1. Alex Preston reviewing the book for the *Guardian* went further, suggesting "Berger's spirit-haunted 2005 novel, *Here Is Where We Meet*, is a clear influence" on Obreht (2019).

2. In this intersectionality, the novel shares much with my discussions of Barry in chapter 3.

3. In 1857 President James Buchanan appointed Beale to survey and build a thousand-mile wagon road from Fort Defiance, Arizona, to the Colorado River, on the border between Arizona and California. The survey experimented by using camels from the Camel Corps imported from Tunis as pack animals during this expedition and on another in 1858–59. His lead camel driver was Hi Jolly (Hadji Ali), a Greek Syrian convert to Islam. Hadji Ali is buried under a pyramid in Quartzsite, Arizona. He died in 1902.

4. Note the parallels to *Days Without End* on this point and the links between the Irish and Native people (see chapter 3).

5. David Shields reports that Donald Trump was told by his father "to be a 'king,' to be a 'killer'" (2018, 21). Crace has echoes of Trump throughout the novel.

6. Merrion Crace's initials suggest something of his assumed role as "master of ceremonies."

7. "I realized there would be no getting away from this narrative of land-grabbing, and boom and bust cycles, and range wars, all these tropes we've come to associate with the genre in modern times.…The first draft of the book was completed sometime in September of 2016, and shortly thereafter things changed. And I was surprised then to find myself editing the book while watching our country slip back into some of these patterns, and recognize the degree to which warring newspapers moved to prominence, and to see these age-old cycles being played out again in 2018, 2019" (Obreht in Farwell 2019).

8. Speaking of her first novel, *The Tiger's Wife*, Obreht commented on "the intersection of truth and myth; collective versus individual memory, and the general unreliability of both; the tension between individual, sometimes selfish and cruel impulse and the requirements imposed by a functioning society" (https://www.womensprizeforfiction.co.uk/reading-room/in-conversation-with/qa-with-tea-obreht).

9. On February 17, 2017, President Donald Trump declared on Twitter that the

New York Times, NBC News, ABC, CBS, and CNN were "fake news" and the "enemy of the people."

10. See Paul Greengrass's *News of the World* (2020) for a filmic treatment of these issues.

11. Nancy's work is relevant here and best explained in Christopher Fynsk's foreword, "Experiences of Finitude," in *The Inoperative Community*: "The death of the other calls the subject beyond itself and thus delivers it to its freedom. Freedom is necessarily *shared* (partage), and the experience of the other's mortality constitutes something like a condition of this sharing. Like love (itself inseparable from an experience of mortality), it calls the subject out and beyond itself, exposing it to alterity and to its freedom" (Nancy 1991, xv). "Love is known always singularly, though it is the knowledge of an encounter and a relation" (xviii). See the conclusion for more on these ideas of love.

Chapter 5. "A Land of Missing Things"

1. This seems to refer to "Two Tigers," a popular Mandarin nursery rhyme called "Liang Zhi Lao Hu." "Two little tigers, Two little tigers, (They) run fast, (They) run very fast, One has no eye [or: One has no ears], One has no tail, Very weird, Very weird."

2. As Zhang explained, her admiration for Ondaatje's novel *Divisadero* is because it "breaks rules and that's where the magic comes in—through the cracks and bends" (Winnette 2020). The same might be said of *How Much of These Hills Is Gold*.

3. Ba insists he was "born" in America. The book suggests he washed ashore with his dead parents.

4. Teacher Leigh seems to owe something to Toni Morrison's Schoolteacher in *Beloved* with his obsessive desire for measuring and defining others as a means of rationalizing racism. Zhang commented, "A key, inspirational book in my life is *Beloved* by Toni Morrison" (Jurczyk 2020). The word "monograph" carries within it the sense of "one-voiced" and so underpins the type of book he is writing. Zhang's novel is, therefore, "heterographic."

5. Zhang, like Diaz, Barry, and Obreht, is concerned with expanding the histories of the West as world histories.

6. Abraham and Torok, and psychoanalysis generally after Freud, consider that successful mourning operates at the level of introjection of the other. Derrida suggests paradoxical associations exist between introjection/incorporation. As Joan Kirkby puts it, "Incorporation acknowledges the other as other, while the so-called normal process of mourning (introjection) merely assimilates the other into the self in a kind of psychic plagiarism" (2006, 470).

7. For Derrida, "Introjection could be seen as an act of assimilation and consummation of the other, another kind of 'repetitive' death cycle, a refusal of the alterity and radical difference of the other. And this, for Derrida, implies an act of duplicity with respect to the other" (O'Connor 2011, 115).

8. Of course, adding to the secrets in the novel is the fact that Ma does not die after giving birth but rather leaves the family, never to be seen again.

9. The emphasis on wealth through gold links to Diaz's dark vision of Clangston's mines in *In the Distance*.

10. This is similar to Diaz's use of repetition and rhythm in the latter sections of *In the Distance*.

11. Judith Butler explains how frames are a "strategy of containment, selectively producing and enforcing what will count as reality" (2010, xiii). In *Gender Trouble*, Butler refers to the "compulsory frames…that police" gender (1990, 33).

12. Interiorization is, according to Derrida, the equivalent to introjection as described by Abraham and Torok (1988, 58).

13. Zhang commented: "What I wanted to do with this book was skewer the myth of the American dream, which states that there is equal and ample opportunity for everyone. And as a young person and as an immigrant myself, I believed very deeply in this idea, as my parents believed in it. And…as I got older…I realized how pernicious this myth is because the dark flipside is the assumption that if you don't make it, that reflects a personal moral failure rather than the systemic failure of a country that is racist and sexist and bigoted" (Simon 2020).

14. The photograph referred to is A. J. Russell's Promontory Summit, Utah, May 10, 1869. Often left out of the storytelling about the effort is the labor of an estimated fifteen to twenty thousand Chinese migrants who laid the tracks of the western half of the railroad. They are invisible in this famous image.

15. To cite the title of the French edition of Derrida's *The Work of Mourning*, "Chaque fois unique, la fin du monde," gives a stronger sense of how he views the process of death and mourning, that is, "each time unique or uniquely, the end of the world."

16. Writing in the face of the COVID-19 crisis in March 2020, Zhang commented about grief and writing, in words that echo Lucy at the end of the novel, grieving at the loss of her sister, Sam, returned to China, for her parents, and to her own life lost to the "writing" of others. "If you are grieving, then I give you permission to write in the best way you can—which is to say, to live" (2020a).

Chapter 6. To Remember Otherwise and Against

1. See Kirwan 2018; and Howe and Kirwan 2020. Kirwan argues it is a sign of their "cotemporal experiences of colonial rule" (Howe and Kirwan 2020, 23). See also Godin 2020.

2. Chadwick Allen maintains that "the trans-Indigenous names a productive set of methodologies for developing Indigenous literary studies that can move among and fully engage registers of inquiry, contextualization, interpretation, understanding, appreciation, and enjoyment marked not only as tribal, local, regional, or national, but also as hemispheric and oceanic, and as aspiring toward the global" (Lyons 2017, 240).

3. The *Guardian* newspaper in the United Kingdom has featured Kimmerer several times in recent years. See Cooke 2021; and Yeh 2020.

4. The line from the heading comes from Howe's poem "Post-Mortem" in *Evidence of Red* (2005, 95).

5. Howe told Squint, "Americans have trouble articulating Natives in the national narrative other than to say that we have vanished" (2010, 219).

6. Howe, like Haraway and Macfarlane, discusses the work of Lynn Margulis on symbiogenesis (see Howe 2013, 19–20; and Haraway 2016, 60, 188–89), claiming that her science "adopted a Choctawan way of looking at the world" (Howe 2013, 20).

7. Like the ending of *How Much of These Hills Is Gold*, Howe emphasizes the importance of alliances in her work. The Covenant Chain is the name given to the complex system of alliances between the Haudenosaunee (also known as the Six Nations and Iroquois League) and Anglo-American colonies originating in the early seventeenth century.

8. As Romero explains, "Howe's writing does not deny the importance of sovereign nation status to Native tribes, but it advocates a form of Native nationalism that allows for pluralities of experience, identity, and alliance, pluralities prohibited by groups like the Nazis and Ku Klux Klan. Through its focus on international alliances and identities, tribalography upholds Native sovereignty while resisting national separatism" (2014, 20–21).

9. The ambiguity of the exchange is such that the Indian may be "in her mind" or a spirit presence. As he says when quoting Shakespeare and the Bible to her, if what the doctors say is true and "I am all in your head," then "I know what you know" (Howe 2019, 70). The ambiguity adds to the text's surreal and oneiric quality.

10. In July 2020 Trump claimed to have done more for Black Americans than anyone with a "possible exception" of former president Abraham Lincoln (https://www.nbcnews.com/now/video/trump-says-he-has-done-more-for-black-people-than-anyone-with-possible-exception-of-lincoln-88141381811).

11. Gar Woman because these fish "feed at night / Sometimes eat their own eggs" (Howe 2019, 15), suggesting Mary's possible killing of her own children (see viii, in which she speculates that Mary suffered from Munchausen syndrome). Throughout, Savage Indian refers to the "fishy" smell surrounding Mary, suggesting both the idea of the Gar and her dubious and corrupt past.

12. Letter of John Pope to Henry H. Sibley, http://historymaking.org/textbook/items/show/255.

13. Howe also refers to Bakhtin's *The Dialogic Imagination*: "I sit with my dog-eared copy of *The Dialogic Imagination*" (2008, 328).

14. See Phillips 2020.

15. "I feel like it's where hope and realism meet…but while I was finishing the book, we were watching elders getting hit with rubber bullets on national TV while trying to pray for clean water. And then we are getting attacked by dogs. That just felt true to me at the time" (Orange in Shotten 2019). "Trump has been on the record many times saying really dumb things about Native people. And his favorite president is Andrew Jackson, the worst president for Native people. So it's not in the past. Trump is a representation of it not being in the past" (Orange in Goldstein 2019). Terese Marie Mailhot, a close friend of Orange's, wrote, "The age of Trumpism seems hell-bent on walking back progress to a time when white people enjoyed the benefit of even more brutal and explicit discrimination than they do today" (2018).

16. Recall Howe's fascination with Bakhtin's dialogism and, therefore, by implication, Orange's.

17. Orange told Mailhot, "I wanted to create a fast-moving vehicle to drive somebody to some brutal truth" (Mailhot and Orange 2018).

Chapter 7. "The Story and the Archive of the Story"

1. This episode is in the section "Westerns" and involves telling Border Patrol officers they are scriptwriters working on "a spaghetti western" (2019a, 130). Ironically, the officer turns out to be an expert on the genre!

2. Note the similarities with *How Much of These Hills Is Gold* (discussed in chapter 5), in particular ideas about mourning. As Joan Kirkby comments, "Certainly history has demonstrated that cultures that foreclose mourning have tended towards violence to others" (2006, 470).

3. Luiselli uses the word "Trumpland" in the coda to *Tell Me How It Ends* (2017, 101). The novel makes it clear that successive US administrations from Reagan to Obama have been keen on a border wall.

4. Like many of the writers discussed in this book, Luiselli is "worldly" in her background, too, born in Mexico City in 1983 and living in Costa Rica, Korea, South Africa, India, Spain, and the United States. She studied for a PhD in comparative literature at Columbia University.

5. Elsewhere in a description of Aaron Copland's *Appalachian Spring*, the phrase "programmatic composition" suggests a similarly controlled approach.

6. I borrow this idea once again from Glissant's *Poetics of Relation* (1997, 91–96) where *écho-monde* suggests the world of things resonating with one another, in patterns, "constituent (not conclusive) elements and its expressions" (94). In any place, no matter how small, there is a potential resonance or echo of all the other places of the world.

7. The idea of "foreignizing" comes from translation and intends "making it more complex and layered." It is "retaken by Walter Benjamin in his essay on translation" (Floyd 2019).

8. Benjamin calls this "the interlinear version" (1992, 82), and Homi Bhabha explained it more broadly as "the foreign element in the midst of the performance of cultural translation" (1994, 227).

9. The novel self-consciously employs references to Derrida, for example, when the mother explains her preparation for the trip: "I read and read, long sleepless nights reading about archive fevers, about rebuilding memory in diasporic narratives, about being lost in 'the ashes' of the archive" (2019a, 23). As with all the references to other writings in the novel, this relates to Luiselli's comment, "My books are like machines for thinking about other books" (Hodkinson 2015).

10. An archive can be private and public, since "it keeps, it puts in reserve, it saves" and is the "law of the house…of the house as place, domicile, family, lineage, or institution" (Derrida 1998, 7).

11. The idea of interruption connects Luiselli's approach with that of Diaz (see chapter 2) and to Jean-Luc Nancy's notion of the interruption of myth (see chapter 1).

12. In the novel she criticizes certain photographers and authors, namely, Robert Frank and Jack Kerouac, for "imposing a point of view" (2019a, 87), yet she and her husband are both guilty of this too.

13. The idea of "a dense, porous novel" appears in Luiselli's earlier novel *Faces in the Crowd* (2012, 28). Luiselli often mentions Benjamin in interviews, he appears in

the lists in *Lost Children Archive*, and he is a definite presence in her essays in *Sidewalks* in which *flanerie* is a central concern and practice.

14. In *An Archive of Feelings*, Ann Cvetkovich describes an "archive of feelings" as "an exploration of cultural texts as repositories of feelings and emotions, which are encoded not only in the content of the texts themselves but in the practices that surround their production and reception" (2003, 7).

15. "A horizontal novel, told vertically. A novel which has to be told from the outside in order to be read from within" is characteristic of Luiselli's *Faces in the Crowd* (2012, 61).

16. There are parallels here with Glissant's use of the storm or the volcanic eruption as a marker of something bubbling within the apparently ordered surface of things (in his case the Caribbean landscape). Here the quaking of the earth suggests a similar eruption.

17. Clearly, this refers to the Black Lives Matter campaigns started in 2013 as an online community to help combat anti-Black racism across the globe. See https://blacklivesmatter.com/.

18. *Elegies for Lost Children* is an invented book by Ella Camposanto, translated and partly based on the historical *Children's Crusade* and made from a series of quotations "recombined" (Luiselli 2019a, 143) from other writers whose works deal with "voyages, journeying, migrating." These include Conrad's *Heart of Darkness*, Eliot's *The Waste Land*, and Ezra Pound's "Canto I," itself an allusion to Homer's *Odyssey*. Together, they suggest an "analogy between migrating and descending into the underworld" (382). In other words, this novel within the novel is, like *Lost Children Archive*, an echo chamber of translations and dialogic voices. The imagined text is not geographically or temporally specific, although it has clear references to current migration in the Southwest, such as the children traveling on a "beastly" train ("La Bestia"). Such local and global concerns add to the sense of worldliness created in Luiselli's novel because this could happen anywhere at any time to anyone.

19. In her essay on Tombstone, Luiselli made the direct parallel between Indian history and the migration crisis: "the nineteenth-century narrative of the 'savage Indian' is not so different from that of the 'illegal immigrant' today" (2019b).

20. "Error" shares the same root as the word and concept "errance," discussed above and elsewhere in this book. Hence, the making of errors links to wandering and journeying, straying from a path and so on.

21. This relates to the father's preferred books: *The Cantos*, *The Waste Land*, *Heart of Darkness*, Kerouac's *On the Road*, Bolano's *2666*, and Golding's *Lord of the Flies* (Luiselli 2019b, 43).

22. Instrumentalism equates to "light pedagogic material, moralistic young-adult novels, boring art in general" (Luiselli 2019a, 79).

23. This is a device borrowed from Virginia Woolf's *Mrs. Dalloway* when Clarissa looks up at the airplane in the sky at the same time as several other characters. Luiselli comments on this in a 2015 interview: "An airplane appears in the sky when, in Regent's Park, an elderly woman is observing a younger woman. The narrator enters this elderly woman's mind as she thinks about the younger one, taking note of her gestures and demeanor, until the airplane interrupts her thoughts—and the

reader can almost see the airplane gliding across the page, its trajectory punctuated by an 'it' sprinkled here and there. The woman's thoughts then venture elsewhere, the narrator leaves her mind, follows the airplane up on the sky. Then, suddenly, the narrator, after just a semi colon, is no longer looking at the airplane, but at London *from* the airplane, and at the countryside beyond London, where there is a forest, where there is a snail. And Woolf continues in this way, weaving a kind of ultimate tapestry of landscape and human thought, intertwined" (Hodkinson 2015).

Chapter 8. Exit West

1. Naomi Klein argues persuasively that the rise of Donald Trump was all about "becoming the ultimate brand" and harnessing the support of neoliberal multinationals in a deregulated nation (2017, 15).

2. The portrayal of Marin shares much with "The Bridge" sections of William Gibson's *Virtual Light* (1993), in which the San Francisco–Oakland Bay Bridge is repurposed as a sheltering shantytown for the dispossessed, described as "an accretion of dreams," "amorphous, startlingly organic," a "patchwork carnival of scavenged surfaces," and "none of it done to any plan.…Not like a mall," whose inhabitants "looked to be as mixed a bunch as their building materials: all ages, races, colors" (58–59, 162–63). The bridge contrasts with the urban expanse of San Francisco, where transnational corporations are in the process of rebuilding the city with advanced technology to create "self-sufficient" skyscrapers.

3. In keeping with the scope of this book, Hamid's wider vision in the novel sees the danger of such nostalgic politics in the world: "Donald Trump says, 'Make America great again.' Brexit is taking back control to a time before the EU came. ISIS is going back to the Caliphate. Modi wants to take India back to an imagined pre-Muslim, pre-colonization Hindu utopia" (Chandler 2017).

4. Donald Trump was referred to as an autocrat in a similar sense to that used by Glissant. See Gessen 2020.

5. Nancy works through ideas in George Bataille's writing: "I can imagine a community with as loose a form as you will—even formless: the only condition is that an experience of moral freedom be shared in common, and not reduced to the flat, self-cancelling, self-denying meaning of particular freedom" (quoted in Nancy 1991, 21).

6. One of Cohen's images in *Darkened Cities* is of the San Francisco–Oakland Bay Bridge with the night sky taken in the Mojave Desert. It both seems to mirror Hamid's use of Marin in the novel and my comments on Gibson's *Virtual Light* above.

7. By "overworked" I echo Nancy's use of "unworked" in *The Inoperative Community* to indicate how community is not a fixed thing, but a more open process, or a spontaneous, "unworked" inclination to come together that has no object or purpose other than itself: "not in a work that would bring it to completion, even less in itself as work (family, people, church, nation, party, literature, philosophy), but in the unworking and as the unworking of all its works" (1991, 72). Notions of community (as nostalgic unity, for example) cannot, according to Nancy, be put in the service of, or assimilated as a founding principle for, a determinate politics or political projects (as in the case of nostalgic myths of community discussed in chapter 1 or Trump's MAGA "work" as a political project).

8. See Packer 2018. In employing Howe and Anzaldúa, I am reclaiming tribalism in a more positive light.

9. Anzaldúa explains *nos/otras* as *nos* (us) and *otras* (others) divided by a slash to show how the "majority" still maintains this separation (see 2000, 254). In the future, she argues, it may become *nosotras* by forging a hybrid consciousness, "bridging the extremes of our cultural realities" (255).

10. "Succinctly put, new tribalism refers to and promotes the ethnically diverse groups that coexist and work together with revolutionary democratic aims. A self that is open to being altered by the other—be it an emotion or another person—is a self with both poetic and queer qualities" (Núñez-Puente 2018, 52).

11. Gregory Cajete insists that the "ancient idea of relationship [found in Native sciences and worldviews] must be allowed to arise in our collective consciousness once again. In this perilous world of the twenty-first century, it may well be a matter of our collective survival" (2000, 105).

12. In *Culture and Imperialism*, Edward Said used a musical metaphor to express a similar approach to the revision of the cultural archive: "As we look back at the cultural archive, we begin to reread it not univocally but contrapuntally, with a simultaneous awareness both of the metropolitan history that is narrated and of those other histories against which (and together with which) the dominating discourse acts. In the counterpoint of Western classical music, various themes play off one another, with only a provisional privilege being given to any particular one; yet in the resulting polyphony there is concert and order, an organized interplay that derives from the themes, not from a rigorous melodic or formal principle outside the work" (1994, 59–60).

13. Nancy's ideas often echo those of Glissant. He writes of place like the idea of the West in this book, where its "proper name" is unimportant or too containing, full of assumptions, and he prefers the melee, "a mixture of syllables stirred on the brink of a semantic identity that is both gently and obstinately deferred" (2000, 151, 146). Only one critic to my knowledge has linked Glissant and Nancy; see Kaiser 2014.

14. See Pamela Sue Anderson's development of Judith Butler's work on the "new imaginary" linked to "relational ontology" and the rethinking of myths of vulnerability as "a first step towards transforming our reciprocal affections—of either violence, and fear due to that violence, or love, and confidence in that love" (P. Anderson, Lovibond, and Moore 2020, 10).

15. Glissant redefines utopia as "bringing together…all the beauties, all the suffering and all the values of the world…a keen sense of the poetics of Relation" (2020b, 110).

16. According to Iain Chambers, "Unfolding the artistic configuration of time and space, of our being and becoming, allows us to harvest the essential truth of the complex ambivalence of a historical constellation that does not merely mirror our passage. It is the oblique gaze, sustained in the excessive and *errant* languages of art, that also allows us to travel beyond the rational conclusions of the human and social sciences" (2014, 19, 11–21; emphasis added).

17. Glissant too talks of interdependence, differentiating it from a "meaningless melting pot…a mush of identities" (2020b, 112).

18. Glissant also uses the term "Chaos-World" to suggest the unpredictable, varied, and turbulent nature of the "Whole-World," although it does not signify disorder as much as potential, as in chaos theory with its insistence upon underlying patterns, interconnectedness, constant feedback loops, repetition, self-similarity, fractals, and self-organization. It is the science of surprises, of the nonlinear and the unpredictable. Karen Barad states, "To be entangled is not simply to be intertwined with another, as in the joining of separate entities, but to lack an independent, self-contained existence. Existence is not an individual affair. Individuals do not preexist their interactions; rather, individuals emerge through and as part of their entangled intra-relating" (2007, ix).

19. "Rather, Glissant conceptualizes the Tout-monde as interconnected layers. The correspondence goes from a detail in the individual's reading of landscape to another detail in the collectively shared landscape, to other details in other landscapes in the world. There is never any transcendent grasping of the entire totality, only interrelations and interfaces between here and there" (Christina Kullberg in Bydler and Sjöholm 2014, 59).

20. See Roberts and Stephens 2017.

21. Mathew Abbott explains that "shattering" is an imperfect rendering of the French *éclater*, which possesses further connotations of bursting, brilliance, shining, and sparking. For Nancy, this shattering "has to be understood as originary: being is always already shattered; to put it a little awkwardly, we might say that the shard precedes the break....The fragments or shards in play here are not pieces of some larger puzzle; rather they are absolutely fragmentary, and do not refer back to some prior whole. Being's multiplicity is not the result of its lacking unity; it is absolute in its plurality, completely incomplete. Existence is 'infinitely finite'" (2011, 149).

22. Love for Nancy is a promise, but one uncompleted, and it is this that is its attraction: "Thus love is at once the promise of completion—but a promise always disappearing—and the threat of decomposition, always imminent. An entire modern eroticism and an entire modern spirituality, those of romantic love, of savage love, of transgressive love, are determined according to this dialectic…the excess or the lack of this completion, which is represented as the truth of love" (1991, 93). Pamela Sue Anderson asserts that vulnerability is also about "love's capability," or what she calls "openness to mutual affection" (P. Anderson, Lovibond, and Moore 2020, 19).

23. Anderson, following Butler, writes, "'We' are both created and dispossessed by our relations to others" (P. Anderson, Lovibond, and Moore 2020, 12).

24. "Being singular plural means the essence of Being is only as coessence" (Nancy 2000, 30), and so we exist with others or not at all.

25. In *Being Singular Plural*, Nancy states, "From now on, we, we others are charged with this truth—it is more ours than ever—the truth of this paradoxical 'first-person plural' which makes sense of the world as the spacing and intertwining of so many worlds (earths, skies, histories) that there is a taking place of meaning, or the crossing through [passages] of presence" (2000, 5).

References

Abbott, Mathew. 2011. "On Not Loving Everyone: Comments on Jean-Luc Nancy's 'L'amour en éclats [Shattered love].'" *Glossator* 5:139–62. https://solutioperfecta .files.wordpress.com/2011/10/g5-ma.pdf.

Abraham, Nicolas, and Maria Torok. 1994. *The Shell and the Kernel*. Edited and translated by Nicholas T. Rand. Vol. 1. Chicago: University of Chicago Press.

Allen, Chadwick. 2017. "Productive Tensions: Trans/national, Trans-/Indigenous." In *The World, the Text, and the Indian: Global Dimensions of Native American Literature*, edited by Scott R. Lyons. Albany: SUNY Press.

Allen, Paula Gunn. 1992. *The Sacred Hoop: Recovering the Feminine in American Indian Traditions*. Boston: Beacon Press.

Alter, Cathy. 2018. "David Shields Interview." November 27, 2018. http://www .washingtonindependentreviewofbooks.com/index.php/features/an-interview -with-david-shields.

Anderson, Ben, and Paul Harrison, eds. 2010. *Taking-Place: Non-representational Theories and Geography*. Farnham: Ashgate.

Anderson, Pamela Sue, Sabina Lovibond, and A. W. Moore. 2020. "Towards a New Philosophical Imaginary." *Angelaki* 25:1–2, 8–22.

Anzaldúa, Gloria. 2000. *Interviews / Entrevistas*. Edited by AnaLouise Keating. London: Routledge.

———. 2015. *Light in the Dark / Luz en lo oscuro: Rewriting Identity, Spirituality, Reality*. Durham, NC: Duke University Press.

Anzaldúa, Gloria, and AnaLouise Keating, eds. 2002. *This Bridge We Call Home: Radical Visions for Transformation*. London: Routledge.

Arola, Adam. 2007. "A Larger Scheme of Life: Deloria on Essence and Science (in Dialogue with Continental Philosophy)." *American Philosophical Association* 7 (1): 1–11.

———. 2011. "Native American Philosophy." In the *Oxford Handbook of World Philosophy*, edited by William Edelglass and Jay L. Garfield, 554–65. Oxford: Oxford University Press.

Augé, Marc. 1995. *Non-Places: Introduction to an Anthropology of Supermodernity*. London: Verso.

Bady, Aaron. 2017. "Subverting the Western: A Conversation with Hernan Diaz." *Nation*, November 20, 2017. http://www.thenation.com/article/subverting-the -Western-a-conversation-with-hernan-diaz/.

Bahng, Aimee. 2018. *Migrant Futures: Decolonizing Speculation in Financial Times*. Durham, NC: Duke University Press.

Bakhtin, Mikhail. 1990. *The Dialogic Imagination: Four Essays*. Austin: University of Texas Press.

———. 1997. *Problems in Dostoevsky's Poetics*. Minneapolis: University of Minnesota Press.

Baldwin, James. 1981. *The Fire Next Time*. Harmondsworth: Penguin.

Barad, Karen. 2007. *Meeting the Universe Halfway: Quantum Physics and the Entanglement of Matter and Meaning*. Durham, NC: Duke University Press.

Barenbaum, Rachel. 2019. "Ghosts Are Always There: An Interview with Téa Obreht on *Inland*." *Los Angeles Book Review*, October 28, 2019. https://lareviewofbooks.org/article/ghosts-are-always-there-an-interview-with-tea-obreht-on-inland/.

Barry, Sebastian. 2016a. *Days Without End*. London: Faber and Faber.

———. 2016b. "You Get Imprisoned in a Kind of Style, I Could Feel It Leaning on Me." October 21, 2016. https://www.theguardian.com/books/2016/oct/21/sebastian-barry-interview-days-without-end.

———. 2017a. "RTE Podcast with Sean O'Rourke." http://www.rte.ie/radio/utils/radioplayer/rteradioweb.html#!rii=b9%5F21074956%5F15036%5F20%2D10%2D2016%5F.

———. 2017b. "Sebastian Barry on His Costa-Winning Novel *Days Without End*—Books Podcast." February 3, 2017. https://www.theguardian.com/books/audio/2017/feb/03/sebastian-barry-on-his-costa-winning-novel-days-without-end-books-podcast.

———. 2020. *A Thousand Moons*. London: Faber and Faber.

Barthes, Roland. 1976. *Mythologies*. London: Paladin.

———. 2002. *A Lover's Discourse: Fragments*. London: Vintage.

Bateman, Geoffrey W. 2016. "Queer Wests: An Introduction." Special issue, *Western American Literature* 51 (2): 129–41.

Belcourt, Billy-Ray. 2019. *This Wound Is a World*. Minneapolis: University of Minnesota Press.

Benjamin, Walter. 1992. *Illuminations*. London: Fontana.

———. 1997. *One-Way Street*. London: Verso.

———. 1999. *The Arcades Project*. Cambridge, MA: Harvard University Press.

Berenson, Tessa. 2016. "John Wayne's Daughter Endorses Trump." *Time*, January 19, 2016. https://time.com/4185378/donald-trump-john-wayne-iowa/.

Berger, John. 1972. *Ways of Seeing*. Harmondsworth: Penguin.

———. 2005. *Here Is Where We Meet*. London: Bloomsbury.

Bergland, Rénee L. 2000. *The National Uncanny: Indian Ghosts and American Subjects*. Hanover, NH: Dartmouth University Press.

Bhabha, Homi. 1994. *The Location of Culture*. London: Routledge.

Biro, Sasha L. 2019. "Disrupting Symmetry: Jean-Luc Nancy and Luce Irigaray on Myth and the Violence of Representation." *Eidos: A Journal for Philosophy of Culture* 3 (2 [8]): 62–74.

Bolling, Eric. 2016. "Donald Trump and the Resurrection of the American Cowboy." *Washington Post*, June 28, 2016. https://www.washingtontimes.com/news/2016/jun/28/donald-trump-and-resurrection-american-cowboy/.

Bowden, Charles. 1998. *Juarez: The Laboratory of Our Future*. London: Aperture.

Breen, Claire. 2019. "Valeria Luiselli Tackles One of the Country's Largest Debates in Her Latest Novel—All While Defying Narrative Convention." April 9, 2019. https://www.thelily.com/valeria-luiselli-tackles-one-of-the-countrys-largest-debates-in-her-latest-novel-all-while-defying-narrative-convention/.

Britton, Celia M. 2009. "Globalization and Political Action in the Work of Édouard Glissant." *Small Axe* 13 (3 [30]): 1–11.

Brook, Pete. 2014. "What Cities Would Look Like If Lit Only by the Stars." *Wired*, November 13, 2014. https://www.wired.com/2014/11/thierry-cohen-darkened-cities/.

Broughton, Lee, ed. 2016. *Critical Perspectives on the Western*. London: Rowman & Littlefield International.

Broun, Elizabeth. 1991. Foreword to *The West as America: Reinterpreting Images of the Frontier, 1820–1920*, edited by William H. Truettner. Washington, DC: National Museum of American Art.

Buck-Morss, Susan. 1993. *The Dialectics of Seeing: Walter Benjamin and the Arcades Project*. Cambridge, MA: MIT Press.

Butler, Judith. 1990. *Gender Trouble*. London: Routledge.

———. 1993. *Bodies That Matter*. London: Routledge.

———. 2004. *Precarious Life: The Powers of Mourning and Violence*. London: Verso.

———. 2010. *Frames of War: When Is Life Grievable?* London: Verso.

———. 2020. *The Force of Nonviolence*. London: Verso.

Butler, Judith, and Athena Athanasiou. 2013. *Dispossession: The Performative in the Political*. London: Verso.

Butler, Judith, and Gayatri Chakravorty Spivak. 2010. *Who Sings the Nation State? Language, Politics, Belonging*. London and New York: Seagull Books.

Bydler, Charlotte, and Cecilia Sjöholm, eds. 2014. *Regionality/Mondiality: Perspectives on Art, Aesthetics and Globalization*. Huddinge: Södertörn Studies in Art History and Aesthetics.

Byrd, Jodi. 2011. *The Transit of Empire: Indigenous Critiques of Colonialism*. Minneapolis: University of Minnesota Press.

———. 2014. "Tribal 2.0: Digital Natives, Political Players, and the Power of Stories." In "Tribalography." Special issue, *Studies in American Indian Literatures* 26 (2): 55–64.

Cajete, Gregory. 2000. *Native Science: Natural Laws of Interdependence*. Santa Fe, NM: Clear Light.

Campbell, Neil. 2000. *The Cultures of the American New West*. Edinburgh: Edinburgh University Press.

———. 2008. *The Rhizomatic West: Representing the American West in a Transnational, Global, Media Age*. Lincoln: University of Nebraska Press.

———. 2016. *Affective Critical Regionality*. London: Rowman & Littlefield International.

———. 2020. "'New Blood Time Now': The American West in Marlon James' *A Brief History of Seven Killings*." In *The New American West in Literature and the Arts: A Journey Across Boundaries*, ed. Amaia Ibarraran-Bigalondo, 103–19. London: Routledge.

———. 2022. "Into the Errant West: Carys Davies's *West*." In *The Literary Western in the Global Imagination*, edited by Christopher Conway, Marek Paryż, and David Rio. Leiden: Brill.

Cantú, Francisco. 2018. *The Line Becomes a River*. London: Bodley Head.

———. 2019. "Téa Obreht Reimagines the Western." *New Yorker*, August 12, 2019. https://www.newyorker.com/magazine/2019/08/19/tea-obreht-reimagines-the -western.

Carter, Josephine. 2020. "How Far Are We Prepared to Go? Mohsin Hamid's *Exit West* and the Refuge Crisis." *Textual Practice* 35 (4): 619–38. tandfonline.com/doi/full/10.1080/0950236X.2020.1745877.

Cary, Alice. 2020. "Interview with C Pam Zhang." April 2020. https://bookpage.com/interviews/25002-c-pam-zhang-fiction#.XrwFDmgzY2w.

Chambers, Iain. 1994. *Migrancy, Culture, Identity*. London: Routledge.

———. 1996. "Waiting on the End of the World." In *Stuart Hall: Critical Dialogues in Cultural Studies*, edited by D. Morley and K. Chen. London: Routledge.

———. 2014. "A Fluid Archive." CIDOB (April 2014). https://www.cidob.org/en/articulos/monografias/transculturality_and_interdisciplinarity/a_fluid_archive.

———. 2018. *Location, Borders and Beyond: Thinking with Postcolonial Art*. N.p.: Worlding the Word.

Chandler, Caitlin L. 2017. "We Are All Refugees: A Conversation with Mohsin Hamid." *Nation*, October 30, 2017. https://www.thenation.com/article/archive/we-are-all-refugees-a-conversation-with-mohsin-hamid/.

Chang, Alexandra. 2020. "Can Two Chinese American Orphans Find Home in the Wild West?" April 7, 2020. https://electricliterature.com/can-two-chinese-american-orphans-find-home-in-the-wild-west/.

Chapman, Ryan. 2019. "'Nobody in This Book Is Going to Catch a Break': Téa Obreht on *Inland*." August 2019. https://longreads.com/2019/08/28/tea-obreht-on-inland/.

Cheah, Pheng. 2014. "World Against Globe: Toward a Normative Conception of World Literature." *New Literary History* 45, (3): 303–29.

———. 2016. *What Is a World? On Postcolonial Literature as World Literature*. Durham, NC: Duke University Press.

Cixous, Helene. 1981. "The Laugh of the Medusa." In *New French Feminisms: An Anthology*, edited by Elaine Marks and Isabelle de Courtivron, 245–64. London: Harvester Wheatsheaf.

Clifford, James. 1986. "Introduction: Partial Truths." In *Writing Culture: The Poetics and Politics of Ethnography*, edited by James Clifford and George Marcus. Berkeley: University of California Press.

———. 1988. *The Predicament of Culture: Twentieth-Century Ethnography, Literature, and Art*. Cambridge, MA: Harvard University Press.

Comer, Krista. 2007. "West." In *Keywords for American Cultural Studies*, edited by Bruce Burgett and Glenn Hendler. https://keywords.nyupress.org/american-cultural-studies/essay/west/.

———. 2019. "Thinking Otherwise Across Global Wests: Issues of Mobility and Feminist Critical Regionalism." *Occasion: Interdisciplinary Studies in the Humanities* 10 (1): 1–18. https://arcade.stanford.edu/occasion/thinking-otherwise-across-global-wests-issues-mobility-and-feminist-critical-regionalism.

Cooke, Rachel. 2021. "Robin Wall Kimmerer: 'Mosses Are a Model of How We Might Live.'" *Guardian*, June 19, 2021. https://www.theguardian.com/science/2021/jun/19/robin-wall-kimmerer-gathering-moss-climate-crisis-interview.

Coulthard, Glen, and Leanne Betasamosake Simpson. 2016. "Grounded Normativity/Place-Based Solidarity." *American Quarterly* 68 (2): 249–55.

Crenshaw, Kimberlé. 1991. "Mapping the Margins: Intersectionality, Identity Politics, and Violence Against Women of Color." *Stanford Law Review* 43 (6): 1241–99.

Cumings, Bruce. 2009. *Dominion from Sea to Sea: Pacific Ascendancy and American Power*. New Haven, CT: Yale University Press.

Curtis, Adam. 2016. *HyperNormalisation*. BBC Films.

Cvetkovich, Ann. 2003. *An Archive of Feelings: Trauma, Sexuality, and Lesbian Public Cultures*. Durham, NC: Duke University Press.

Davies, Carys. 2017. "Crossing Borders." https://granta.com/crossing-borders/.

———. 2018. *West*. London: Granta.

Davis, Colin. 2005. "État présent: Hauntology, Spectres and Phantoms." *French Studies* 59 (3): 373–79.

Davis, Mike. 1998. *Ecology of Fear: Los Angeles and the Imagination of Disaster*. New York: Metropolitan Books.

de Certeau, Michel. 1988. *The Writing of History*. New York: Columbia University Press.

Deckard, Sharae. 2012. "Peripheral Realism, Millennial Capitalism, and Roberto Bolano's 2666." *Modern Language Quarterly* 73 (3): 351–72.

Deleuze, Gilles. 1989. *Cinema 2*. London: Athlone Press.

Deleuze, Gilles, and Felix Guattari. 1986. *Kafka: Toward a Minor Literature*. Minneapolis: University of Minnesota Press.

———. 1996. *A Thousand Plateaus*. London: Athlone Press.

Deleuze, Gilles, and Claire Parnet. 1987. *Dialogues II*. London: Athlone Press.

Deloria, Vine. 1999. *Spirit & Reason: The Vine Deloria, Jr. Reader*. Golden, CO: Fulcrum.

de Man, Paul. 2002. *The Resistance to Theory*. Minneapolis: University of Minnesota Press.

Derrida, Jacques. 1986a. "*Fors*: The Anglish Words of Nicolas Abraham and Maria Torok." In *The Wolf Man's Magic Word: A Cryptonomy*, edited by Nicolas Abraham and Maria Torok. Minneapolis: University of Minnesota Press.

———. 1986b. *MEMOIRES for Paul de Man*. New York: Columbia University Press.

———. 1988. *The Ear of the Other*. Lincoln: University of Nebraska Press.

———. 1994. *Specters of Marx: The State of Debt, the Work of Mourning and the New International*. London: Routledge.

———. 1997. *The Politics of Friendship*. New York: Verso.

———. 1998. *Archive Fever: A Freudian Impression*. Chicago: University of Chicago Press.

———. 2001. *The Work of Mourning*. Chicago: University of Chicago Press.

Devisch, Ignaas. 2000. "A Trembling Voice in the Desert: Jean-Luc Nancy's Rethinking of the Space of the Political." *Cultural Values* 4 (2): 239–56.

Diawara, Manthia. 2011. "Conversation with Édouard Glissant." *Journal of Contemporary African Art* 28 (Spring): 4–19.

Diaz, Hernan. 2017a. "Book Notes: Hernan Diaz's *In the Distance*." *Largehearted Boy* (blog), October 23, 2017. http://www.largeheartedboy.com/blog/archive/2017/10/book_notes_hern.html.

———. 2017b. "Great Artists Steal: *In the Distance* by Hernan Diaz." *Fiction Advocate*, October 12, 2017. https://www.fictionadvocate.com/2017/10/12/great-artists-steal-in-the-distance-by-hernan-diaz/.

———. 2017c. *In the Distance*. London: Daunt Books.

Doerfler, Jill. 2009. "An Anishinaabe Tribalography: Investigating and Interweaving Conceptions of Identity During the 1910s on the White Earth Reservation." *American Indian Quarterly* 33 (3): 295–324.

———. 2013. "Radical Migrations through Anishinaabewaki Spirit Island." Interview. http://midwestcompass.org/wp-content/uploads/2013/01/Jill-Doerfler.pdf.

———. 2014. "Making It Work: A Model of Tribalography as Methodology." In "Tribalography." Special issue, *Studies in American Indian Literatures* 26 (2): 65–74.

Drabinski, John. 2019. "Sites of Relation and 'Tout-monde': Reflections on Glissant's Late Work." *Angelaki* 24 (3): 157–72.

Dubow, Jessica. 2007. "Case Interrupted: Benjamin, Sebald, and the Dialectical Image." *Critical Inquiry* 33 (Summer): 820–36.

Edwards, J. A. 2018. "Make America Great Again: Donald Trump and Redefining the U.S. Role in the World." *Communication Quarterly* 66 (2): 176–95.

Elam, J. Daniel. 2018. "'The Temporal Order of Modernity Has Changed': A Conversation with Amitav Ghosh." *Boundary 2* 45 (2): 243–52.

Emmons, David M. 2010. *Beyond the American Pale: The Irish in the West, 1845–1910*. Norman: University of Oklahoma Press.

Etter, Sarah Rose. 2020. "Fool's Gold: C Pam Zhang Interviewed." *Bomb Magazine*, April 16, 2020. http://bombmagazine.org/articles/c-pam-zhang/.

Evans, Kate. 2017. Interview with Sebastian Barry, Australian Radio (ABC), January 22, 2017. http://www.abc.net.au/radionational/programs/booksplus/sebastian-barrys -new-novel-days-without-end/8115364.

Farge, Arlette. 1989. *The Allure of the Archive*. New Haven, CT: Yale University Press.

Farwell, Eric. 2019. "Who Gets to Reinvent Themselves in the West?" *Electric Lit*, August 22, 2019. https://electricliterature.com/who-gets-to-freedom-to-reinvent -themselves-in-the-west/.

Fazzino, Jimmy. 2016. *World Beats: Beat Generation Writing and the Worlding of U.S. Literature*. Hanover, NH: Dartmouth College Press.

Flaherty, E. 2015. "Rundale and 19th Century Irish Settlement: System, Space, and Genealogy." *Irish Geography* 48 (2): 3–38.

Floyd, E. P. 2019. "Telling the Story of Now: A Conversation with Valeria Luiselli." February 15, 2019. https://therumpus.net/2019/02/the-rumpus-interview-with -valeria-luiselli-2/.

Friedman, Susan Stanford. 2018. *Planetary Modernisms: Provocations on Modernity Across Time*. New York: Columbia University Press.

Gates, Marlena. 2018. "Tommy Orange Gives Voice to Urban Native Americans." https://electricliterature.com/tommy-orange-gives-voice-to-urban-native -americans/.

Gessen, Masha. *Surviving Autocracy*. New York: Riverhead Books, 2020.

Ghanayem, Eman, and Rebecca Macklin. 2019. "Indigenous Narratives: Global Forces in Motion." *Transmotion* 5 (1): 1–10.

Ghosh, Amitav. 2016. *The Great Derangement: Climate Change and the Unthinkable*. Chicago: Chicago University Press.

Gibson, William. 1993. *Virtual Light*. New York: Viking.

Giles, Paul. 2013. *Antipodean America: Australasia and the Constitution of U.S. Literature*. Oxford: Oxford University Press.

Gilloch, Graeme. 1997. *Myth and Metropolis: Walter Benjamin and the City*. Oxford: Polity Press.

Giroux, Henry A. 2007. "Democracy's Promise and the Politics of Worldliness in the Age of Terror." *CLCWeb: Comparative Literature and Culture* 9 (1). https://docs.lib .purdue.edu/cgi/viewcontent.cgi?article=1016&context=clcweb.

Glissant, Édouard. 1996a. *Caribbean Discourse*. Charlottesville: University Press of Virginia.

———. 1996b. *Faulkner, Mississippi*. Chicago: University of Chicago Press.

———. 1997. *Poetics of Relation*. Ann Arbor: University of Michigan Press.

———. 2002. "The Unforeseeable Diversity of the World." In *Beyond Dichotomies: Histories, Identities, Cultures, and the Challenge of Globalization*, edited by Elisabeth Mudimbe-Boyi, 287–95. Albany: SUNY Press.

———. 2020a. *The Baton Rouge Interviews with Alexandre Leupin*. Liverpool: Liverpool University Press.

———. 2020b. *Introduction to a Poetics of Diversity*. Liverpool: Liverpool University Press.

———. 2020c. *Treatise on the Whole-World*. Liverpool: Liverpool University Press.

Godin, Melissa. 2020. "Irish Donors Are Helping a Native American Tribe Face the Coronavirus Crisis: Here's the Historical Reason Why." *Time*, May 8, 2020. https:// time.com/5833592/native-american-irish-famine/.

Goldstein, Jessica. 2019. "Native Novelist Tommy Orange Talks 'Straight-Up Facts About This Country That People Try to Ignore.'" February 7, 2019. https://archive .thinkprogress.org/native-novelist-tommy-orange-talks-straight-up-facts-about -this-country-that-people-try-to-ignore-3d32f031a038/.

Gorenberg, Gershom. 2016. "Gunslinger Trump: 'Saving America' by Going Back to the Wild West." *Haaretz*, June 23, 2016. https://www.haaretz.com/opinion /.premium-saving-america-by-going-back-to-the-wild-west-1.5400146.

Grandin, Greg. 2019. *The End of the Myth: From Frontier to the Border Wall in the Mind of America*. New York: Metropolitan Books.

Greenblatt, Stephen. 2001. "Racial Memory and Literary History." *PMLA* 116 (1): 48–63.

Greengrass, Martha. 2019. "The Waterstones Interview: Téa Obreht on *Inland*." August 8, 2019. https://www.waterstones.com/blog/the-waterstones-interview-tea -obreht-on-inland.

Gross, Terry. 2017. "An Irish Immigrant Fights on the Great Plains in *Days Without End*." NPR, February 20, 2017. https://www.npr.org/2017/02/20/515806702/an-irish -immigrant-fights-on-the-great-plains-in-days-without-end?t=1581414598138&t =1585734871798.

Haas, Lidija. 2019. "New Books." *Harper's Magazine*, February 2019. https://harpers .org/archive/2019/02/new-books-february-2019-how-to-hide-an-empire-immer wahr-lost-children-archive-valeria-luiselli-territory-of-light-tsushima/.

Hall, Stuart. 1992. "The West and the Rest." In *Formations of Modernity*, edited by S. Hall and B. Gieben. Cambridge: Polity Press.

———. 1995. "New Cultures for Old." In *Place in the World*, edited by Doreen Massey and Pat Jess, 175–213. Oxford: Open University Press.

Hamid, Mohsin. 2017. *Exit West*. London: Penguin.

———. 2018a. "Author Mohsin Hamid Talks Influence, Optimism and Magical Realism." *Nashville Scene*, April 5, 2018. https://www.nashvillescene.com/arts-culture/books/article/20999297/exit-west-author-mohsin-hamid-talks-influence-optimism-and-magical-realism.

———. 2018b. "Writing Fiction Is a Form of Travel: Mohsin Hamid on *Exit West*, Migration, Empathy and a Certain Fantastic Fox." *Five Dials* (43): 4–13. https://fivedials.com/interviews/writing-fiction-is-a-form-of-travel-mohsin-hamid-exit-west-interview/.

Hanson, Victor Davis. 2018. "Donald Trump, Tragic Hero." *National Review*, April 12, 2018. https://www.nationalreview.com/2018/04/donald-trump-tragic-hero/.

Haraway, Donna. 2008. "Companion Species, Mis-recognition, and Queer Worlding." In *Queering the Non/Human*, edited by N. Giffney and M. J. Hird, xxiii–xxvi. London: Routledge.

———. 2016. *Staying with the Trouble: Making Kin in the Chthulucene*. Durham, NC: Duke University Press.

Harvey, David. 2003. *The New Imperialism*. Oxford: Oxford University Press.

Hayot, Eric. 2012. *On Literary Worlds*. Oxford: Oxford University Press.

Heidegger, Martin. 1975. "The Origins of the Work of Art." In *Poetry, Language, Thought*. New York: Harper Colophon.

———. 2013. *The Question Concerning Technology, and Other Essays*. New York: Harper Perennial.

Higgins, MaryEllen, Rita Keresztesi, and Dayna Oscherwitz, eds. 2015. *The Western in the Global South*. London: Routledge.

Hodkinson, Ted. 2015. "Valeria Luiselli: 'A Writer Is a Social Climber.'" *LitHub*, April 29, 2015. https://lithub.com/valeria-luiselli/.

Holmes, Oliver Wendell. 1859. "The Stereoscope and the Stereograph." *Atlantic*, June 1859. https://www.theatlantic.com/magazine/archive/1859/06/the-stereoscope-and-the-stereograph/303361/.

Howe, LeAnne. 1999. "Tribalography: The Power of Native Stories." *Journal of Dramatic Theory and Criticism*: 117–26.

———. 2005. *Evidence of Red: Poems and Prose*. Cambridge: Salt.

———. 2008. "Blind Bread and Business of Theory Making." In *Reasoning Together: The Native Critics*, edited by Craig S. Womack, Daniel Heath Justice, and Christopher B. Teuton. Norman: University of Oklahoma Press.

———. 2013. *Choctalking on Other Realities*. San Francisco: Aunt Lute Books.

———. 2019. *Savage Conversations*. Minneapolis: Coffee House Press.

Howe, LeAnne, and Padraig Kirwan, eds. 2020. *Famine Pots: The Choctaw-Irish Gift Exchange 1847–Present*. East Lansing: Michigan State University Press.

Hughey, Jesse. 2019. "Author Interview: Tommy Orange." July 24, 2019. https://www.cowboysindians.com/2019/07/author-interview-tommy-orange/.

Hunt, Alex. 2011. "Postcolonial West." In *A Companion to the Literature and Culture of the American West*, edited by Nicolas Witschi, 229–43. Chichester: Wiley-Blackwell.

Ignatiev, Noel. 1995. *How the Irish Became White*. London: Routledge.

Irving, Washington. 1976 [1836]. *Astoria*. Boston: Twayne.

Johnson, Susan Lee. 2000. *Roaring Camp: The Social World of the California Gold Rush*. New York: W. W. Norton.

Jurczyk, Eva. 2020. "Panning for Gold: A Conversation with C Pam Zhang." April 8, 2020. https://therumpus.net/2020/04/the-rumpus-interview-with-c-pam-zhang/.

Kaiser, Birgit Mara. 2014. "Worlding CompLit: Diffractive Reading with Barad, Glissant and Nancy." *Parallax* 20 (3): 274–87.

Kim, Hyunjin. 2017. "A Thousand Asian Tigers: Contested Modernity and the Image of History." "2 or 3 Tigers Exhibition." April 21–July 3, 2017. https://www.hkw.de/media/texte/pdf/2017_2/203tiger/170523_203Tiger_pdf_Hyunjin_Kim_press.pdf.

Kimmerer, Robin Wall. 2013. *Braiding Sweetgrass: Indigenous Wisdom, Scientific Knowledge, and the Teachings of Plants*. Minneapolis: Milkweed Editions.

Kirkby, Joan. 2006. "'Remembrance of the Future': Derrida on Mourning." *Social Semiotics* 16 (3): 461–72.

Kirwan, Padraig. 2016. "Choctaw Tales: An Interview with LeAnne Howe." *Women: A Cultural Review* 27 (3): 265–79.

———. 2018. "How a Small American Indian Tribe Came to Give an Incredible Gift to Irish Famine Sufferers." *Conversation*, August 23, 2018. https://theconversation.com/how-a-small-american-indian-tribe-came-to-give-an-incredible-gift-to-irish-famine-sufferers-98742.

Klein, Naomi. 2017. *No Is Not Enough*. London: Allen Lane.

Kollin, Susan. 2001. *Nature's State: Imagining Alaska as the Frontier*. Chapel Hill: University of North Carolina Press.

———. 2011. "The Global West: Temporality, Spatial Politics, and Literary Production." In *A Companion to the Literature and Culture of the American West*, edited by Nicolas Witschi, 514–27. Chichester: Wiley-Blackwell.

———. 2015a. *Captivating Westerns: The Middle East in the American West*. Lincoln: University of Nebraska Press.

———. 2015b. "Introduction: Historicizing the American Literary West." In *A History of Western American Literature*, edited by Susan Kollin. New York: Cambridge University Press.

Korpez, Esra Coker. 2020. "*Exit West* to a Borderless Frontier." In *The New American West in Literature and the Arts*, edited by Amaia Ibarraran-Bigalondo, 161–76. London: Routledge.

Krivokapić, Marija. 2019. "Traveling for Reciprocity: LeAnne Howe's *Choctalking on Other Realities*." *Neohelicon* 46:521–41.

Lahti, Janne. 2019. *The American West and the World: Transnational and Comparative Perspectives*. London: Routledge.

Lamont, Victoria. 2016. *Westerns: A Women's History*. Lincoln: University of Nebraska Press.

Lapointe, Annette. 2019. Review of *Savage Conversations*, by LeAnne Howe. *New York Journal of Books*. https://www.nyjournalofbooks.com/book-review/savage-conversations.

Latour, Bruno. 2007. *Reassembling the Social: An Introduction to Actor-Network-Theory*. Oxford: Oxford University Press.

———. 2010. "An Attempt at a Compositionist Manifesto." *New Literary History* 41 (3): 471–90.

———. 2017. *Facing Gaia: Eight Lectures on the New Climatic Regime*. Cambridge: Polity Press.

———. 2018. *Down to Earth: Politics in the New Climactic Regime*. Cambridge: Polity Press.

Latour, Bruno, Denise Milstein, Isaac Marrero-Guillamón, and Israel Rodríguez-Giralt. 2018. "Down to Earth Social Movements: An Interview with Bruno Latour." In "Reassembling Activism, Activating Assemblages." Special issue, *Social Movement Studies* 17 (3).

Leblanc, Lauren. 2019. Interview in *Poets & Writers Magazine* 47 (2).

Le Menager, Stephanie. 2003. "Trading Stories: Washington Irving and the Global West." *American Literary History*, 15 (4): 683–708.

———. 2004. *Manifest and Other Destinies: Territorial Fictions of the Nineteenth-Century United States*. Lincoln: University of Nebraska Press.

Lewis, Nathaniel, and Stephen Tatum. 2017. *Morta Las Vegas: "CSI" and the Problem of the West*. Lincoln: University of Nebraska Press.

Leyshon, Cressida. 2016. "This Week in Fiction: Mohsin Hamid on the Migrants in All of Us." *New Yorker*, November 7, 2016. https://www.newyorker.com/books/page-turner/this-week-in-fiction-mohsin-hamid-2016-11-14.

Limerick, Patricia Nelson. 1987. *The Legacy of Conquest*. New York: W. W. Norton.

———. 2020. "Limerick: Trump Drains the History of the American West of Dignity and Meaning." *Denver Post*, February 14, 2020. https://www.denverpost.com/2020/02/14/limerick-trump-drains-the-history-of-the-american-west-of-dignity-and-meaning/.

Lippard, Lucy R. 2014. *Undermining: A Wild Ride Through Land Use, Politics, and Art in the Changing West*. New York: New Press.

Lowe, L., and David Lloyd, eds. 1997. *The Politics of Culture in the Shadow of Capital*. Durham, NC: Duke University Press.

Lowe, Lisa. 1997. *Immigrant Acts: On Asian American Cultural Politics*. Durham, NC: Duke University Press.

Loxley, James. 2007. *Performativity*. London: Routledge.

Luiselli, Valeria. n.d. Penguin Random House Open Book Event, Luiselli Lecture. https://www.youtube.com/watch?v=1auQ1_snZUY.

———. 2012. *Faces in the Crowd*. London: Granta.

———. 2013. *Sidewalks*. London: Granta.

———. 2017. *Tell Me How It Ends: An Essay in Forty Questions*. Minneapolis: Coffee House Press.

———. 2018. "Valeria Luiselli (*Lost Children Archive*)." Penguin Random House Open Book Event, December 2018. https://www.youtube.com/watch?v=1auQ1_snZUY&t=127s.

———. 2019a. *Lost Children Archive*. London: 4th Estate.

———. 2019b. "The Wild West Meets the Southern Border." *New Yorker*, June 3, 2019. https://www.newyorker.com/magazine/2019/06/10/the-wild-west-meets-the-southern-border.

Lyons, Scott R., ed. 2017. *The World, the Text, and the Indian: Global Dimensions of Native American Literature*. Albany: SUNY Press.

Macfarlane, Robert. 2019. *Underland: A Deep Time Journey*. London: Hamish Hamilton.

Macklin, Rebecca. 2017. "An Interview with LeAnne Howe." May 9, 2017. https://www.wasafiri.org/article/interview-leanne-howe/.

Maguire, James H. 2002. "Western Literary Regionalism and Globalizing Literary Studies." *Western American Literature* 36 (4): 48–116.

Mailhot, Terese Marie. 2018. "Native American Lives Are Tragic, but Probably Not in the Way You Think." *Mother Jones*, November–December 2018. https://www.motherjones.com/media/2018/11/native-american-story-tragic-terese-mailhot-tommy-orange-poverty-porn/.

———. 2019. *Heart Berries: A Memoir*. London: Bloomsbury.

Mailhot, Terese Marie, and Tommy Orange. 2018. "In Conversation with Two Rising Voices in Native American Literature." *Time*, May 22, 2018. https://time.com/5286693/tommy-orange-terese-marie-mailhot-books/.

Malik, Nesrine. "The Rotten State of American Politics Made Trump Smell Fresh." *Guardian*, November 8, 2020. https://www.theguardian.com/commentisfree/2020/nov/08/american-politics-trump-broken-system.

Martínez, Óscar. 2013. *The Beast: Riding the Rails and Dodging the Narcos on the Migrant Trail*. London: Verso.

Massey, Doreen. 1994. *Space, Place and Gender*. Cambridge: Polity.

———. 2005. *For Space*. London: Sage.

McCarthy, Stella. 2019. "One-to-One with Téa Obreht." October 15, 2019. https://tv.cuny.edu/show/onetoone/PR2008697.

Meland, Carter. 2014. "Talking Tribalography: LeAnne Howe Models Emerging Worldliness in 'The Story of America' and Miko Kings." In "Tribalography." Special issue, *Studies in American Indian Literatures* 26 (2): 26–39.

Meurs, Pieter, Nicole Note, and Diederik Aerts. 2009. "This World Without Another: On Jean-Luc Nancy and *la mondialisation*." *Journal of Critical Globalisation Studies* (1): 31–46.

———. 2011. "The 'Globe' of Globalization." *Kritike* 5 (2): 10–25.

Mignolo, Walter. 2000. *Local Histories / Global Designs: Coloniality, Subaltern Knowledges, and Border Thinking*. Princeton, NJ: Princeton University Press.

———. 2005. *The Idea of America*. Oxford: Blackwells.

Montgomery, Sarah Fawn. 2019. "Native Ghosts Genocide and Madness Collide in a Reinterpretation of Mary Todd Lincoln." Poetry Foundation, February 18, 2019. https://www.poetryfoundation.org/articles/149201/native-ghosts/.

Morito, Bruce. 2012. *An Ethic of Mutual Respect: The Covenant Chain and Aboriginal-Crown Relations*. Vancouver: University of British Columbia Press.

Moss, Stephen. 2017. "Sebastian Barry: 'My Son Instructed Me in the Magic of Gay Life.'" *Irish Times*, February 2, 2017. https://www.irishtimes.com/culture/books/sebastian-barry-my-son-instructed-me-in-the-magic-of-gay-life-1.2960757.

Muthyala, John. 2006. *Reworlding America: Myth, History, and Narrative*. Athens: Ohio University Press.

Naas, Michael. 2014. "When It Comes to Mourning." In *Jacques Derrida Key Concepts*, edited by Claire Colebrook. London: Routledge.

Nancy, Jean-Luc. 1991. *The Inoperative Community*. Minneapolis: University of Minnesota Press.

———. 1997. *The Sense of the World*. Minneapolis: University of Minnesota Press.

———. 2000. *Being Singular Plural*. Stanford, CA: Stanford University Press.

———. 2007a. *The Creation of the World; or, Globalization*. Albany: SUNY Press.

———. 2007b. "Nothing but the World: An Interview with Vacarme." *Rethinking Marxism* 19 (4): 521–35.

———. 2008. *Dis-Enclosure: The Deconstruction of Christianity*. New York: Fordham University Press.

———. 2015. "The Singular Plural Art: Interview by M. Casolaro and L. Romano." http://logoi.ph/edizioni/numero-i-1-2015/ricerca/filosofia-e-arte/larte-singolare-plurale-intervista-a-cura-di-m-casolaro-e-l-romano.html.

Neary, Lynn. 2019. "Téa Obreht's Latest Is Steeped in the Supernatural—Also, There Are Camels." NPR, August 2019. https://www.npr.org/2019/08/11/749438304/t-a-obrehts-latest-is-steeped-in-the-supernatural-also-there-are-camels.

Nguyen, Tina. 2017. "This Television Show Predicted Donald Trump…in 1958." *Vanity Fair*, February 9, 2017. https://www.vanityfair.com/news/2017/02/tv-show-predicts-donald-trump.

Núñez-Puente, Carolina. 2018. "Queeremos a Gloria Anzaldúa: Identity, Difference, New Tribalism, and Affective Eco-Dialogues." *Camino Real* 10 (13): 47–62.

Obreht, Téa. 2019a. *Inland*. London: Weidenfeld and Nicolson.

———. 2019b. "Last Camp." August 14, 2019. https://www.powells.com/post/original-essays/last-camp.

O'Connor, Maria. 2011. "Canopy of the Upturned Eye: Writing on Derrida's Crypt." *Mosaic* 44 (4): 109–23.

Oliva, Alejandra. 2019. "American Purgatory: An Interview with Valeria Luiselli." https://www.bookforum.com/print/2601/an-interview-with-valeria-luiselli-20819.

Orange, Tommy. 2018a. "*Friday Black* Paints a Dark Portrait of Race in America." Review of *Friday Black*, by Nana Kwame Adjei-Brenyah. https://www.nytimes.com/2018/10/23/books/review/-nana-kwame-adjei-brenyah-friday-black.html.

———. 2018b. *There There*. London: Vintage.

O'Rourke, Sean. 2017. "RTE Podcast with Sebastian Barry." https://www.rte.ie/radio/radio1/clips/21074956/.

Owens, Jill. 2019. "Powell's Interview: Valeria Luiselli, Author of *Lost Children Archive*." February 28, 2019. https://www.powells.com/post/interviews/powells-interview-valeria-luiselli-author-of-lost-children-archive.

Packer, George. 2018. "A New Report Offers Insights into Tribalism in the Age of Trump." *New Yorker*, October 13, 2018. https://www.newyorker.com/news/daily-comment/a-new-report-offers-insights-into-tribalism-in-the-age-of-trump.

Page, Benedicte. 2016. "Sebastian Barry: 'It's Terrifying, but Fascinating That Human Groups Have These Impulses.'" October 10, 2016. http://www.thebookseller.com/profile/sebastian-barry-407676.

Palladini, Giulia, and Marco Pustianaz, eds. 2017. *Lexicon for an Affective Archive*. Bristol: Intellect.

Papanikolas, Zeese. 2007. *American Silence*. Lincoln: University of Nebraska Press.

Papastergiadis, Nikos. 2000. *The Turbulence of Migration*. Cambridge: Polity Press.

Paryż, Marek, and John R. Leo, eds. 2015. *The Post-2000 Film Western*. New York: Palgrave Macmillan.

Phillips, Katrina. 2020. "Longtime Police Brutality Drove American Indians to Join the George Floyd Protests." *Washington Post*, June 6, 2020. https://www.washing tonpost.com/outlook/2020/06/06/longtime-police-brutality-drove-american -indians-join-george-floyd-protests/.

Pinckney, Joel. 2017. "Feeling Foreign: An Interview with Hernan Diaz." *Paris Review*, October 10, 2017. https://www.theparisreview.org/blog/2017/10/10/feeling-foreign -an-interview-with-hernan-diaz/.

Plunkett, John. 2013. "'Feeling Seeing': Touch, Vision and the Stereoscope." *History of Photography* 37 (4): 389–96.

Pratt, Mary-Louise, 1995. *Imperial Eyes*. London: Routledge.

Preston, Alex. 2019. "*Inland* by Téa Obreht Review—the Wild West Just Got Wilder." *Guardian*, August 11, 2019. https://www.theguardian.com/books/2019/aug/12 /inland-tea-obreht-review.

Prieto, Eric. 2010. "Édouard Glissant, Littérature-monde, and Tout-monde." *Small Axe* 33 (November): 111–20.

Raffoul, François. 2012. "The Creation of the World." In *Jean-Luc Nancy and Plural Thinking: Expositions of World, Ontology, Politics, and Sense*, edited by P. Gratton and M. Morin, 13–26. Albany: SUNY Press.

Rand, Nicholas T. 1994. "Introduction: Renewals of Psychoanalysis." In Nicolas Abraham and Maria Torok, *The Shell and the Kernel*, vol. 1. Chicago: University of Chicago Press.

Rash, Felicity. 2017. *The Discourse Strategies of Imperialist Writing: The German Colonial Idea and Africa*. London: Routledge.

Rashkin, Esther. 1992. *Family Secrets and the Psychoanalysis of Narrative*. Princeton, NJ: Princeton University Press.

Roberts, Brian Russell, and Michelle Ann Stephens, eds. 2017. *Archipelagic American Studies*. Durham, NC: Duke University Press.

Rogers, K., and N. Fandos. 2019. "Trump Tells Congresswomen to 'Go Back' to the Countries They Came From." *New York Times*, July 14, 2019. https://www.nytimes .com/2019/07/14/us/politics/trump-twitter-squad-congress.html.

Rollenhagen, Luisa. 2019. "Valeria Luiselli Discusses Migrant Children and Other Lost Souls." February 12, 2019. https://www.vulture.com/2019/02/lost-children -archive-author-valeria-luiselli-q-and-a.html.

Romero, Channette. 2014. "Expanding Tribal Identities and Sovereignty Through LeAnne Howe's 'Tribalography.'" In "Tribalography." Special issue, *Studies in American Indian Literatures* 26 (2): 13–25.

Rosemberg, Muriel. 2016. "Édouard Glissant's Geopoetics, a Contribution to the Idea of the World as the World." *L'Espace Géographique* 4 (45): 1–14.

Ross, Stephen, and Steven Sexton. 2020. "Digital Tribalography." *PMLA* 23 (October): 581–88.

Said, Edward W. 1991. *Orientalism: Western Conceptions of the Orient*. Harmondsworth: Penguin.

———. 1994. *Culture and Imperialism*. London: Vintage.

———. 2000. *Reflections on Exile*. Cambridge: Cambridge University Press.

Scutts, Joanna. 2019. "Téa Obreht: 'In America, We Make Progress, Then Revert in Horrific Ways.'" *Guardian*, August 24, 2019. https://www.theguardian.com/books/2019/aug/24/tea-obreht-in-america-we-make-progress-then-revert-in-horrific-ways.

Seaman, Donna. 2017. "An Interview with Mohsin Hamid, Author of *Exit West*." October 24, 2017. https://penguinrandomhouselibrary.com/2017/10/24/an-interview-with-mohsin-hamid-author-of-exit-west/.

Sebald, W. G. 2001. *Austerlitz*. New York: Modern Library.

———. 2002. *The Emigrants*. London: Vintage.

Sedgwick, Eve Kosofsky. 1990. *Epistemology of the Closet*. Berkeley: University of California Press.

———. 1994. *Tendencies*. London: Routledge.

Sherman, Gabriel. 2019. "'There Is No Endgame': White House Aides Fear Trump Has Turned the Border Wall into His Alamo." *Vanity Fair*, January 8, 2019. https://www.vanityfair.com/news/2019/01/trump-aides-fear-the-wall-will-be-his-alamo.

Shields, David. 2018. *Nobody Hates Trump More than Trump: An Intervention*. New York: Thought Catalog Books.

Shotten, Heather J. 2019. "Resisting Violence Through Writing." https://www.worldliteraturetoday.org/2019/autumn/resisting-violence-through-writing-conversation-tommy-orange-heather-j-shotton.

Simon, Scott. 2020. "Into the West, from the Far East: *How Much of These Hills Is Gold*." NPR, April 4, 2020. http://www.npr.org/2020/04/04/827241624/into-the-west-from-the-far-east-how-much-of-these-hills-is-gold.

Slotkin, Richard. 1973. *Regeneration Through Violence*. Middletown, CT: Wesleyan Press.

———. 1993. *Gunfighter Nation: The Myth of the Frontier in Twentieth-Century America*. New York: Harper-Perennial.

Solnit, Rebecca. 2004. *Hope in the Dark: Untold Histories, Wild Possibilities*. New York: Nation Books.

———. 2010. *Infinite City: A San Francisco Atlas*. Berkeley: University of California Press.

———. 2014. "Disasters and the Landscape of Public Love." October 2014. https://commonthreads.sgi.org/post/140414840583/disasters-and-the-landscape-of-public-love.

———. 2017a. "The Loneliness of Donald Trump." *LitHub*, May 30, 2017. https://lithub.com/rebecca-solnit-the-loneliness-of-donald-trump/.

———. 2017b. "Protest and Persist: Why Giving Up Hope Is Not an Option." *Guardian*, March 13, 2017. https://www.theguardian.com/world/2017/mar/13/protest-persist-hope-trump-activism-anti-nuclear-movement.

———. 2020. "Trump's Response to the Pandemic Has Always Been Dishonest and Cruel." *Guardian*, October 8, 2020. https://www.theguardian.com/commentisfree/2020/oct/08/trump-coronavirus-pandemic-dishonest-cruel.

Spivak, Gayatri Chakravorty. 1985. "The Rani of Sirmur: An Essay in Reading the Archives." *History and Theory* 24 (3): 247–72.

———. 1990. *The Post-colonial Critic: Interviews, Strategies, Dialogues.* London: Routledge.

Squint, Kirstin L. 2010. "Choctawan Aesthetics, Spirituality, and Gender Relations: An Interview with LeAnne Howe." *MELUS* 35 (3): 211–24.

Steedman, Carolyn. *Dust: The Archive and Cultural History.* New Brunswick, NJ: Rutgers University Press, 2002.

Stegner, Page. 2003. *Winning the Wild West: The Epic Saga of the American Frontier, 1800–1899.* New York: Simon and Schuster.

Stewart, Kathleen. 2013. "The Achievement of a Life, a List, a Line." In *The Social Life of Achievement,* edited by N. J. Long and H. L. Moore. New York: Bergahn.

Stewart, Susan. 1993. *On Longing: Narratives of the Miniature, the Gigantic, the Souvenir, the Collection.* Durham, NC: Duke University Press.

Suchak, Aakash M. 2018. "The Place of Consignation; or, Memory and Writing in Derrida's Archive." *Journal of Comparative Literature and Aesthetics* 41 (1–2): 55–69.

Tatum, Stephen. 2007. "Spectrality and the Postregional Interface." In *Postwestern Cultures: Literature, Theory, Space,* edited by Susan Kollin, 3–29. Lincoln: University of Nebraska Press.

Teo, Stephen. 2017. *Eastern Westerns: Film and Genre Outside and Inside Hollywood.* London: Routledge.

Truettner, William H. 1991. "Ideology and Image." In *The West as America: Reinterpreting Images of the Frontier, 1820–1920,* edited by William H. Truettner. Washington, DC: National Museum of American Art.

Trump, Donald. 2019. "Remarks by President Trump to the 74th Session of the United Nations General Assembly." September 24, 2019. https://trumpwhite house.archives.gov/briefings-statements/remarks-president-trump-74th-session -united-nations-general-assembly/.

———. 2020. "State of the Union Address." https://www.govinfo.gov/content/pkg /CREC-2020-02-04/pdf/CREC-2020-02-04-pt1-PgH758-6.pdf.

Trump, Donald, and Tony Schwartz. 1987. *The Art of the Deal.* New York: Ballantine Books.

Tsing, Anna Lowenhaupt. 2005. *Friction: An Ethnography of Global Connection.* Princeton, NJ: Princeton University Press.

———. 2015. *The Mushroom at the End of the World.* Princeton, NJ: Princeton University Press.

Turner, Frederick Jackson. 1961. *Frontier and Section.* Englewood Cliffs, NJ: Prentice-Hall.

Viala-Gaudefroy, Jérôme. 2018a. "In Trump's America, Immigrants Are Modern-Day 'Savage Indians.'" Conversation, July 16, 2018. https://theconversation.com/in -trumps-america-immigrants-are-modern-day-savage-indians-99809/.

———. 2018b. "President Trump and the Virtue of Power." *Revue Lisa* 16 (2). https:// journals.openedition.org/lisa/9861?lang=en.

Vizenor, Gerald. 1994. *Manifest Manners: Postindian Warriors of Survivance.* Hanover, NH: Wesleyan University Press.

———. 1998. *Fugitive Poses: Native American Scenes of Absence and Presence.* Lincoln: University of Nebraska Press.

Vizenor, Gerald, and A. Robert Lee. 1999. *Postindian Conversations*. Lincoln: University of Nebraska Press.

Wander, Ryan. 2016. "Heterochronic West: Temporal Multiplicity in Bret Harte's Regional Writing." Special issue, *Western American Literature* 51 (2): 143–73.

Washington, John. 2019. "'How Do You Address Disappearance?': A Q&A with Valeria Luiselli." *Nation*, April 1, 2019. https://www.thenation.com/article/valeria-luiselli-interview-lost-children-archive/.

Watson, Alexandra. 2020. "Making Space for Imaginative Empathy in the Historical Record." *Apogee*, April 7, 2020. https://apogeejournal.org/2020/04/07/making-space-imaginative-empathy-historical-record/.

Watson, David. 2007. Preface to *The Worlding Project: Doing Cultural Studies in the Era of Globalization*, edited by Rob Wilson and Christopher Leigh Connery. Berkeley, CA: North Atlantic Books.

Wheatstone, Charles. 1838. "Contributions to the Physiology of Vision—Part the First. On Some Remarkable, and Hitherto Unobserved, Phenomena of Binocular Vision." *Philosophical Transactions of the Royal Society of London* 128: 371–94.

Wilson, Rob. 2007. "Afterword: Worlding as Future Tactic." In *The Worlding Project: Doing Cultural Studies in the Era of Globalization*, edited by Rob Wilson and Christopher Leigh Connery, 209–23. Berkeley, CA: North Atlantic Books.

———. 2008. "Worlding Space, Worlding Time: On the Making of the Worlding Project." November 12, 2008. https://www.boundary2.org/2008/11/worlding-space-worlding-time-on-the-making-of-the-worlding-project/.

———. 2018. "Worlding Asia/Oceania: Concepts, Tactics, and Transfigurations Inside the Anthropocene." Plenary talk, Inter-Asia Cultural Studies Conference, July 28–30, 2017, Seoul. http://culturalstudies.kr/wpcontent/uploads/2018/03/WorldingAsiaOceania2018.pdf?ckattempt=1.

———. 2019. "On Thinking Literature Across Continents." "More than Global? A Roundtable Discussion." *New Global Studies* 13 (1). https://www.researchgate.net/publication/332232064_More_than_Global_A_Roundtable_Discussion.

Wilson, Rob, and Christopher Leigh Connery, eds. 2007. *The Worlding Project: Doing Cultural Studies in the Era of Globalization*. Berkeley, CA: North Atlantic Books.

Winnette, Colin. 2020. "Read This One: C Pam Zhang on Michael Ondaatje's *Divisadero*." *Believer*, March 6, 2020. https://believermag.com/logger/read-this-one-c-pam-zhang-on-michael-ondaatjes-divisadero/.

Womack, Craig S. 2005. Review of *Evidence of Red*, by LeAnne Howe. *Studies in American Indian Literatures* 7 (4): 158–61.

Womack, Craig, and Daniel Heath Justice, eds. 2008. *Reasoning Together: The Native Critics Collective*. Norman: University of Oklahoma Press.

Wright, Robert. 2019. "How Trump Could Wind up Making Globalism Great Again." *Wired*, January 17, 2019. https://www.wired.com/story/trump-style-nationalism-make-globalism-great-again/.

Yang, Mimi. 2018. "Trumpism: A Disfigured Americanism." *Palgrave Communications* 4 (117). https://www.nature.com/articles/s41599-018-0170-0.

Yeh, James. 2020. "Robin Wall Kimmerer: 'People Can't Understand the World as a Gift Unless Someone Shows Them How.'" *Guardian*, May 23, 2020. https://www

.theguardian.com/books/2020/may/23/robin-wall-kimmerer-people-cant-understand-the-world-as-a-gift-unless-someone-shows-them-how.

Young, Clara. 2018. "How Donald Trump Caused the Wild West to Reappear on the Spring Runways." *Fashion*, March 19, 2018. https://fashionmagazine.com/fashion/wild-west-donald-trump-spring-2018/.

Zhang, C Pam. 2020a. "C Pam Zhang on Writing in a Time of Grief." *LitHub*, March 31, 2020. https://lithub.com/c-pam-zhang-on-writing-in-a-time-of-grief/.

———. 2020b. *How Much of These Hills Is Gold*. London: Virago.

———. 2020c. "When Your Inheritance Is to Look Away." *New Yorker*, April 7, 2020. https://www.newyorker.com/culture/personal-history/when-your-inheritance-is-to-look-away.

About the Author

235

Neil Campbell is emeritus professor of American studies at the University of Derby, United Kingdom. He has published widely on the American West in articles, book chapters, and monographs. He has published an interdisciplinary trilogy of books on the postwar American West: *The Cultures of the American New West*, *The Rhizomatic West*, and *Post-Westerns: Cinema, Region, West*. He is coeditor of the book series Place, Memory, Affect and has a volume within it, *Affective Critical Regionality*. He edited *Under the Western Sky*, a collection of essays on the fiction and music of Willy Vlautin, published by the University of Nevada Press.